Gateway to Business Analytics with Microsoft Excel®

Gateway to Business Analytics with Microsoft Excel®

HUMBERTO BARRETO

PALNI OPEN PRESS
INDIANAPOLIS, INDIANA

This book was produced with Pressbooks (https://pressbooks.com) and rendered with Prince.

Dedication

For Simon

Contents

Publisher's Note

This textbook was peer-reviewed, copyedited, and published through the Private Academic Library Network of Indiana (PALNI) PALSave Textbook Creation Grants Program. For more information about the PALSave Affordable Learning Program, visit the PALSave website: https://palni.org/palsave.

If you have comments, suggestions, or corrections for this textbook, please send them to palsave@palni.edu.

Acknowledgments

While they did not work with me closely on this book, the materials bear the imprint of my long-time colleagues: Frank Howland, Kealoha Widdows, and Michele Villinski.

Tami Barreto copyedited the working draft of this manuscript, like almost everything else I have written. She has fixed countless mistakes and greatly improved the exposition.

I received encouraging, helpful suggestions from two reviewers.

This work was funded by a PALSave Textbook Creation Grant. The editorial team at PALNI was organized and supportive.

I thank Amanda Hurford, Heather Myers, Victoria Peters, and I especially want to thank Jennifer Boeree for her outstanding editorial assistance.

My students in BUS 110 at DePauw University used these materials as the textbook for the course as we launched our new School of Business and Leadership in fall 2023. They gave me valuable and constructive feedback. I hope this book helps future students, at DePauw and everywhere around the world.

Thank you all.

Preface

If you think of business analytics as a big city, then this book is a gateway to a crowded downtown with bright, neon lights. There is so much to see and do! *Gateway to Business Analytics with Microsoft Excel* shows you the sights via spreadsheets. This allows you to acquire a great deal of sophisticated, advanced Excel skills while sampling from a variety of engaging topics at an introductory level.

The use of Excel drives other innovations in this book. Spreadsheets require concrete, numerical problems instead of abstract functions and graphs. Constructing models takes time and effort, but the payoff is that you are able to see how changes in cells affect graphs and other results.

Business analytics is a rapidly growing subdiscipline that is not well defined. Content and level of presentation vary widely. This book delivers a coherent set of topics appropriate for first- or second-year college students. *No specialized training in Excel, calculus, statistics, or programming is needed.*

For example, instead of using calculus to solve optimization problems, we use Excel's Solver. Instead of reading a description of gross domestic product (GDP) and national income accounting, we use the FRED Excel add-in to download data and show that equations like GDP = C + I + G + NX are really true.

I am a veteran economics professor, and I have written several books and many articles using Excel to teach economics. Excel-based teaching has really helped my students learn economic theory and econometrics. I am excited to try this approach to deliver content in business analytics.

May your intellectual journey be as rewarding and fun as it has been for me.

Humberto Barreto
hbarreto@depauw.edu
Greencastle, Indiana

User Guide

Which Excel?

This book is a manual for actively working with and manipulating content in Excel. There are, however, many versions of Excel—which one is needed?

Use *Windows* (not Mac) *desktop* (not browser) *Excel*.

Some of the files will work on a Mac, but the best solution for Mac users is to emulate Windows with software such as Parallels or Boot Camp. For students at an educational institution, accessing a Windows machine from a server (see, for example, VMWare's Horizon software or Windows App) is an easy solution for Mac users. Students at my university, DePauw, can log in at virtualdesktops.depauw.edu
from a Mac, Chromebook, or tablet (anything that has a browser) to access a Windows machine with desktop Excel (and other Office applications).

Online versions of Excel do not support Visual Basic and other advanced features. Thus, you cannot get full functionality using Excel within a web browser. Do not use Excel in a browser to do the work in this book.

In addition to Windows desktop Excel, you need your brain. This book presumes that you have seen a spreadsheet before. You can open Excel and write a formula that adds cells together. As you will see, however, Excel is much more than a simple adding machine. You will learn how to use Excel in much more advanced ways. In addition to analyzing data and learning many new Excel functions, you will learn how to use special Excel files called *add-ins* that solve optimization problems and run simulations.

The most important thing you can do as you read this book is *experiment*. You might find yourself wondering, "What would happen if this cell was 10 instead of 1?" Do not just wonder, change the cell and see what happens! There is deep neuroscience at work here. When you are in control and making up your own questions, you learn best. The beauty of this approach is that everything is alive, and you can make points move and lines shift. Take full advantage. Be engaged.

> **EXCEL TIP** Never settle for passive reading. Always do the steps and experiment as you work, changing things to see what happens.

Finally, if something is not working the way you expect, there are many possible causes. It is always a good idea to close Excel completely and reopen it. Even if this does not fix the problem, slowly repeating the steps will help you debug or describe what is happening.

In addition to generative AI (such as ChatGPT), I recommend these websites for Excel tips, tricks, and problem-solving:

- Tushar Mehta: www.tushar-mehta.com/excel/
- Chip Pearson: www.cpearson.com/excel
- Jon Peltier: peltiertech.com/Excel/
- Andy Pope: www.andypope.info

Paths Through This Book

You can read and do the activities in this book in a straightforward way from beginning to end, but you can also skip around. The chapters are mostly stand-alone, and within chapters, the sections are also somewhat independent.

Chapters 2 and 6 are an exception. The former introduces Excel's Solver add-in with simple optimization problems. The latter chapter covers constrained optimization and introduces elasticity via another add-in, the Comparative Statics Wizard.

While these two chapters are paired together, they are separated in the book to enable the reader to digest the material. Allowing ideas to sit for a while and then dredging them back up is an effective way to learn.

After reading and doing the opening section of Monte Carlo simulation in chapter 3, you can do the remaining sections in any order. They all apply the MCSim add-in to different problems.

The FRED add-in is introduced in chapter 5 on unemployment. It is used again in chapter 7 on the yield curve and chapter 8 on national income accounting.

PED—process, explain, and decide—is embedded throughout the book. Excel is used in different ways to download and organize data, to visualize and communicate results, and to find optimal solutions. No matter the path you take through this book, you will learn a great deal about business analytics and Excel.

Book Website

This book is open access and is distributed through many outlets. If you did not get it from the book's website, see dub.sh/gbae.

This site has the latest version of the book, along with all of the add-ins and finished files. You should build your own Excel workbooks, but you can always check your work by downloading files and comparing them to yours.

The book website also has an Instructor Resources section with materials specifically dedicated to teaching a course in business analytics.

Visit and bookmark dub.sh/gbae to begin your journey.

1. Defining Business Analytics

> Someday soon, say predictive analytics experts, it will be possible for companies to know our tastes and predict our habits better than we know ourselves.
>
> Charles Duhigg

What exactly is business analytics? The business part is easy; it means a commercial operation or a company. Business is often associated with entrepreneurship and management.

Analytics is a little harder—it is the systematic computational analysis of data. So, simply put, it is number crunching. Figure 1.1 shows how the word *analytics* has exploded in use, according to Google's Ngram Viewer.

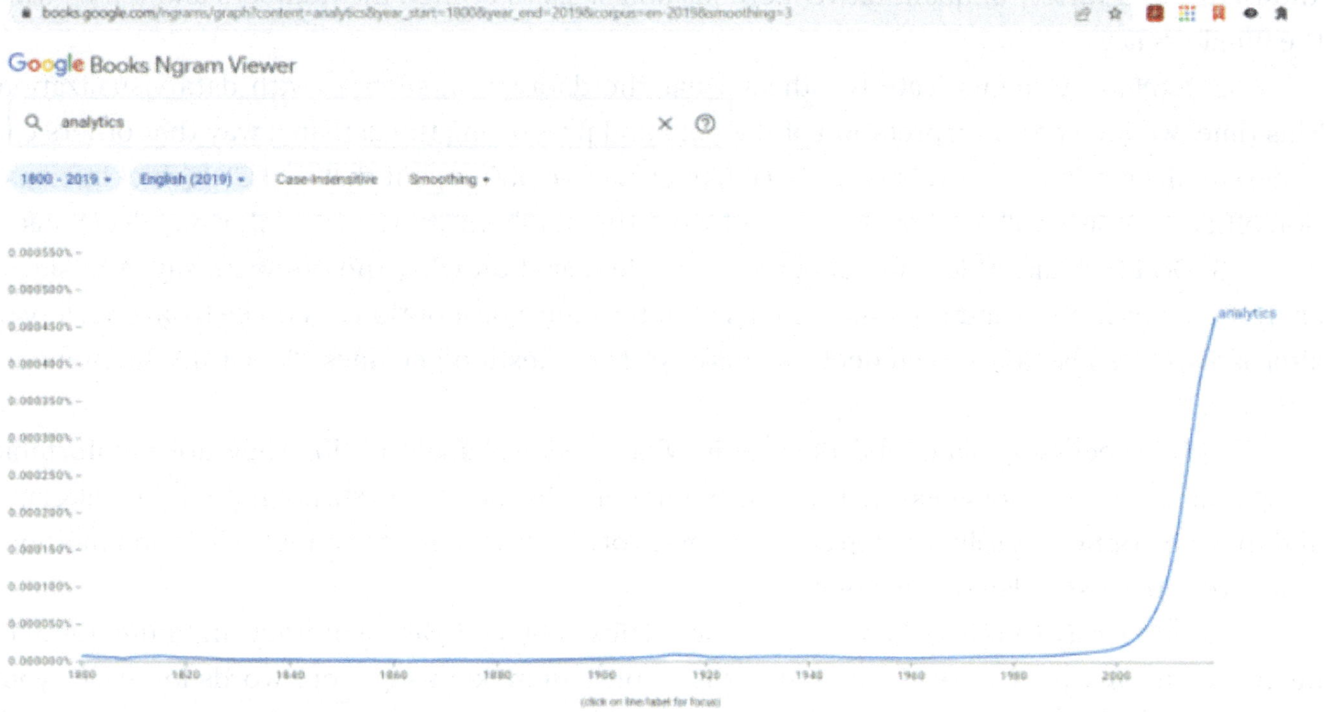

Figure 1.1: Use of the word analytics in a large corpus of books over time.
Source: Google Books Ngram Viewer / License.

Before this century, it was not often used, but now analytics is applied to many different fields, such as marketing analytics or baseball analytics. The word *analytics* is shorthand to indicate the use of quantitative or statistical methods to study something.

Putting the two words together, business analytics **is the study of business with a special emphasis on numbers, data, and quantitative information**.

More succinctly, business analytics is all about this question:

"What do the numbers say?"

The answer can be approached in three different ways:

1. Process
2. Explain
3. Decide

1. *Process*: Decode and analyze data to extract information. Most people do this constantly without even realizing it. For example, when reading a menu at a restaurant, the numbers tell you the prices of different dishes, and you can add items together to estimate the total cost of your meal. You would, however, be unlikely to figure out how much revenue the restaurant made from each item if you were handed a stack of receipts for an entire year! A business analyst has specific knowledge of a variety of quantitative methods and skills to crunch the numbers and tell us what the numbers say.

2. *Explain*: Communicate to others what the data show, such as with data visualization. This time, we focus on interpretation of the data and presenting the data in a way that others can understand. Our role is not that of a CEO (chief executive officer) but that of a CIO (chief information officer). Others will use how we present what the numbers say to make informed decisions.

3. *Decide*: Make a decision about what to do based on what the numbers say. A business analyst creates models and runs simulations to determine a best option or choice from a variety of alternatives. This is data-driven decision-making. The question becomes, "What do the numbers say to do?"

PED—process, explain, and decide—is what business analysts do. They are comfortable using a variety of technologies and think with numbers. Business analysts are not mathematicians, and they do not necessarily develop software or algorithms; instead, they apply tools and methods to answer business-related questions.

Another way to think about business analytics is by comparing literacy and numeracy. To be literate means you can read and write. It is a continuum; knowing more words increases your literacy. Numeracy is the ability to work with numbers and the mastery of mathematical tools. Business analytics is built on numeracy—we process, explain, and decide with numbers as a foundation and guide.

Business analytics is an interdisciplinary area of study that borrows from mathematics, statistics, computer science, finance, economics, and anywhere else that emphasizes quantitative analysis in the study of business. The borders of business analytics are not well defined, and the field easily blends into other areas, such as data science (which is more aligned with computer science). It can be difficult to pin down exactly what falls under the broad umbrella of this exciting new area, since it accepts input from any source.

A critical, underappreciated aspect of business analytics is ethics. Just because you can do something does not mean you should—no matter how technically sophisticated and impressive. Or, put another way, what the numbers say to do may be the wrong thing to do because it is unethical or immoral. This is worth remembering.

References

The epigraph is from the chapter on Target in Charles Duhigg's *The Power of Habit*. Duhigg tells the story of how Target was one of the first retailers to monetize customer data. Target's success is also an early cautionary tale, as it faced intense backlash when its customers learned that Target somehow knew before family members that someone in the house was pregnant.

2. Optimization with Solver

> The first way of thinking that made the law about the behavior of light evident was discovered by Fermat in about 1650, and it is called *the principle of least time*, or *Fermat's principle*. His idea is this: that out of all possible paths that it might take to get from one point to another, light takes the path which requires the *shortest time*.
>
> Richard Feynman

2.1 The Lifeguard Problem

You are a lifeguard on a beach. You are standing on the shore; the water laps at your feet as the sun shines on your face. You timed yourself the other day, and you ran 100 meters in 20 seconds. You are much slower than the other lifeguards, but you are a superfast swimmer. You can swim 100 meters in 50 seconds—that's only a few seconds off the freestyle world record! You like numbers, and a thought pops into your head: "It's funny that I'm a slow runner and fast swimmer, yet I can still run 2.5 times faster than I swim—my run speed is 5 m/sec, while my swim speed is 2 m/sec."

Suddenly, you see someone frantically waving in the water and hear cries of "Help!" They are exactly 100 meters to your right and 100 meters from the shore. Figure 2.1 shows the positioning. Your training kicks in, and you take off running along the shore toward the drowning person. Your goal is to get to them as quickly as you can. Your mind is consumed by a critical question: "When do I dive in and start swimming?"

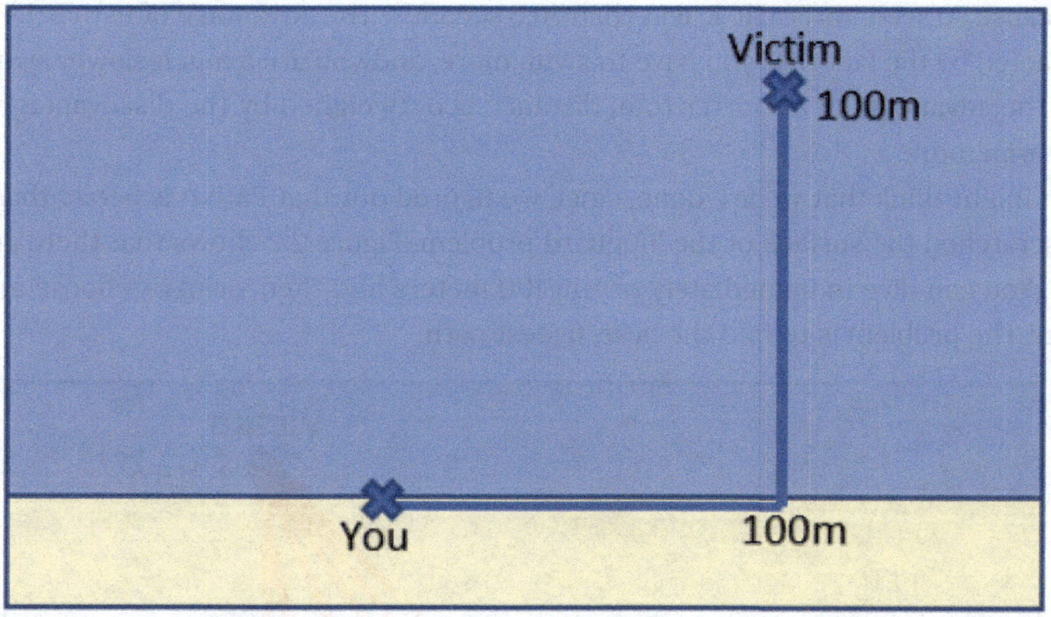

Figure 2.1: Initial positions of the lifeguard and victim.

Before we implement and solve this problem in Excel, let's agree that you do have a decision to make. Consider these two paths:

(A) Based on the logic that you're a faster runner than a swimmer, you could run 100 meters along the shoreline in 20 seconds and then swim 100 meters in 50 seconds, and you would reach the drowning person in 70 seconds. This path is the shortest swimming distance.

(B) On the other hand, you could argue that it is better to just dive into the water and make a beeline for the victim because this is the shortest total distance. The Pythagorean Theorem says that the hypotenuse is about 141 meters (sqrt(100^2 + 100^2)). This distance is much shorter than the 200 meters total distance required by running 100 and swimming 100 meters.

The problem, however, is to minimize not swimming distance or total distance but time—you have to get to the drowning victim as soon as possible. We know Path A takes 70 seconds, but what about Path B?

Path B takes a little longer than A. Here is the algebra involved in the computation:

$$time = \frac{distance}{speed} = \frac{141m}{2\frac{m}{sec}} = 70.5\text{seconds}$$

Thus, running 100 meters and swimming 100 meters is better than swimming about 141 meters because 70 seconds is a little less than 70.5 seconds. The advantage of Path B, less distance, is counteracted by the fact that you have to swim more, and you are a much slower swimmer than a runner. The advantage of a shorter total distance is outweighed by the disadvantage or cost of having to swim more.

You might think that we are done, since we figured out that Path A is better than B, but we have just scratched the surface of the lifeguard problem. Figure 2.2 shows that there are not only two paths. You can dive in immediately or run 100 meters and then swim or choose any distance in between! The problem is to find the best, fastest path.

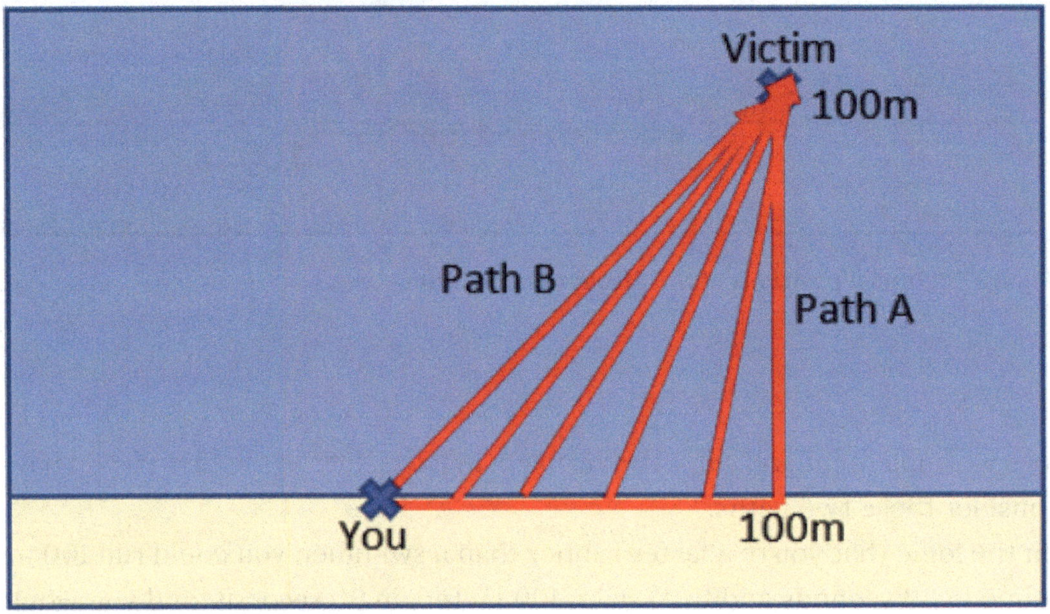

Figure 2.2: Of the many paths, which is the best, fastest path?

The lifeguard problem can be solved analytically, with calculus and algebra, but we will not do that. Instead, we will use *numerical methods*: An algorithm is used to get an approximate result. We will implement the problem in Excel and use Excel's Solver add-in to find the correct answer.

STEP Open a blank Excel workbook and save it as *LifeguardProblem.xlsx*. Enter the numbers and labels shown in Figure 2.3. Make sure your Excel workbook looks exactly like Figure 2.3 because we will be referencing those specific cell addresses.

	A	B	C	D
1	Exogenous Variables			
2	100	Distance Away on Sand, m		
3	100	Distance Away in Water, m		
4	5	Max Run Speed, m/sec		
5	2	Max Swim Speed, m/sec		
6				
7	Endogenous Variables			
8	0	Distance Run, m		
9	141.4214	Distance Swim, m		
10				
11	Goal			
12	70.71068	min Time to Victim, sec		

Figure 2.3: Setting up the problem in Excel.

Exogenous variables cannot be changed by the decision-maker. From the Greek, *exo* means "outside," like a lobster's exoskeleton. Exogenous variables are outside or beyond our control. They are also known as independent, given, or constant variables. They are parameters that are part of the decision-maker's environment.

You certainly cannot control where the victim is drowning. If you could, the problem would be trivial—you would put them right at your feet and pull them out. So the location of the drowning swimmer is exogenous: 100 meters away on the sand and 100 meters from the shore in the water.

Your run and swim speeds are also exogenous. You might think you can control how fast you run and swim, but these are not the actual variables. As the labels show, "Max Run Speed" and "Max Swim Speed" are your fastest run and swim speeds. We are assuming you are going all out to save the victim. Sure, you could train to get faster, but at that moment when you are trying to save the victim, your max speeds are given. The fastest you can (and will) run is 5 m/sec, and the fastest you can (and will) swim is 2 m/sec.

To really cement the concept of exogenous variables, ponder this: If you were waiting to order at the drive-thru at your favorite fast-food restaurant, could you think of a few exogenous variables? What makes the variables you chose exogenous?

Endogenous variables are the ones the decision-maker sets and determines. Since *endo* means "inside" in Greek (you have an endoskeleton), endogenous variables are within your control.

They are also known as choice or dependent variables. What to drink is endogenous to you at the fast-food restaurant.

You decide how far you will run from zero (dive right in and start swimming, Path B) to 100 meters (Path A), so this is the endogenous variable in this problem. Notice that deciding how far to run immediately determines how much you will swim, since you will always swim in a straight line along the hypotenuse formed by the triangle of where you entered the water (see Figure 2.2). We can use Excel to demonstrate this.

STEP Enter the formula =SQRT((A2-A8)^2+A3^2) in cell A9 and press *Enter*. You will know you did it correctly if Excel displays something close to 141.4217. The formula computes the hypotenuse for any value of cell A8. Excel treats the value of the blank cell A8 as zero, so A2 – A8 is 100 and we get the hypotenuse of Path B (shortest total distance).

> **EXCEL TIP** Maximize the flexibility of your spreadsheets.
>
> It would have been easier to enter and read the formula if we *hard-coded* the distance away on sand and in water like this: =SQRT((100-A8)^2+100^2), but we would lose the flexibility of being able to change these variables and have the formula automatically update. In general, you want to develop spreadsheets that depend on other cells and not on numbers.

STEP To make sure the formula works well, let's check Path A: Enter 100 in cell A8. Cell A9 should also display 100. If not, return to the previous step and fix the formula.

In addition to exogenous and endogenous variables, every optimization problem has to have a *goal*, known more formally as an *objective function*. For the lifeguard problem, this is minimizing the time it takes to get to the victim. The goal always has to be a function (in Excel, a formula) that depends on the endogenous variables.

STEP Enter the formula =A8/A4+A9/A5 in cell A12 and press *Enter*. You will know you did it correctly if Excel displays 70 (with cell A8 at 100), since we know this is how long it takes for Path A.

Having set up the optimization problem in Excel with exogenous and endogenous variables, along with a goal, we are now ready to find the best path. We begin by manually trying a few different paths.

STEP Set cell A8 to 50 and notice the time to victim. Try 25 and 75. Keep playing with cell A8 until you think you've found the best answer.

Cell A8 should now be in the mid-50s, and the time to victim should be around 65.8 seconds. That's several seconds better than Path A or B—this could mean the difference between life and death!

Not many people try fractional distances, but this is perfectly acceptable. Of course, we are not going to hunt and peck for hours, changing A8 by 0.001 to see the effect on A12. Instead, we will use Excel's Solver. Hunting and pecking (or its twin, plugging and chugging), but really fast, is exactly what Solver does.

Excel's Solver is an optimization algorithm. It tests many trial solutions very quickly, converging to an answer. Later, we will explore how it works in more detail. Right now, let's see it in action.

STEP Click the *Data* tab (in the *Ribbon* across the top of the screen), then Solver (in the Analysis group) to bring up the *Solver Parameters* dialog box. If Solver is not available, then use the Add-in Manager to install it. Use Excel's Help if you are having trouble or visit support.office.com.

EXCEL TIP Press *Alt*, *t*, *i* to access the Add-in Manager. Press the *Alt* key, then release it and press the letter *t*, then release it and press the letter *i* to quickly bring up the Add-in Manager.

The *Solver Parameters* dialog box is initially empty. You need to give it the appropriate information before asking it to search for a solution. It always needs specific cell addresses for the Objective and Changing Variable Cells inputs. Some problems are constrained and require further input, but the lifeguard problem does not.

STEP Do these three things: (1) Click in the *Set Objective* input field and select cell A12 by clicking on it. (2) Click the *Min* radio button. (3) Click the *By Changing Variable Cells* input field and select cell A8. Your screen should look like Figure 2.4. If not, make it so.

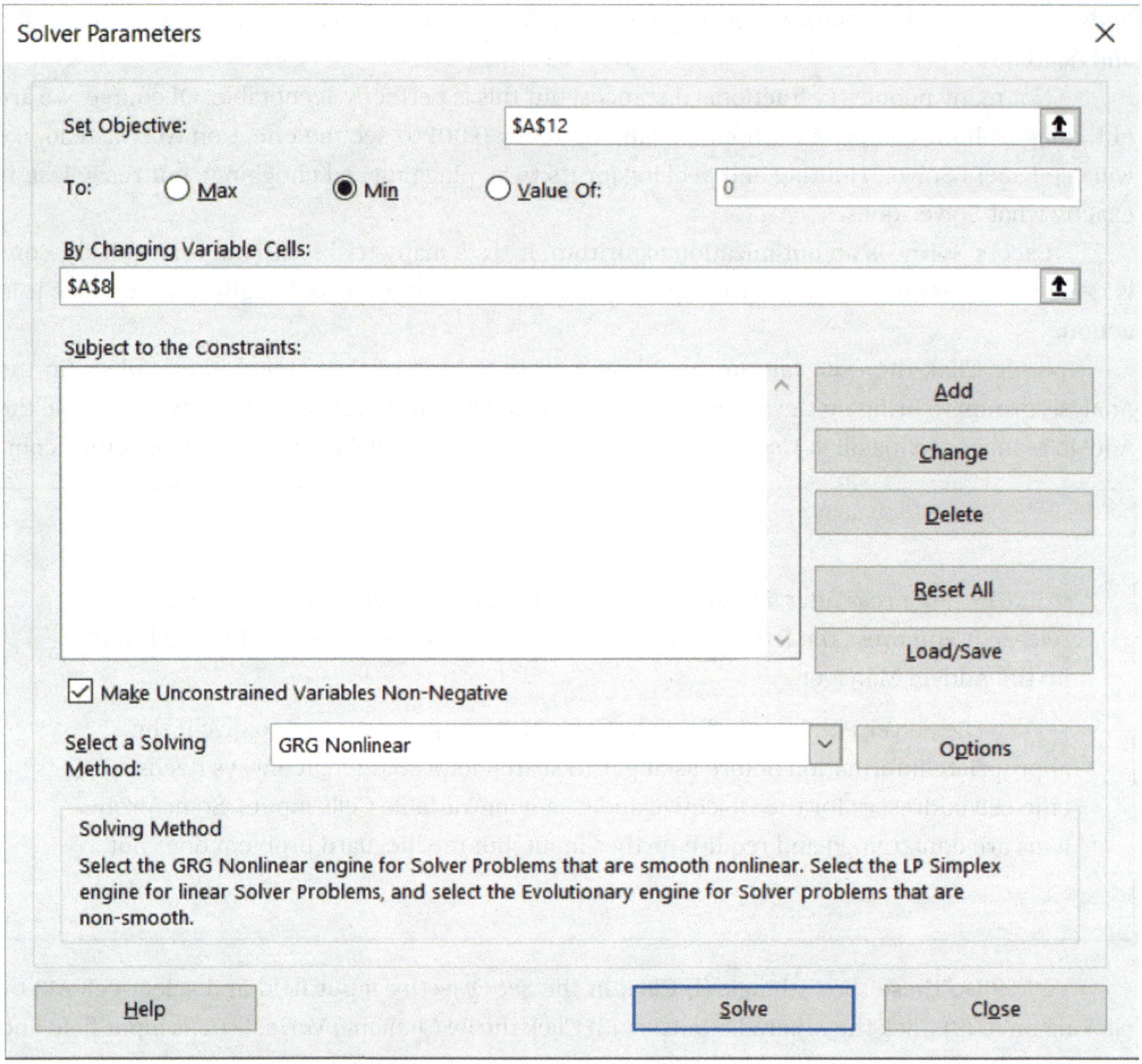

Figure 2.4: The Solver Parameters dialog box.
Source: Screenshot of Excel interface, © Microsoft Corporation.

STEP Click the Solve button in the bottom-right corner of the *Solver* dialog box, read the *Solver Results* dialog box, and click OK.

You did it! You found the correct answer to the lifeguard problem! By running about 56 meters before jumping in, you will reach the victim in a little under 66 seconds, and this is the shortest possible time. We can see that this is a true minimizing solution by exploring a small move away from Solver's solution.

STEP Change cell A8 to 57 and you can see that cell A12 increases a little bit. Decrease cell

A8 to 55 and, once again, cell A12 goes up. That is pretty convincing evidence that Solver has the correct answer, since the values around it yield higher times to reach the drowning person.

There is more to do, but let's recap. We modeled an optimization problem, implemented it in Excel, and used Excel's Solver to find the optimal solution. There are other ways to solve optimization problems, but Solver offers a pretty simple approach—as long as you can set up the problem in Excel, Solver has a shot at solving it. We will see in future work that Solver is not perfect, but on a simple problem like this one, it is reliable.

Excel's Solver is an example of numerical methods. Its answer is not exactly correct, but it is so close that, practically speaking, it is the right answer. This problem can be solved analytically to get an exact solution, and doing so yields something called Snell's Law. Physicists have known for a long time that light refracts when it goes through a different medium than air, like water. As Pierre de Fermat realized in 1650, light is taking the fastest path, and this is why it bends when it hits water.

There are some pretty mind-boggling applications of minimizing time across different media from the natural world. Some people think dogs can find the optimal path (Pennings, 2003; Perruchet and Gallego, 2006) and so can ants, as shown in Figure 2.5. As described in the caption, the green area is rough felt that is harder to walk on. The ants do not go in a straight line to the food (like they do in a control setting with only the white, smooth surface). The authors call this *decentralized optimization* because the ants are working together without any direction from an authority telling them what to do.

Figure 4. "Refracted" trail of *W. auropunctata* workers at the medium border between smooth (white) and rough (green) felt.
The position of the food is on the rough felt. Note that the density of workers on the rough felt is higher than on the smooth felt because travel speed is lower. In addition it appears, although not very obvious, as if the ants on the rough felt 'float' on top of the felt hairs, indicating the difficulty of walking on this substrate. Photograph kindly provided by Simon Tragust.

Figure 2.5: Ants solving the lifeguard problem.
Source: Oettler et al., 2013 / CC-BY.

Let's close with a crazy thought experiment. What would happen if you were suddenly transformed from a slow runner and near-Olympic swimmer to a freakish mix of Usain Bolt and Michael Phelps? Not only are you a really fast swimmer, but you also can run 100 meters in 10 seconds, so your maximum run speed is a blazing 10 m/sec. How does this shock (change in the maximum run speed exogenous variable) affect your decision of how far to run?

STEP Change cell A4 to 10 and run Solver.

Does Solver's new optimal solution make sense when compared to the initial answer?

Takeaways

We introduced and solved the lifeguard problem: To get to a drowning swimmer as quickly as possible, the lifeguard has to choose the best path.

This is a well-known problem in physics and optics because light bends (refracts) when it goes through a different medium, like when it hits water.

There are several different analytical formulas, but we used Solver (a numerical method) to find the fastest path.

We had to implement the problem in Excel, creating an objective function that depended on a changing (endogenous variable) cell and constant (exogenous variable) cells. We then called Solver, and it generated the correct solution.

References

The epigraph of this chapter can be found in section 26-3 of the online edition of Feynman's famous *Lectures on Physics*. He explains what Fermat did and gives the analytical solution. The lectures are freely available from Caltech's website (where he taught for many years): https://www.feynmanlectures.caltech.edu/.

For a fun visualization of the lifeguard problem, see geogebra.org/m/wBcKASpN.

Oettler, J., Schmid, V., Zankl, N., Rey, O., Dress, A., and Heinze, J. (2013). "Fermat's Principle of Least Time Predicts Refraction of Ant Trails at Substrate Borders." PLOS *One*, open access: doi.org/10.1371/journal.pone.0059739.

Pennings, T. (2003). "Do Dogs Know Calculus?" *College Mathematics Journal* 34, no. 3 (May 2003), pp. 178–182, jstor.org/stable/3595798.

Perruchet, P., and Gallego, J. (2006). "Do Dogs Know Related Rates Rather Than Optimization?" *College Mathematics Journal* 37, no. 1 (Jan. 2006), pp. 16–19, www.jstor.org/stable/27646266.

2.2 Visualizing Comparative Statics

When maximum run speed increases from 5 to 10 m/sec, you run longer and dive in after running nearly 80 meters. Thus, you run roughly 23 meters more than when your max speed was 5 m/sec. This is about a 40% increase (=23/56). Running more (and swimming less) makes sense—after all, you are much faster running now that you are a world-class sprinter, so you should take advantage of this.

Changing an exogenous variable while holding everything else constant (called ceteris paribus) is known as *comparative statics analysis*. It is comparative because you are comparing the new to the initial optimal solution, and it is statics because you focus only on the beginning and the end, ignoring any kind of adjustment process (which, if not ignored, would be dynamic analysis).

One way to understand what we are doing is by creating a simple graph to show the optimal solution. The x-axis will be how far we run before diving in, and the y-axis will be the corresponding time.

STEP Using the initial problem (make sure cell A4 is set to 5), enter the labels Distance Run, Distance Swim, and Time to Victim in cells G1, H1, and I1, respectively. Create a series from 0 to 100 by 5 by entering 0 in cell G2, 5 in cell G3, and then filling it down by selecting cells G2 and G3, clicking on the bottom righthand corner of cell G3, and dragging down. In cell H2, enter the formula for the hypotenuse based on the value in cell G2. Fill down. Compute the Time to Victim in cell I2 and fill it down. Check your numbers with Figure 2.6, and if there are any discrepancies, fix your formulas or, if you cannot do it, proceed to the appendix to get help.

Now that we have data for how Time to Victim responds to Distance Run, we can visualize the lifeguard problem by creating a chart. You may know how to make a chart in Excel, but it is worth reviewing basic charting principles before diving in.

STEP Watch this three-minute video on making a chart in Excel: vimeo.com/econexcel/how-to-chart-in-excel.

Selecting data, clicking the desired chart type, and cleaning up the chart are the three steps. Always check the axes and titles and avoid the dreaded "Series 1" legend text like the plague. Stay away from chart junk (wild colors and crazy fonts). Best practice is minimalist—let the data speak for itself (Tufte, 1983).

STEP Make a *Scatter* chart of Time to Victim as a function of Distance Run. Check that your chart looks like Figure 2.6.

Distance Run	Distance Swim	Time to Victim
0	141.4213562	70.71067812
5	137.9311422	69.96557112
10	134.5362405	69.26812024
15	131.2440475	68.62202374
20	128.0624847	68.03124237
25	125	67.5
30	122.0655562	67.03277808
35	119.2686044	66.63430221
40	116.6190379	66.30951895
45	114.1271221	66.06356105
50	111.8033989	65.90169944
55	109.658561	65.8292805
60	107.7032961	65.85164807
65	105.9481005	65.97405025
70	104.4030651	66.20153254
75	103.0776406	66.53882032
80	101.9803903	66.99019514
85	101.1187421	67.55937104
90	100.4987562	68.24937811
95	100.124922	69.06246099
100	100	70

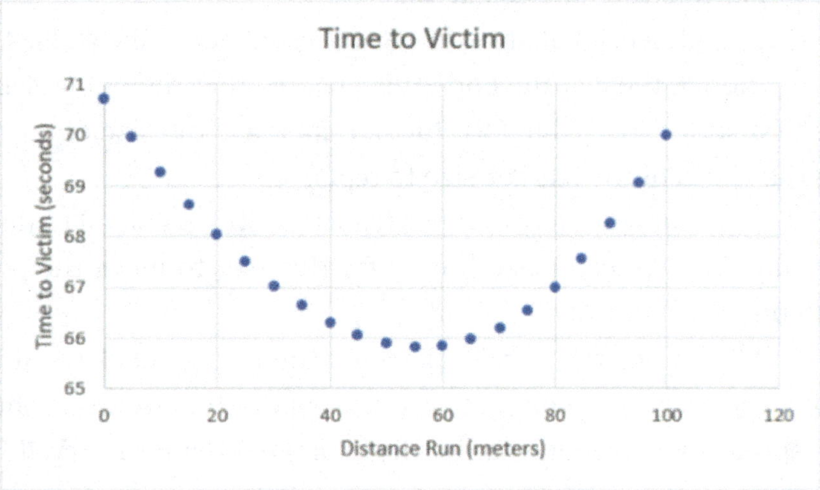

Figure 2.6: Visualizing the lifeguard problem.

Figure 2.6 shows pretty clearly that the optimal solution is at the bottom of the U-shaped Time to Victim function. The lifeguard really does face an optimization problem. Correctly solving it means the lifeguard will get to the drowning person as fast as possible.

We can highlight the optimal solution and learn how to add controls to a spreadsheet. The *Developer* tab needs to be visible on the *Ribbon*. If it is not, click *File*, then click *Options*, then click *Customize Ribbon*, and check the Developer item.

With the *Developer* tab available in the *Ribbon*, we are ready to add a scroll bar. First, we will get a coordinate point, then we will add it to the chart, and finally, we will connect it to a *Scroll Bar* control.

STEP Select cell range G22:I22 and copy (*Ctrl-c*), select cell G24, and paste (*Ctrl-v*). In cell G24, enter the formula =A8 so that we have the optimal solution.

To add this single point to the chart, we will use a powerful, advanced method: We will directly edit the SERIES formula. This approach allows you to easily and quickly reuse or update a chart.

STEP Watch this five-minute video on how to modify the SERIES formula in a chart: vimeo.com/econexcel/using-series-formula.

We can now add the single point to the chart by copying the existing SERIES formula and editing it, replacing the x– and y-axes data with the cell addresses of the single point.

STEP Click on the Time to Victim series (click on one of the points), copy, press the Esc key (to clear the formula bar), click on the northwest corner of the chart, paste, and then edit the SERIES formula so it looks like this:

=SERIES(Sheet1!$I$1,Sheet1!$G$24:$G$24,Sheet1!$I$24:$I$24,2)

Notice the 2 at the end—this ensures that the point is always visible because it is on top of the first series. To highlight it further, increase the size of the point by clicking on it and increasing the width of the marker size to 5 pts.

You can enter any number from 0 to 100 in cell A8 to display that point on the Time to Victim function. We can make it easy for the user to move the point on the chart by adding a scroll bar connected to cell A8.

STEP Click the *Developer* tab on the *Ribbon*, click the down arrow in the Insert button, and select the scroll bar icon (in the top, *Form Control* group) as shown in Figure 2.7. Click and drag on the spreadsheet (roughly under the chart) to create the *Scroll Bar* control.

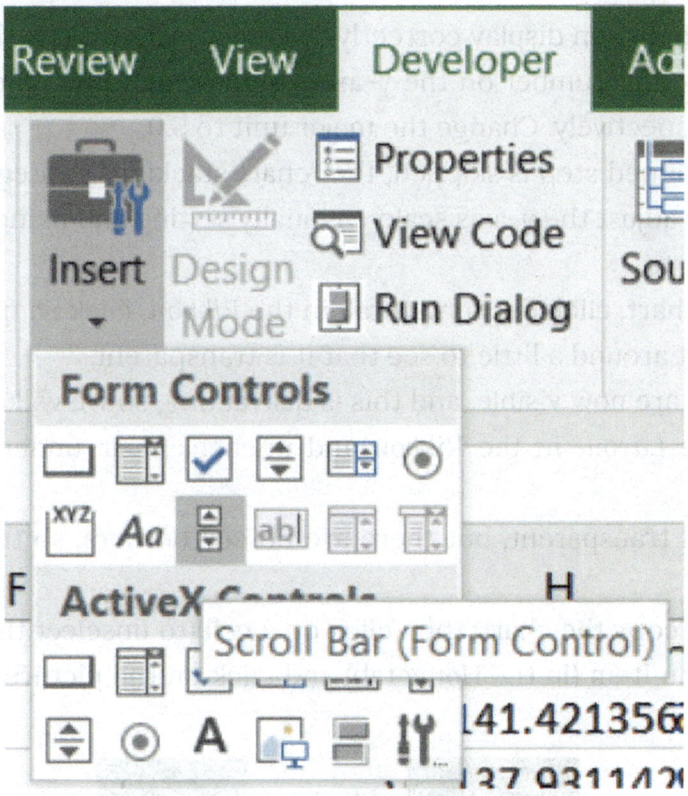

Figure 2.7: Accessing the scroll bar form control.
Source: Screenshot of Excel interface, © Microsoft Corporation.

STEP Right-click the *Scroll Bar* control (that you just created), click the *Control* tab, click in the *Cell link* field, and click cell G24 (it appears in the field). Click OK and click on a cell in the spreadsheet. Click a few times on the scroll bar to make the red dot on the chart move along the Time to Victim function.

You can also click the scroll box itself (sometimes called a thumb) and drag it. You can also manually change the value in cell G24, and the scroll bar box will reflect that value.

STEP Enter the formula =A8 in cell G24 to display the optimal solution and see that the scroll box moves to this value.

We now have a clear display of the optimal solution and understand that it minimizes Time to Victim, but the correct solution depends on the exogenous variables. What happens, for example, when you become Usain Bolt and can run not 5 m/sec but 10 m/sec?

STEP Change cell A4 to 10 and watch what happens.

Excel immediately updates the chart, and the changes are dramatic. It is clear that the function has shifted down, and there is a new minimum to the right of the initial solution.

How can we compare the two situations? One way is by displaying the two environments (initial with 5 m/sec and new with 10 m/sec) on the same chart. We can do this with a clever trick that has many applications: Create a transparent image and lay it on top of the chart.

To make the comparison display correctly, we need to lock down the *y*-axis in the chart.

STEP Right-click any number on the *y*-axis, and change the minimum and maximum axis bounds to 55 and 75, respectively. Change the major unit to 5.0.

If the aforementioned step is skipped, the "chart stacking" strategy will not work because Excel will automatically adjust the *y*-axis scale. Manually setting and fixing the scale is a necessary step when stacking charts.

STEP Click the chart, click the *Format* tab in the *Ribbon*, click *Shape Fill*, and select *No Fill*. Click and drag the chart around a little to see that it is transparent.

The cell borders are now visible, and this is distracting, so we will remove them.

STEP Click *Page Layout* in the *Ribbon* and uncheck *View* under *Gridlines* (in the *Sheet Options* group).

The chart is still transparent, but there are no cell borders, so the chart's background is white.

STEP Select and copy the chart, then click on a cell (to unselect the chart). Click the down arrow on the *Paste* menu item (in the *Home* tab) and click on the picture icon as shown in Figure 2.8.

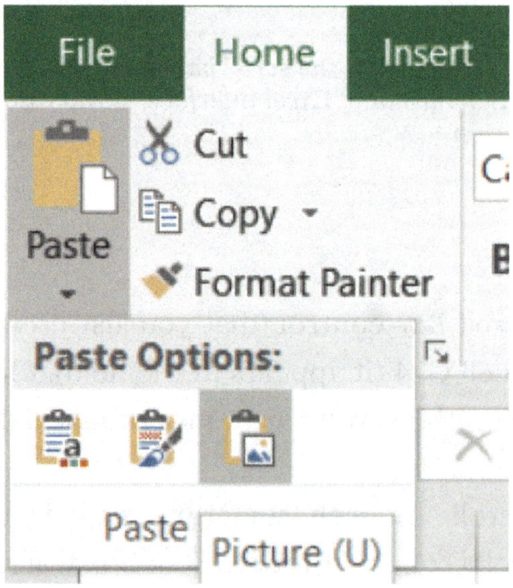

***Figure 2.8*: Pasting as a picture.**
Source: Screenshot of Excel interface, © Microsoft Corporation.

The chart you just pasted is "dead" in the sense that it is a fixed image and is not connected to the data like the original chart. It can be pasted into a doc or slide and will not change even if you alter the data.

STEP Drag the chart you just pasted so it is exactly on top of the live, original chart. Add text boxes to label the initial and new solutions (remove the border and fill of the text boxes to improve the display).

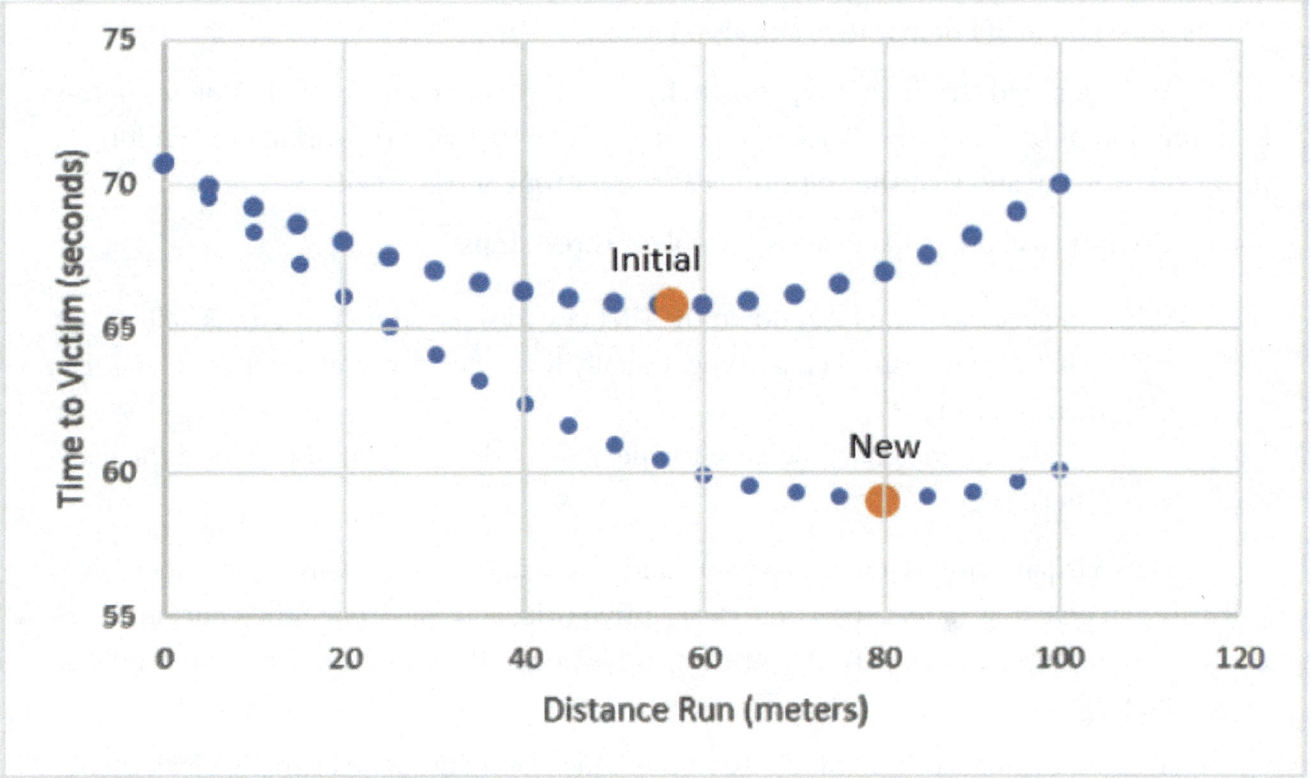

Figure 2.9: Comparative statics visualization.

Your final product should look like Figure 2.9. It clearly shows the impact of the shock to running speed on the lifeguard problem. The entire function shifts down, and the minimum moves to the right.

What other exogenous variables are there in the lifeguard problem that we ignored? Imagine yourself as a real lifeguard on a crowded beach, perched on a chair, looking out over the ocean. What else would influence your decision of where to enter the water?

Takeaways

We shocked the lifeguard problem by changing max run speed from 5 m/sec to 10 m/

sec, ceteris paribus, and found that the optimal distance to run on the sand increased. This is an example of comparative statics analysis.

We visualized the lifeguard problem by creating a chart in Excel of Time to Victim as a function of Distance Run. This made it easy to see that we are working on a minimization problem and that the solution is at the bottom of the bowl.

Creating a chart in Excel always involves three steps:

1. Select the data: Hold down the *Ctrl* key to select noncontiguous cells.
2. Insert the desired chart type: Usually it is a *Scatter* chart, but Excel has many chart types.
3. Clean up the chart: Be sure to check the title, the legend text, and the axes labels.

Data visualization is a mixture of art and science. In Excel, always remember the third step in charting: label axes, add a descriptive title, and make sure the chart is clear and easy to understand. Be sure that the legend is needed and makes sense. A minimalist approach is best.

The bible of chart design is Tufte (1983). This classic preaches simple, clean chart design. Excel allows you to do all kinds of word art and color schemes. You should avoid this.

Excel is complicated software with many features and capabilities. Understanding that a chart is really a SERIES formula is a big step forward. Directly editing the SERIES formula has many powerful applications.

The transparency trick is also quite useful. You are slowly building a library of skills and knowledge. There is not a single, specific thing that makes you an Excel expert. It is like a wall; every brick matters.

References

Barreto, H. (2013, July 2). *How to Chart in Excel* [Video]. Vimeo. vimeo.com/econexcel/how-to-chart-in-excel.

Barreto, H. (2012, March 9). *Using SERIES Formula* [Video]. Vimeo. vimeo.com/econexcel/using-series-formula.

Tufte, E. (1983). *The Visual Display of Quantitative Information* (Cheshire, CT: Graphics Press), open access: archive.org/details/visualdisplayofq0000tuft.

For more on how graphs and data visualization evolved, see Friendly, M., and Wainer, H. (2021). *A History of Data Visualization and Graphic Communication* (Cambridge, MA: Harvard University Press).

Appendix

To replicate Figure 2.6, follow the steps here, but think about the formulas you are entering and what each cell is doing instead of mindlessly typing:

(1) In cell H2, enter the formula =SQRT(($A$2-G2)^2+$A$3^2) and fill it down. Note that if you do not use absolute references (the $ before cell column and row), then the formula does not work when you fill it down.

An absolute reference, like $A$2, means when you copy and paste the cell (or fill it down), the formula remains unchanged and will continue to refer to $A$2. A relative reference, like G2 (no $ signs), means the formula will change because entering =G2 in cell H2 means "the cell one column to the left of this cell."

(2) In cell I2, enter the formula =G2/$A$4+H2/$A$5 and fill it down. Again, note the use of absolute references.

Both formulas were used earlier and neither hard-code the variables—in other words, cell addresses are used instead of numbers. This maximizes spreadsheet flexibility.

Use the *Ctrl* key to select noncontiguous data to make the chart.

2.3 Solver Pros and Cons

We know Solver is a numerical methods (as opposed to analytical) approach to solving an optimization problem. We saw it in action as it minimized the time it takes to reach the victim in the lifeguard problem for running speeds of 5 m/sec and 10 m/sec.

This section is devoted to these two questions:

1. How does Solver actually work?
2. Can we always count on it giving us the correct answer?

The answer to the first question is explored in more detail in the next section, but in a nutshell, Solver hunts and pecks really fast and converges to a solution. The answer to the second question is shorter: no. We will see that Solver can fail in two ways: *miserable* and *disastrous*. It can announce that it cannot find the answer (that is miserable), or worse, it can claim to have an answer that is wrong. This is disastrous because you think it is right, but it is not. The bottom line is that you always need to be on high alert when using Solver—it is not a silver bullet.

How Does Solver Actually Work?

We begin our explanation of how Solver works with a simple profit maximization problem. A firm sells its product at \$4/unit, and it has costs of production given by the square of the number of units it produces. So it costs \$9 to make 3 units and \$25 to make 5 units. Since the price is \$4, the firm's revenue function is 4x. If it sells 3 units, it makes \$12, while 5 units generate \$20 of revenue.

The firm seeks to maximize profits (denoted by convention with the Greek letter pi, π), which are equal to revenues minus costs. The following profit function says that 3 units produce \$3 of profit (\$12 of revenue minus \$9 of costs), and 5 units leave the firm with a loss of \$5, since 20 - 25 = -5.

$$\underset{x}{max}\pi = 4x - x^2$$

If you know calculus, you could solve this problem analytically by taking the derivative with respect to x, setting it equal to zero, and solving for x^*. But even without calculus, the solution is obvious if you tabulate (a single-entry table that lists the values of a function at discrete points) and graph the profit function.

STEP Create data and make a chart of the profit function with the x-axis going from 0 to 5 in increments of 0.5. If you have trouble, see the appendix.

Both the data you created and the corresponding chart show that the answer is $x^* = 2$, leading to maximum profits of $4. Can Solver also find the optimal solution? Yes, it can.

STEP Use cell A17 for x, and enter the profit formula in cell A18. Next, call Solver and fill in the dialog box and click *Solve*. Again, if you have trouble, see the appendix.

As expected, Solver finds the optimal solution, but how does Solver do it? In a word, *iteration*, which means repetition. Solver runs the following three steps over and over until it cannot improve much:

1. Using the starting value in cell A17 (this is zero if left blank), it evaluates cell A18.
2. It then moves away from the starting value. The amount it moves is determined by the particular recipe—a popular one (and Solver's default) is called Newton-Raphson steepest descent.
3. It compares the new value of profits to the original. If profits are higher, it continues in that direction. If lower, it goes in the opposite direction.

Solver continues iterating, changing cell A17 and checking how profits respond, until the improvement in profits is "small," an amount determined by the convergence criterion. The last change it made to cell A17 is the answer.

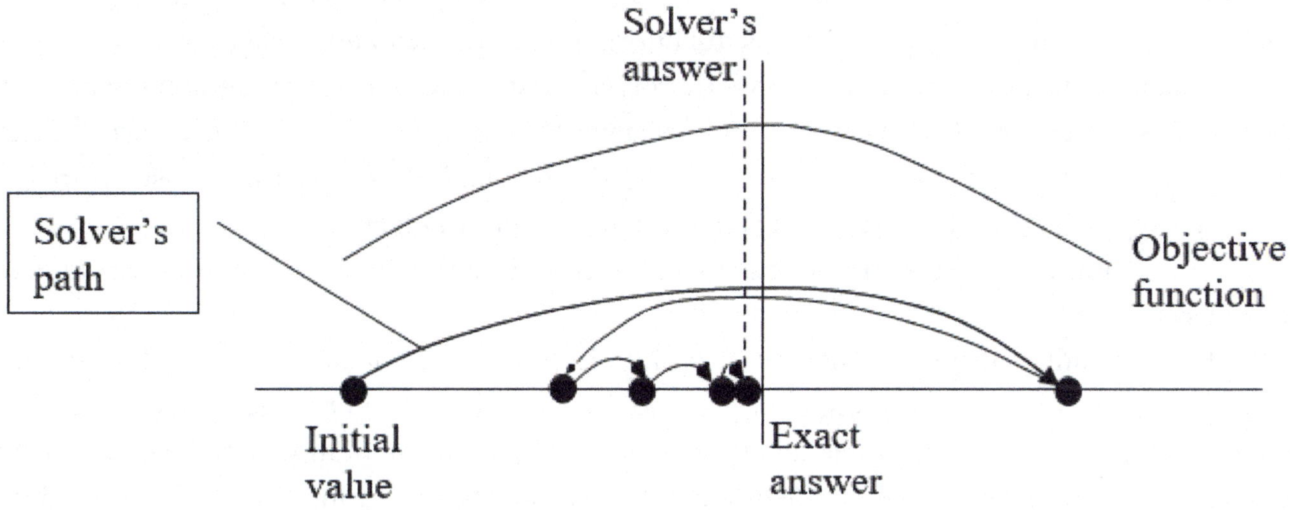

Figure 2.10: Solver in action.

The *stylized graph* (which means it represents an idea without using actual data) in Figure

2.10 shows that Solver works by trying different values and seeing how much improvement occurs. The path of the choice variable (on the x-axis) is determined by Solver's internal optimization algorithm. See FrontlineSolvers at https://www.solver.com/excel-solver-online-help to learn more about Excel's Solver.

When Solver takes a step that improves the value of the objective function by very little, determined by the convergence criterion (adjustable via the Options button), it stops searching and announces success. In Figure 2.10, Solver is missing the optimal solution by a little bit because, if we zoomed in on the graph, the objective function would be almost flat at the top. When Solver computes minuscule additional improvement, it stops and announces it has found a solution.

This is all too abstract. Let's see it in action.

STEP Set cell A17 to 1.1 and widen column A to make sure it displays many decimal points. Call Solver, but this time, click the Options button and check *Show Iteration Results* (in the *All Methods* tab). Click *Solve*. Click *Continue* as many times as needed and watch the values on the spreadsheet.

Excel displays each trial solution. Solver might (this is not guaranteed) even hit 2 as a trial solution, but then it moves off it because it does not know this is the exactly correct answer.

It is quite likely that, starting from 1.1, Solver's answer is not exactly 2. You might have a result like this: 1.99999999467892. When we say Solver got the answer, we mean this in a practical sense. If Solver is off from the exact answer by a tiny amount, that is success, for all practical purposes.

There is a danger to avoid when using Solver (or any numerical optimization method that relies on convergence): It is easy to conclude that Solver must give an exact answer because it displays so many decimal places. This is incorrect. Solver's solution is an example of *false precision*. It is not true that the many digits provide useful information. The exact answer is 2.

Usually, Solver does not find the exactly correct answer, yet it displays a number with many digits. This is *Solver noise* (a less technical way of saying "false precision"). You must learn to interpret Solver's results as inexact and not report all the decimal places. You must use words like *roughly* or *approximately* when reporting answers produced by Solver.

In general, there are two reasons for really tiny disagreements between Solver and the exact answer.

1. Excel cannot display a number to an infinite number of decimal places. Most modern Excel software has 15 significant digits of precision. If the solution is a repeating decimal or irrational number, there is no exact decimal representation. Even if the number can be expressed as a decimal—for example, one-half is 0.5—precision error may occur during the computation of the final answer.

STEP Click in any cell and enter the formula =pi(). Now select the cell displaying π and add decimal places by repeatedly clicking the Increase Decimal button , in the *Home* tab of the *Number* group in the *Ribbon*. When Excel displays "######," it means the number does not fit in the column, so you need to widen the column. Keep adding decimal places until you start seeing zeroes. You have reached Excel's maximum precision.

2. Even if the answer is an integer, like 2, Excel's Solver often misses the exactly correct answer by small amounts. Solver's convergence criterion (that you can set via the Options button in the *Solver Parameters* dialog box) determines when it stops hunting for a better answer. Excel treats all numbers the same—it has no way of saying, "Oh, that's really close to 2, so the answer must be 2."

False precision or Solver noise is a serious issue. Be aware that Solver's answer is likely not the exactly right answer. There are other ways in which Solver can fail us that are more serious than misunderstanding precision.

Solver Behaving Badly

A *miserable result* (an actual technical term in the numerical methods literature) occurs when an algorithm reports that it cannot find the answer or displays an obviously erroneous solution. We can easily create an example.

STEP Copy your existing sheet (right-click the sheet tab in the bottom left-hand corner, select *Move or Copy . . .* and check *Create a copy*). Select cell B2 and delete the -A2^2 part of the formula so you have only =4*A2. Fill down.

The chart updates and you have a straight line. You are graphing total revenue now instead of profits.

STEP Select cell A18 and change the formula to =4*A17 (just like you did to the chart). Call Solver and click *Solve*.

You are looking at a miserable result. Solver cannot find a solution, so it announces (loudly, with a red exclamation mark) that it cannot find an answer.

In this case, that is actually reasonable. After all, this function does not have a well-defined maximum, unless you want to argue that the answer is positive infinity.

Solver will also give a message like this if it cannot perform a computation such as dividing by zero or taking the square root of a negative number. The algorithm fails, which is bad news, but at least it tells you that it cannot solve the problem.

When Solver fails like this, there are three basic strategies to get Solver to find a solution (but nothing is guaranteed):

1. Try different initial values in the changing cells. If you know roughly where the solution lies, start near it. Always avoid starting from zero or a blank cell.
2. Add more structure to the problem. Include nonnegativity constraints on the endogenous variables, if appropriate.

3. Completely reorganize the problem. Instead of directly optimizing, you can put Solver to work on conditions that must be met.

None of these approaches will work on this problem because it does not have a solution.

There is a second way in which Solver can behave badly, and it is much worse than a miserable result. Solver can give an answer that is wrong, yet it thinks it is right and reports it as the solution. This is called a *disastrous result*. Again, we can create an example to demonstrate this.

Our example requires use of a more complicated cost function. Instead of the simple square we used earlier, we will use a cubic cost function, ax^3+bx^2+cx. By strategically choosing the coefficients a = 1, *b*= −8, and c = 19, we can get a cost curve that will give us a profit function with a trough and a peak, like a sine wave:

$$\max_x \pi = 4x - \left(\left(x^3 - 8x^2 + 19x\right)\right) = 4x - x^3 + 8x^2 - 19x$$

STEP Copy the original sheet again. Change cell B2's formula so it looks like this: =4*A2-A2^3+8*A2^2-19*A2. Fill it down.

The graph updates and now has a clear maximum near *x* = 4 but also has a valley as we increase output starting from zero. Can Solver find the optimal solution with this more complicated cost function?

STEP Edit cell A18 so that it uses the new profit function. The formula should look like this: =4*A17-A17^3+8*A17^2-19*A17. Call Solver and click *Solve*. How did it do?

If you started from the original sheet's optimal solution (x = 2) or near the maximum, then Solver will work fine. Notice that Solver's answer is a little higher than 4, and remember that Solver's answer is not the exact optimal solution, but it is really close (off by 0.000001 or so).

STEP Change cell A17 to 1 and run Solver. What happens now?

You just saw a disastrous result. Solver said it got an answer, but it is wrong. Your spreadsheet is showing that cell A17 is zero, but we know the correct solution is a little over 4. This is really bad and shows that we must always be skeptical of Solver. It is not a silver bullet, and mindless reliance on its output is a recipe for disaster.

Can you figure out why Solver failed?

STEP To help you, look at the chart and remember that we started from *x* = 1. Force your eyes to follow a straight line down from 1 (on the horizontal axis). You can see that you are to the left of the minimum of the profit function.

The fact that we are on a downward-sloping part of the profit function explains why Solver failed. It started from there, and the algorithm led it away from the true max (x becoming smaller) because profits rise (become less negative) as *x* decreases.

We can see that starting from near the maximum generates a good result because the function is a hill around the maximum. Moving away leads you to lower profits so the algorithm can find the correct solution.

STEP Start from 7 (set cell A17 to 7) and run Solver to see that starting values around the top of the hill enable Solver to succeed.

Will any starting value far away from zero work?

STEP Start from 100, then try 10.

This is surprising. If you start too far from the maximum, Solver takes a big first step that leads it to the wrong answer. Notice, however, that Solver does not give any indication that something may be wrong. To be clear, with a disastrous result, the computer's answer is incorrect, but you have no way of knowing this. That means you always have to be skeptical and vigilant when using Solver.

Unlike a miserable result, where we know we have a problem, a disastrous result tricks us into thinking all is well. Even when Solver says it has an answer, you should question it. Try starting from a different place to see if you get the same answer. Always ask yourself if the answer makes sense. Be careful out there.

Takeaways

Solver is an example of a search algorithm. It works by exploring the objective function, like an ant crawling on a surface. If movement in a certain direction improves things, then it keeps going that way. Moves that generate worse results lead to it reversing course.

Usually, this is an effective method. Many problems have solutions that can be found by numerical methods, using a computer to plug and chug through the problem.

Even when Solver finds the solution, always remember that its answer is not likely to be exactly correct. Solver usually suffers from what is formally known as false precision (and we call it, intuitively, Solver noise). This means that the last decimal places are not reliable and do not signal exactitude.

You want to be a sophisticated user and understand that, while powerful, Solver is not perfect. It can fail in two ways:

1. A miserable result is when Solver surrenders and announces that it cannot find an answer. This is disappointing.
2. A disastrous result is much worse. Solver says it has an answer, but it is wrong.

This happens when you have a difficult problem, perhaps like asking an ant to find the highest point on a crumpled piece of paper. It is likely to find a local maximum but not a true, global max.

Solver is a tool, like a chain saw. You can use it to cut down and trim trees really fast. You can also cut your leg off with it. Be careful.

Appendix

Charting the Profit Function

To make a chart of the profit function, begin with x-axis data. Create a label in cell A1 by entering the letter x. Below it, enter a 0, then a 0.5 below that. Select both cells, then fill down to cell A12, which should display 5.

For the y-axis, enter the label, *profits*, in cell B1. In the cell below it, enter the formula =4*A2-A2^2. Fill it down. Format the profit values as $.

Select the data and make a *Scatter* chart. Remember to add labels for the axes and an appropriate title. Your chart should look like Figure 2.11.

Using Solver to Find the Optimal Solution

Enter the labels in cells B17 and B18 shown in Figure 2.11. Enter the formula =4*A17-A17^2 in cell A18. Call Solver (click the *Data* tab in the *Ribbon* and click *Solver*), then click on cell A18 for the objective function and cell A17 for the changing cells (as shown in Figure 2.11). Click *Solve* and click OK when Solver displays its *Results* dialog box.

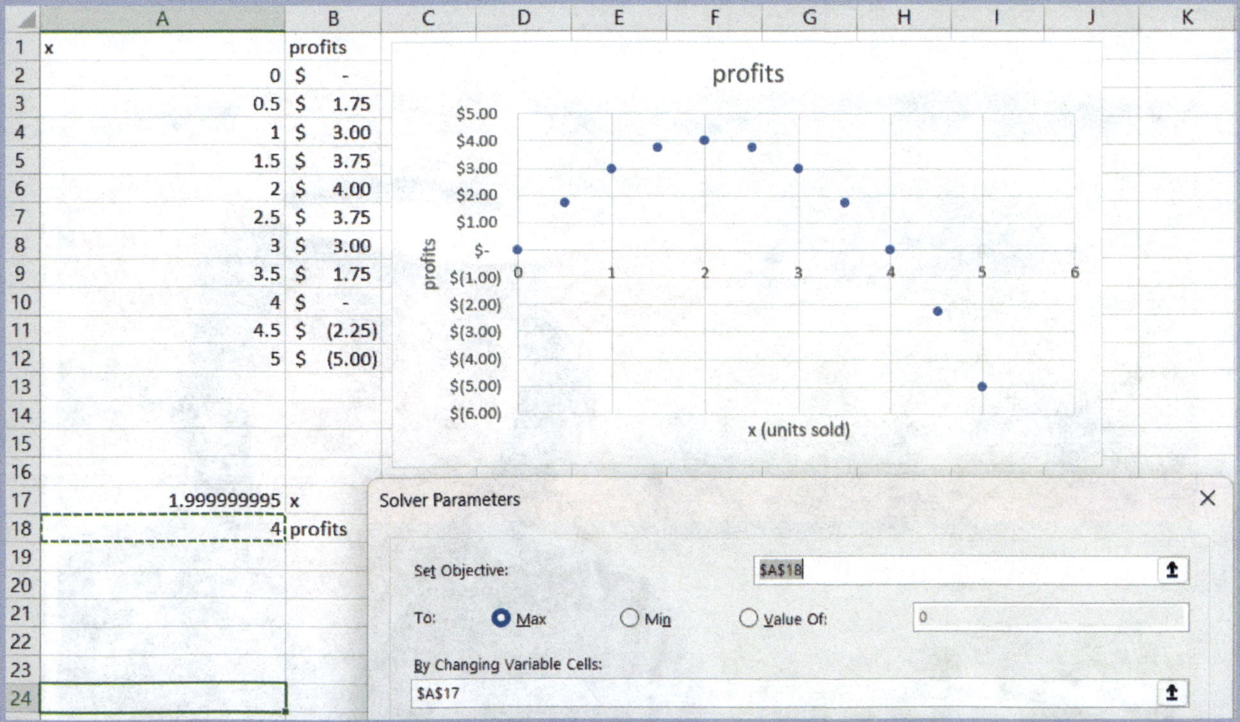

Figure 2.11: Tabulating and charting 4x – x2.
Source: Screenshot of Excel interface, © Microsoft Corporation.

2.4 Profit Maximization Practice Problem

Figure 2.12: Computer-generated image of a farmer.
Source: Stable Diffusion, 2023/ License.

You are a farmer. You buy seed, do a lot of work (till the soil, plant, irrigate, fertilize, and control weeds), then harvest and sell your crop. To keep the optimization problem simple, we assume away almost all of this and ignore all labor, all machinery, and any other costs except seed.

In our toy model, you simply buy seed, S, and it is transformed into output—say, corn—via the function $Q = 100\sqrt{S}$. For example, 64 pounds of seed makes

800 pounds of corn, 100 times the square root of 64. This functional form reflects the fact that you have a fixed amount of land, so planting twice as much seed less than doubles the amount of corn. The square root means that more seed increases output, but at a decreasing rate.

You sell your output at the market-given price, P, of \$8 per pound. You cannot sell at a price higher than this because there are many other farmers willing to sell at \$8 per pound, so no one would buy your harvest at a price above the market price. To be clear, 1,000 pounds of corn generates \$8,000 of total revenue.

The seed costs you \$2 per pound. You can buy as much seed as you want at this price, so your total cost function is linear, $TC = \$cS$, where c is the input price of seed. The total cost function tells us that, for example, 200 pounds of seed has a total cost of \$400.

You want to buy the amount of seed that maximizes profits, which is total revenues minus total costs. You can see that choosing 100 pounds of seed will get you \$8,000 - \$200 = \$7,800 of profits.

The question, however, is whether or not that's the best amount of seed to buy—in other words, is 100 pounds of seed the profit-maximizing solution? The following questions will lead you to an answer to this question and help reinforce what you know about Solver, data visualization, and comparative statics analysis.

STEP Open a blank Excel workbook and save it with an appropriate file name. Answer the following questions in the spreadsheet, saving the file after each question (in case there is a crash or other problem). For questions that require explanation, put your response in a text box (in the *Insert* tab on the *Ribbon*) with the question number.

1. What is the endogenous variable in this problem? Why is it endogenous?
2. Put the values for the output price of corn and the input price of seed in two cells with labels next to them.
3. Implement this problem in Excel so that it is ready for Solver to work on it. You do this by adding other information in cells in addition to the cells you have from the previous question.
4. Use Solver to get the optimal solution.
5. The exactly correct answer is 40,000 pounds of seed with maximum profits of \$80,000. Since Solver does not give this exactly correct answer, do we say it is wrong? Explain.
6. Create a chart that displays the optimal solution.
7. What are the three steps in creating a chart in Excel? Did you do all three steps in the chart you made?
8. We know Solver can give miserable or disastrous results. What do these terms mean?

9. Does your chart give you confidence that Solver is not giving a disastrous result in this case? Explain.
10. Conduct a comparative statics analysis of changing the output price. Explain what you did and what you found.

RAND()

For the last question, you can change the output price to any number you choose, but you could also use Excel to generate a random number for the output price using the RAND() function. We will explain and use RAND() in chapter 3, but it is very easy to use and gives you a way to play with the exogenous variables in this problem, so it is worth doing it now.

STEP In any empty cell, enter the formula =RAND() and press *Enter*. Press the F9 key (you may have to use the function, *fn*, key to access F9 on your keyboard) repeatedly to see the number bounce around.

> **EXCEL TIP** The F9 key is a keyboard shortcut for *Calculate Now* in the *Formulas* tab in the *Ribbon*. It recalculates the sheet and updates functions like RAND(), thereby displaying a new random number.
>
> You cannot run Solver with an objective function that depends on RAND() because every time Solver puts down a trial solution, the cell with RAND() would recalculate. There are, however, several ways to "deaden" RAND() and turn it into a number. Perhaps the easiest uses the F9 key when you are in the formula bar of the cell.

STEP Copy your RAND() cell and paste it into another empty cell. Press F9 repeatedly to see two bouncing numbers. Select one of the cells with RAND() and then click in the formula bar. Press F9 and then *Enter*.

You replaced the formula in that cell with a single number that will no longer change when the sheet recalculates. You could create a cell formula for the output price like =RAND()*4+6 to generate random output prices from 6 to 10. You could get a specific, unchanging price by entering the formula bar of that cell and pressing F9. You can make many practice problems with different output prices with this method.

3. Monte Carlo Simulation

> Anyone who considers arithmetical methods of producing random digits is, of course, in a state of sin.
>
> John von Neumann

3.1 Free Throw Shooting with MCSim

You are the new kid on the block, and it is time to choose teams at the rec center. You think you are pretty good, so you say, "I'm a 90% free throw shooter." This is quite impressive. Someone hands you a basketball and says, "Prove it."

You shoot 100 free throws, but it does not go as well as you hoped. You make only 75. Someone says, "You are not a 90% free throw shooter." You insist, however, that you really are. "It was just bad luck. Honestly," you say, "I really am a 90% free throw shooter."

The question is, Should we believe you? Anyone who has ever shot free throws knows there is luck involved. We would not expect you to make 9 out of every 10 shots like clockwork. So it could be that by chance, you missed a few more than expected. Another way to ask the question is, Can randomness explain this poor outcome? Or, in yet other words, how uncommon is missing this many free throws for a 90% shooter?

We would not be having this conversation if you had made 89 or even 88 out of 100. Then it would be easy to believe you are actually a 90% shooter and it was just bad luck. But how do we handle the fact that you missed 15 more than expected? That seems like a lot, but how rare is that?

There is a way to answer this question analytically—that is, with mathematics. We will not go that route. Instead, we will use the method of simulation.

Monte Carlo simulation simply means the repeated running of a chance process and then direct examination of the results. It can be used in frontier research work, but we will use it just like we used numerical methods to solve optimization problems—simulation enables us to understand complicated concepts without advanced mathematics.

Monte Carlo simulation is based on brute force—repeat the chance process and examine the results. It requires no imagination or mathematics at all. It will be our go-to method for understanding randomness and answering questions like, "Do we believe you are a 90% free throw shooter if you make only 75 out of 100?"

Gauss and Two Approaches

Carl Friedrich Gauss (1777–1855) was perhaps the greatest mathematician of all time. Before the euro, Germany's 10 deutsche mark note featured him along with a graph of the normal curve (which he made famous, called the Gaussian distribution). Look carefully in Figure 3.1 and you can see that it even displays the equation of the normal distribution.

Figure 3.1: German currency featuring Gauss.
Source: YavarPS on Wikimedia / CC BY-SA 4.0.

There is a story, probably apocryphal, of how he amazed his kindergarten teacher. Apparently, the children were especially unruly one day, so the teacher assigned a dreary problem as punishment. He told them to add all the numbers from 1 to 1,000. This starts easily but gets tedious and painful pretty quickly. 1 + 2 = 3, 3 + 3 = 6, 4 + 6 = 10, and 5 + 10 = 15. It will take a long time to get to 1,000.

Gauss waited a minute, then stood up and announced the answer: 500,500. The stunned teacher asked him where he got that number, which is correct, and Gauss said he noticed a pattern. Remember, he was five years old.

If you make a list of the numbers, then create a second list, but flipped, the pairs always add up to 1,001: 1 goes with 1,000, 2 with 999, 3 with 998, and so on until the end, when 998 is with 3, 999 with 2, and 1 with 1,000.

The rest is easy (well, maybe not for the usual five-year-old, but this is Gauss). Multiply 1,001 by 1,000 (since there are 1,000 pairs) and divide by 2 to get 500,500. As they say, QED.

This is clever, remarkable, and beautiful. It is like Michelangelo and the Sistine Chapel. Is Monte Carlo simulation like this? No.

Monte Carlo simulation is a different approach to problems that uses little creativity or subtlety. It is a direct attack on a question.

Monte Carlo simulation is like solving the teacher's tedious problem by using a spreadsheet to add the numbers.

STEP Make a list from 1 to 1000 in cells A1:A1000 (using fill down, of course), and then, in cell B1, enter the formula =SUM(A1:A1000).

Excel displays 500,500. This is nowhere as magnificent as what Gauss did, but it does give the answer.

Monte Carlo simulation was developed during World War II by physicists working on the Manhattan Project. Nicholas Metropolis coined the term because his colleague, Stanislaw Ulam, was an avid poker player. They were simulating how radiation propagates and incorporating randomness. The connection to chance and gambling is why Metropolis named the method after the famous Monte Carlo casino in Monaco.

So Monte Carlo simulation, or "simulation" for short, is an alternative to the analytical approach. Instead of using equations and algebraic manipulations, simulation uses computers to repeat the chance process many times and then directly observe the outcomes.

You can think of simulation as the much younger sibling of analytical methods. Let's apply it to free throw shooting to show how it works.

Are You Really a 90% Shooter?

Our solution strategy will be simulation, but make no mistake: Gauss would not have needed simulation. He would have immediately rejected your claim. He knows a formula can be used, $\sqrt{n}\sigma$, that answers the question quickly. The formula is the product of sophisticated mathematics and can be called beautiful, but most people find it extremely difficult to understand and cannot use it to answer the question.

All Monte Carlo simulations use a random number generator (RNG). Excel's RNG function is RAND(). This draws uniformly distributed random numbers in the interval from zero to one.

STEP Insert a sheet in your Excel workbook and, in cell A1, enter the formula =RAND().

You see a number with several decimal places displayed that is between zero and one. The number is actually much longer.

STEP Widen the column and add decimal places to see this. Keep adding decimal places (widening column A as needed) until you start seeing zeroes.

As you learned when we explained Solver's false precision, most modern spreadsheets use 64-bit double-precision floating point format. If you count carefully, you will see that RAND() has a zero, then a decimal point, and then 15 decimal places with values from zero to nine. After that, they are all zero, so we have reached the maximum precision. It is important to understand that our spreadsheet's random number is finite but also that it has many more decimal digits than what was originally displayed.

STEP Repeatedly press F9 (you may have to hold down the *fn* key on your keyboard). F9 is the keyboard shortcut to recalculate the sheet.

The number in cell A1 changes each time you recalculate the sheet. This is the beating heart of the simulation.

The bouncing numbers show that although RAND() is finite, it has a massive set of numbers to choose from. If it had only one decimal place, RAND() would have 10 possible numbers (from 0.0, 0.1, 0.2, and so on until 0.9). Six decimal places would give it 1 million different numbers. Twelve gives a trillion numbers. Fifteen is a quadrillion!

So you can think of RAND() as plucking a number from a humongous box with a quadrillion numbers in it.

Full disclosure: This is not exactly right because RAND() is using an algorithm to produce the next number. This is why computer-generated random numbers are called *pseudorandom*, where the prefix *pseudo* means "false."

To model a 90% free throw shooter, we use an IF statement.

STEP In cell B1, enter the formula =IF(A1<0.9, 1, 0).

The IF function has three arguments (or inputs) separated by commas. The first argument is the test, the second is what happens if the test is true (or yes), and the third is what happens if it is false (or no). If the random number in cell A1 is less than 90%, then cell B1 shows a one, which means the free throw was made; otherwise, it shows a zero, which means it was missed.

Some students (usually really smart, careful ones) obsess about whether A3 should be less than (<) or less than or equal to (≤) 90%. This does not matter because RAND() has so many random numbers available to it. The chances of drawing exactly 0.900000000000000 are ridiculously small.

When the IF function evaluates to 1, the free throw is made, and when it is 0, it is missed. This is a binomial random variable, since it can only take on two values, 0 or 1.

We do not need to actually see the random number generated, so we can embed RAND() directly in the IF statement.

STEP In cell B2, enter the formula =IF(RAND()<0.9,1,0). Fill down this formula to cell B100. Press F9 a few times to see the 0 and 1 values bouncing around.

We have implemented the *data generation process* (DGP) in Excel. The DGP tells us how our data are produced.

STEP Rename the sheet (double-click on the sheet tab) DGP and save the workbook as *FreeThrowSim*.

As you scroll back up to the top row, you will see many ones and a few zeroes. With a 90% success rate, roughly 1 in 10 cells will have a random number greater than 0.9 and, therefore, show a 0.

The fact that each cell in column B stands alone and does not depend on or influence other cells means we are assuming *independence*. In our model, a miss or make does not affect the chances of hitting the next shot.

If you believe in the hot hand (Cohen, 2020), this implementation of the chance process is wrong. If making the previous shot increases the chances of making the current shot, there is *autocorrelation*, and we cannot use 0.9 as the threshold value for every shot. We assume independence from one shot to the next.

How many shots out of 100 will a 90% shooter make?

STEP Enter the formula =SUM(B1:B100) in cell C1 and the label *Number made* in cell D1.

You will see a number around 90 in cell C1. Each press of F9 gives you the result of a new outcome from 100 attempted free throws.

The number of made free throws from the virtual shooter you have constructed in Excel is not always exactly 90 because you incorporated RAND() in each shot.

STEP Use your keyboard shortcut, F9, to recalculate the sheet a few times to get a sense of the variability in the number of made shots from 100 free throws.

There is no doubt that the number of made shots is a random variable, since it is bouncing around when you recalculate the sheet. It makes common sense that adding 100 bouncing numbers will produce a random outcome.

A *statistic* is a recipe for the data. Cell C1 is a sample statistic because the recipe is to add up the results from a sample of 100 shots. We are interested in the distribution of the sum of 100 free throws from a 90% free throw shooter, including its central tendency, dispersion, and shape of a histogram of outcomes. With this, we can decide if a result of 75 made shots is merely unlikely or so rare that we reject the claim that you are a 90% shooter.

Simulation is simply repeating the experiment many times so we can approximate the center, dispersion, and distribution of the outcomes. Since we are working with a sample statistic, the distribution of the sum of 100 free throws is called a *sampling distribution*.

To process the many outcomes, we need software. A free Excel add-in that does Monte Carlo simulation is available here: dub.sh/addins.

STEP Download the *MCSim.xla* file from the link above and use the Add-ins Manager (File → Options → Add-ins → Go) to install it. Click the *Add-ins* tab and click *MCSim*.

EXCEL TIP The keyboard shortcut to call the Add-ins Manager is *Alt, t, i* (press these keys in order without holding any of them down).

Figure 3.2 shows the MCSim add-in dialog box. On the left are three required choices. You must select a cell to track (C1 in our example), the number of repetitions (the default is 1,000), and the random number generator to use. The MCSim add-in comes with its own RNG, RANDOM. Selecting it will replace all RAND in the sheet with RANDOM. The default is no changes.

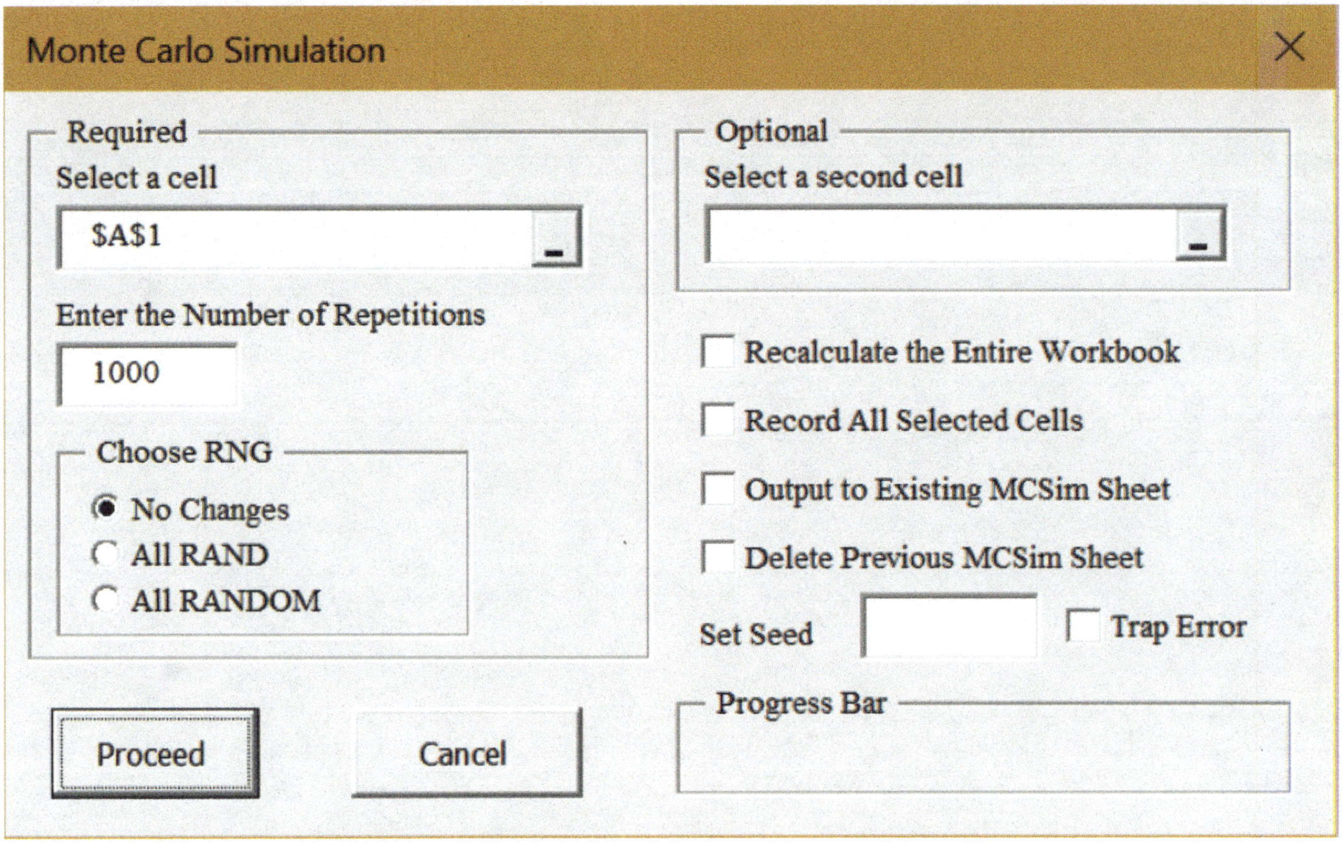

Figure 3.2: The Monte Carlo simulation Excel add-in.
Source: Screenshot of Excel interface, © Microsoft Corporation. Add-in by H. Barreto.

On the right are some advanced options. Some of these will be used in future work. The Set

Seed option forces the RNG to begin from the same initial position, which allows for replication of results.

STEP Click in the *Select a cell* box, clear it, and click cell A1 (displaying RAND()). Click in the *Set Seed* box and enter 123. Click *Proceed.*

A new sheet is inserted in the workbook. It shows the first 100 outcomes in column B, summary statistics, and a histogram. It is roughly, but not exactly, a rectangle. If you ran more repetitions, it would be less jagged.

STEP Return to the DGP sheet and repeat the simulation of cell A1.

The results are exactly the same as before because the *Set Seed* option started the RNG from the same initial value.

STEP Return to the DGP sheet and click the MCSim button in the *Add-ins* tab. Select cell C1 (the sum of made free throws) and clear the *Set Seed* box. Click *Proceed.*

Figure 3.3 shows the results. Yours will be different because we cleared the *Set Seed* box. However, your results will be quite close in the sense that your average is near 90 and the standard deviation (SD) is around 3.

Summary Statistics		Notes
Average	89.955	
SD	3.1523	
Max	98.000	
Min	78.000	

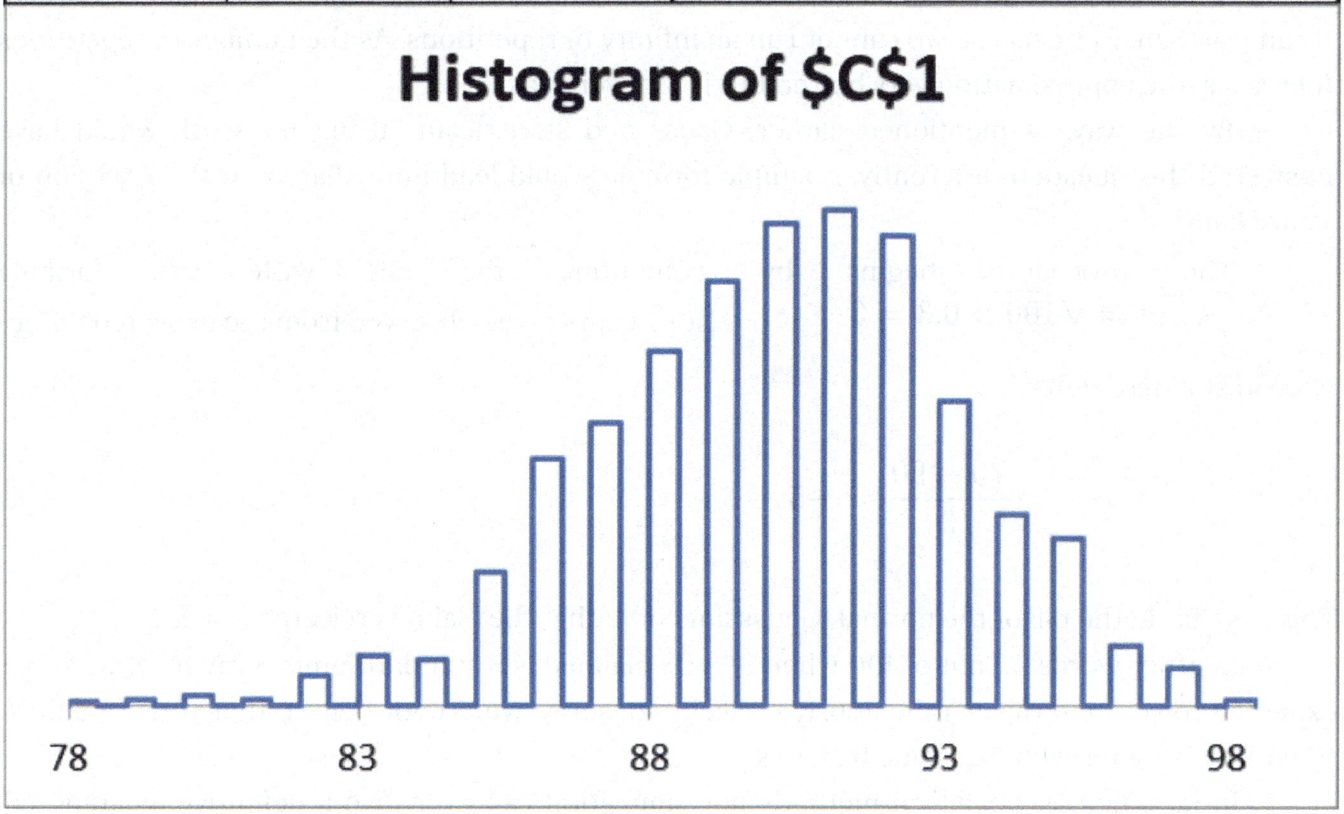

Figure 3.3: Simulation results for sum of 100 attempts from a 90% shooter.

The average and SD are approximations of their true exact analogues, the expected value (EV) is exactly 90, and the standard error (SE) is exactly 3. The EV is the center of the sampling distribution, while the SE is the typical deviation, or bounce, in the statistic.

We would say that we expect a 90% free throw shooter to make 90 out of 100 attempts, plus or minus 3 free throws. The plus or minus is critical because it tells us the variability in the number of made free throws.

The sim also shows the maximum and minimum shots made from 100 free throws in 1,000 repetitions. In Figure 3.3, the max is 98 and the min is 78.

This gives an answer to our question. In 1,000 repetitions, the worst a 90% shooter did was 78. It certainly looks like you are not a 90% free throw shooter.

What if we did more repetitions?

STEP Run a simulation of 10,000 sets of 100 free throws.

Once again, you are unlikely to see 75 or fewer. It seems the bad luck defense is not going to work. While it is possible that you really are a 90% free throw shooter and had an incredibly unlikely run of bad luck, such an outcome is incredibly rare—so rare, in fact, that we do not believe your claim to be a 90% free throw shooter.

The average and SD values changed a little with the second simulation. This shows that simulation always gives an approximate answer with some variability. Simulation can never give us an exact answer because we cannot run an infinity of repetitions. As the number of repetitions increases, the approximation gets better, but it is never exact.

By the way, as mentioned earlier, Gauss and statisticians using his work would have answered this question differently. A simple formula would lead immediately to the rejection of your claim.

The procedure begins by computing the SE with the formula $\sqrt{n}\sigma = \sqrt{100} \times 0.3 = 3$. Next, express the observed from the expected difference in standard units:

$$\frac{75 - 90}{3} = -5$$

This is so far in the tail of the normal (Gaussian) curve that the claim is rejected.

In other words, 75 out of 100 when 90 was claimed is 5 standard units away from what we expected to see, and this is ridiculously unlikely, so, sorry, we do not believe that you are a 90% free throw shooter who had some bad luck.

In fact, neither analytical methods nor simulation can ever give a definitive, guaranteed answer. Both agree that, given the evidence, 75 out of 100 means we do not believe the claim that you are a 90% shooter. Since chance is involved, it is possible that you are a 90% shooter and missed every shot. We are not interested in what is possible. We want to know how to use the evidence to decide whether or not we believe a claim.

If you have taken a statistics course, you might recognize that we are doing hypothesis testing without explicitly saying so. The null is that you are a 90% shooter, and the alternative hypothesis is that you are not. Seventy-five out of 100 produces a test statistic far from the expected 90, so the p-value is really small. Thus, we reject the null.

Max Streak

A second example of simulation involves streaks, also known as runs. A streak in this case is a consecutive set of made shots.

STEP Return to the DGP sheet. Starting from cell B1, find the first 1 (it could be cell B1), and then count how many 1s in a row you see before you encounter a miss. Write that number down and count the next streak. Continue until you reach the 100th shot attempt. The longest streak is the max streak.

The question is, What is the length of the typical max streak in a set of 100 free throws from a 90% free throw shooter?

This is an exceedingly difficult question. It is asking not to count the streaks (also a hard question) but to find the biggest streak in 100 shots. You do not simply add up the number made; you have to find the length of all the streaks and then identify the longest one.

Unlike how many free throws in 100 attempts a 90% shooter will make, you have no easy way to guess the typical max streak. It could be 20, 40, or maybe 50. Who knows? How can we answer this question?

The analytical approach is a bit of a dead end. There are formulas that approximate a solution (Feller, 1968, p. 325), but the math is somewhat complicated. No exact analytical solution has been found.

Simulation can be used if we can figure out a way to ask the question in Excel so that a cell displays the answer. This means simulation requires some ingenuity. We need a cell that computes the max streak so we can use the MCSim add-in. We do this in two steps: first we figure out how to report the current streak, then we use the MAX function to find the longest streak.

STEP In cell E1, enter the formula =B1. In cell E2, enter the formula =IF(B2=1,E1+1,0). Fill it down a few cells.

Now you can see what the formula is doing. If the shot is made, we add it to the previous running sum, but if it is missed, it resets the running sum to 0. The B2=1 part of the formula tests if the current shot is made, and E1 + 1 increases the current streak length by one. The zero means you missed and the streak is now zero.

STEP Fill the formula down to E100 and look at the values as you scroll back up.

You should see several streaks in a set of 100 free throws. We want the longest streak. That is the second step in our implementation of the question in Excel, and it is easy.

STEP In cell F1, enter the formula =MAX(E1:E100) and enter the label *max streak* in cell G1. Press F9 a few times.

Cell F1 displays the max streak from each set of 100 free throws. Max streak is a statistic, just like the sum, because it is a recipe—albeit much more complicated than the sum.

It has an expected value, standard error, and sampling distribution. We can approximate all of these with simulation.

STEP Run a simulation, with 10,000 repetitions, of cell F1.

Figure 3.4 shows the results. Yours will be a little different. The average is an approximate answer to our question: The max streak is about 27 or so. The exact answer is the expected value, but we have no way of computing it.

Summary Statistics		Notes
Average	26.858	
SD	9.5715	
Max	85.000	
Min	9.000	

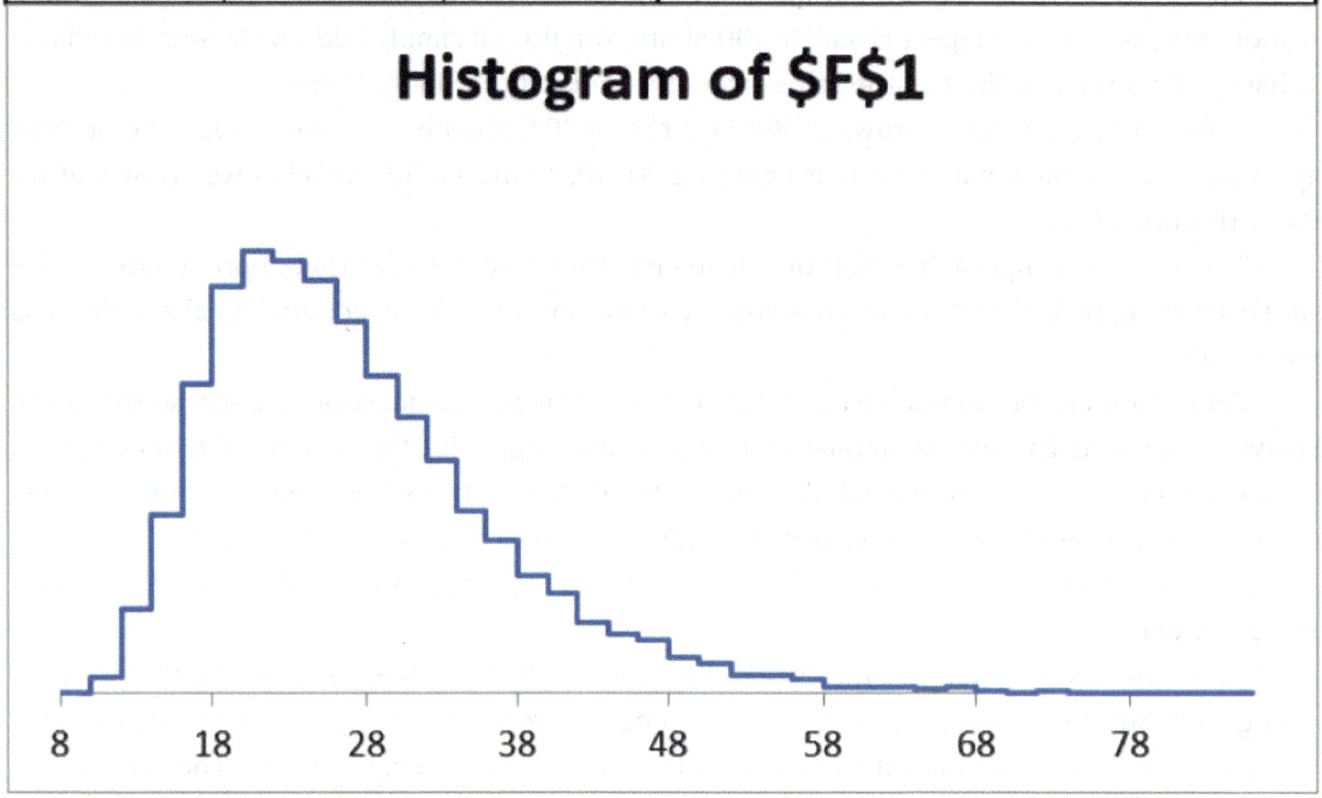

Figure 3.4: Sim results for a max streak in 100 attempts from a 90% shooter.

The histogram is an approximation to the exact sampling distribution (which no one has figured out how to exactly derive). The graph tells us which values are unlikely: roughly 10 or fewer and 50 or more.

Notice that the sampling distribution of the max streak statistic, unlike the sum, does not appear to follow the normal curve. The max streak has a long right tail and is not symmetric.

Takeaways

Sometimes a function or problem is deterministic, but other times we are faced with *stochastic data*—the numbers depend on chance, luck, and randomness. The values we observe are produced by a DGP, and they are volatile.

Monte Carlo simulation is a brute-force approach to answering questions involving stochastic data. A much older alternative, the analytical approach, relies on brainpower to derive formulas.

To run a simulation, the problem must be implemented in Excel (or some software that can generate random numbers). Of course, one can manually flip a coin many times in the real world, but this is tedious. Simulation did not become a powerful tool until modern computers were invented and enabled a great many repetitions in a short period of time.

Simulation is always only an approximation. By running more repetitions, the approximation improves, but it can never give an exact answer because it would have to run forever.

Often, we are searching for the sampling distribution of a statistic. This tells us the chances of each outcome, the typical result (called the expected value), and the dispersion in values (called the standard error, or SE).

The MCSim add-in always produces summary statistics and a histogram. If the cell that is tracked is a statistic, then the average is the approximate expected value and the SD is the approximate SE.

In case you think streaks are a waste of time, look at this headline to an article in *The Wall Street Journal* on July 27, 2023, on page B1:

> Dow Sets Longest Winning Streak Since 87

The Dow's streak of 13 consecutive sessions with gains ended the next day. The longest streak ever (as of this writing) is 14, back in 1897.

References

The epigraph is a famous quote from 1951, when computer science was taking off. In "Various Techniques Used in Connection with Random Digits" (freely available at https://mcnp.lanl.gov/pdf_files/InBook_Computing_1961_Neumann_JohnVonNeumannCollectedWorks_VariousTechniquesUsedinConnectionwithRandomDigits.pdf), von Neumann supported the use of pseudorandom number generation but warned against misinterpreting what these numbers meant. There are many algorithms for random number generation, some are better and others worse. Excel's RAND() is not great.

Cohen, B. (2020). *The Hot Hand: The Mystery and Science of Streaks* (Custom House). Russ Roberts interviews Cohen in an August 10, 2020, episode of EconTalk, available at www.econtalk.org/ben-cohen-on-the-hot-hand.

Feller, W. (1968, 3rd ed.). *An Introduction to Probability Theory and Its Applications* (John Wiley & Sons), archive.org/details/introductiontopr0001fell.

3.2 Simulating Parrondo's Paradox

A paradox is something (such as a situation) with opposing elements that seems impossible but is actually true.

An optical illusion is related to a paradox in that you see something that is not easily explained or can seem impossible. Figure 3.5 is an example. Do you see the old woman, or the young lady, or both? Your age affects what you see in this drawing—older people are more likely to see the old lady (Nicholls et al., 2018).

Figure 3.5: Old woman or young lady?
Source: My Wife and My Mother-In-Law, by the cartoonist W. E. Hill, 1915 / Public domain.

Juan Parrondo is a physicist who discovered the paradox named after him in 1996. Parrondo's Paradox occurs when *two losing games are combined and they produce a winning game.* That is puzzling and counterintuitive.

Almost always, game outcomes are additive, so a losing game plus a losing game equals a losing game just like adding two negative numbers gives an even more negative number. Parrondo found what can be described as a black hole in the parameter space where adding two losers yields a winner.

The paradoxical nature of the result will become apparent when we implement the games in Excel and directly examine the outcomes. Our goal is to show how simulation makes Parrondo's Paradox crystal clear.

Losing Game A

Game A is a coin flip with a slightly negatively biased coin. Heads earns you +1 monetary units (M) and tails −1. The coin is flipped 100 times, and we keep a running sum after each flip. On average, at the end of the game, the result is negative, so we say Game A is a losing game.

STEP In cell A1, enter the label *Game A*. In cell A3, enter the label *epsilon*; and in cell B3, enter the number 0.005. In cell A4, enter the label *p*(H); this is the probability of flipping a head. In cell B4, enter the formula =0.5-B3.

With a probability of heads less than 50%, we will flip heads less often than tails. This is why this game is a loser.

STEP In cell A6, enter the label *Flip #* and create a series from 1 to 100 in cells A7:A106. In cell B6, enter the label *Result*, and in cell B7, enter the formula =IF(RAND()<$B$4,1,0). Fill it down to cell B106.

Column B has our simulated coin flips. We know RAND() is uniformly distributed on the interval [0,1]. It will produce tails slightly more frequently than heads because cell B4<0.5.

We track the money in column C with an IF statement.

STEP In cell C6, enter the label *End M*, and in cell C7, enter the formula =IF(B7=1,1,-1).

The formula for the next cell is different because we have to track how much money we had at the end of the previous flip. Thus, we add the cell above.

STEP In cell C8, enter the formula =IF(B8=1,1,-1)+C7. Fill it down to cell C106. Select C6:C106 and make a *Scatter* chart. Press F9 a few times.

The chart shows the entire game, and cell C106 tells us the outcome of Game A. If it is positive, the game was won; if negative, it was lost. The number tells us how much we won or lost.

We can use the MCSim Excel add-in to examine the sampling distribution of C106. If needed, download and install MCSim from dub.sh/addins.

STEP Select cell range C7:C106 and click MCSim (in the *Add-ins* tab). Check the *Record All*

Selected Cells option and click *Proceed*. The simulation is fast, but Excel may take some time to display the results.

Excel inserts two sheets in the workbook. The MC*Sim* sheet has the result for C7 (the first coin flip), but the MC*Raw* sheet has 1,000 rows and 100 columns of numbers (which is why Excel took so long to display the results).

We can process these numbers to understand Game A. Each row is a game with 100 flips running left to right. Each flip number (column) is called an *ensemble*, and the average of each flip number is called the *ensemble average*.

STEP In cell A1003 of the MC*Raw* sheet, enter the formula =AVERAGE(A2:A1001).

This value will agree exactly with the average in J5 of the MC*Sim* sheet. This value is the average M after one flip. It is slightly negative.

STEP Select cell A1003 in the MC*Raw* sheet and fill it right to the 100th column (CV). With these cells selected, make a chart by clicking *Insert* and choosing *Scatter* with lines and no markers. Title the chart "Flip #" (since the title is right above the x-axis, it labels the axis).

Your chart is an approximation to the exact ensemble average in Figure 3.6. Simulation produces random deviation from the exact object. We could improve the approximation by increasing the number of repetitions. The squiggly graph in the simulation would converge to the line in Figure 3.6.

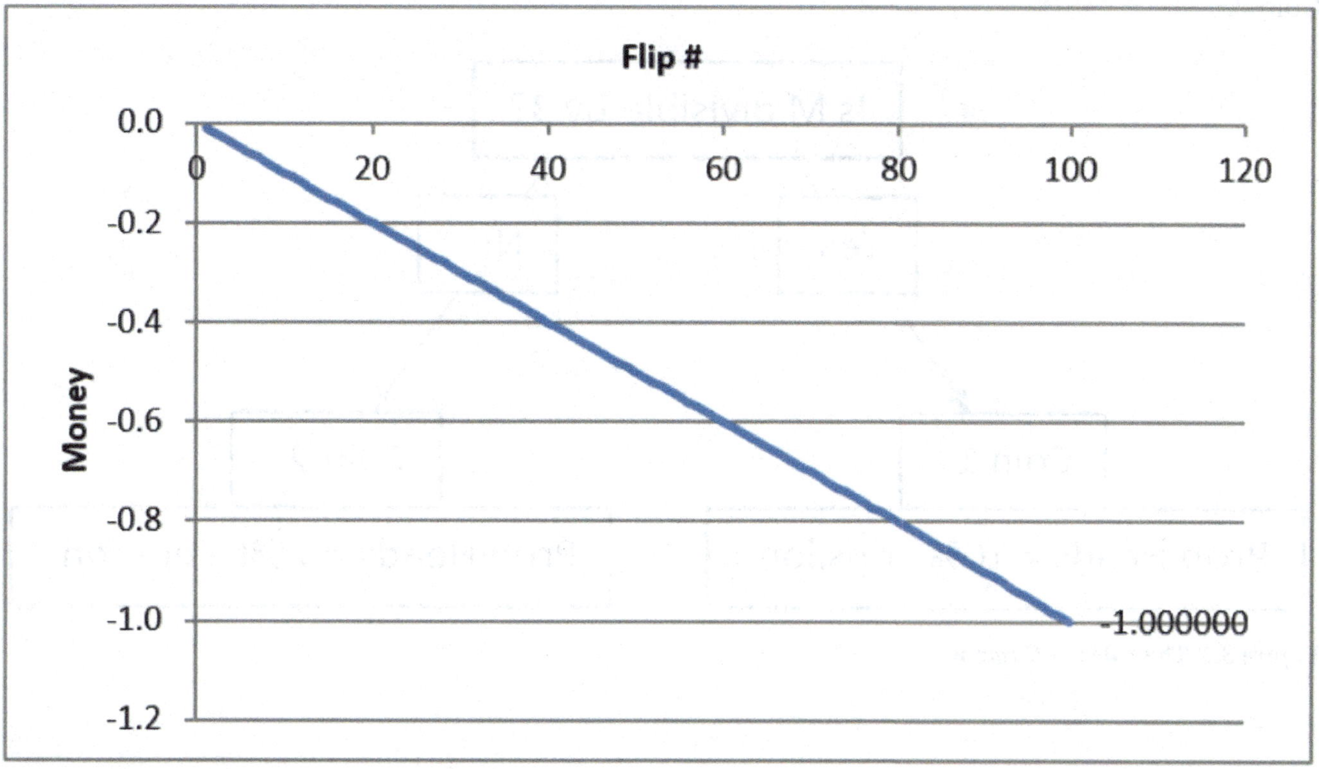

Figure 3.6: The exact evolution of Game A.

Your simulation and Figure 3.6 make clear that Game A is a loser. From the first flip, it gets steadily worse, and by the last flip, you can expect to lose 1 monetary unit.

Of course, not every single game is a loser. Column CV in the MC*Raw* sheet shows many cells that are positive. On average, however, we can expect to lose playing Game A.

Losing Game B

Game B is also a loser, but it is more complicated than Game A. Game B is based on two coins, and you use Coin 1 if your current monetary holding is divisible by 3; otherwise, you use Coin 2. The MOD function enables us to determine which coin to use.

STEP Return to the sheet with Game A, and in cell E1, enter the formula =MOD(13,12).

The cell displays 1 because it is doing modulo arithmetic. Converting military time to a.m./p.m. time uses the modulo operator: 1300 is 1 p.m. because you divide by 12 and the remainder is the answer.

Game B follows the flow chart in Figure 3.7. We will use the MOD function to divide any number by 3, and if the result is 0, we know it is evenly divisible, and we flip Coin 1. If not, we flip Coin 2.

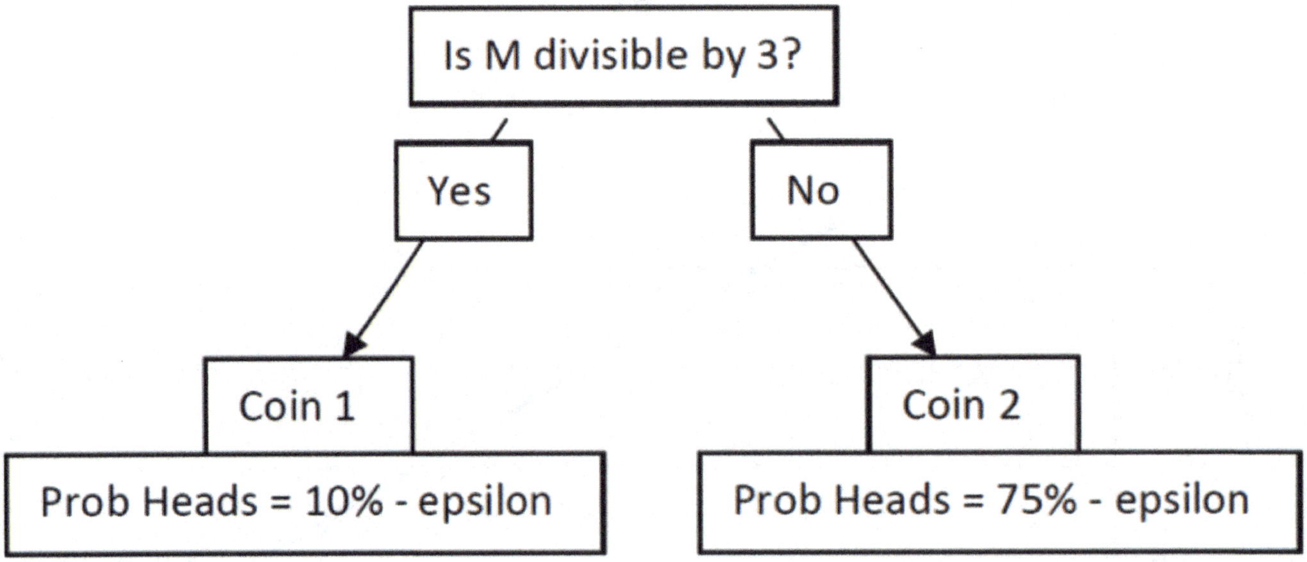

Figure 3.7: The rules of Game B.

STEP In cell G1, enter the label *Game B*. In cells G3 and G4, enter the labels "Coin 1" and "p(H)." In cell H4, enter the formula =0.1-B3. In cells J3 and J4, enter the labels "Coin 2" and "p(H)." In cell K4, enter the formula =0.75-B3.

Obviously, we would rather flip Coin 2. It comes up heads almost 75% of the time, so we win 1 monetary unit. Coin 1 is the opposite. It is strongly biased against heads, so we lose often with Coin 1.

STEP Copy cells A6:A107 and paste in cell G6. In cell H6, enter the label *Start* M, and in cell H7, enter a 0. In cell I6, enter the label *MOD(M,3)*, and in cell I7, enter the formula =MOD(H7,3). In cell J6, enter the label *Coin*, and in cell J7, enter the formula =IF(I7=0,1,2).

You start with 0 monetary units. That is evenly divisible by 3, so we will use Coin 1, but we need a more general formula to determine what happens if it is Coin 1 or Coin 2. An IF statement can handle this.

STEP In cell K6, enter the label *Result*, and in cell K7, enter the formula =IF(J7=1,IF(RAND()<$H$4,1,0),IF(RAND()<$K$4,1,0)).

Next, we report our money position.

STEP In cell L6, enter the label *End* M, and in cell L7, enter the formula =IF(K7=1,1,-1).

In the next row, we walk through the cells in order.

STEP In cell H8, enter the formula =L7 and fill it down. Select cell range I7:K7 and fill it down. In cell L8, enter the formula =IF(K8=1,L7+1,L7−1). Fill it down. Select L6:L106 and make a Scatter chart.

This completes Game B. Cell L106 gives the final result of the game, but as we did before, we can track every flip of the game to better understand it.

STEP Select cell range L7:L106 and click *MCSim* (in the *Add-ins* tab). Check (if needed) *Record All Selected Cells* and click *Proceed.*

As before, two sheets are inserted, and we will process the data in the *MCRaw* sheet to show how Game B works.

STEP Return to the *MCRaw*3 sheet and copy row 1003. Go to the *MCRaw*5 sheet, select cell A1003, and paste. Make a chart of row 1003.

Your results are surprising. In the first few flips of the ensemble average, it jaggedly oscillates and then settles down to a downward-sloping relationship.

The exact ensemble average is given by Figure 3.8. The simulation is correct in that there is an oscillation in the expected value in the first few flips before convergence to a single line that heads downward.

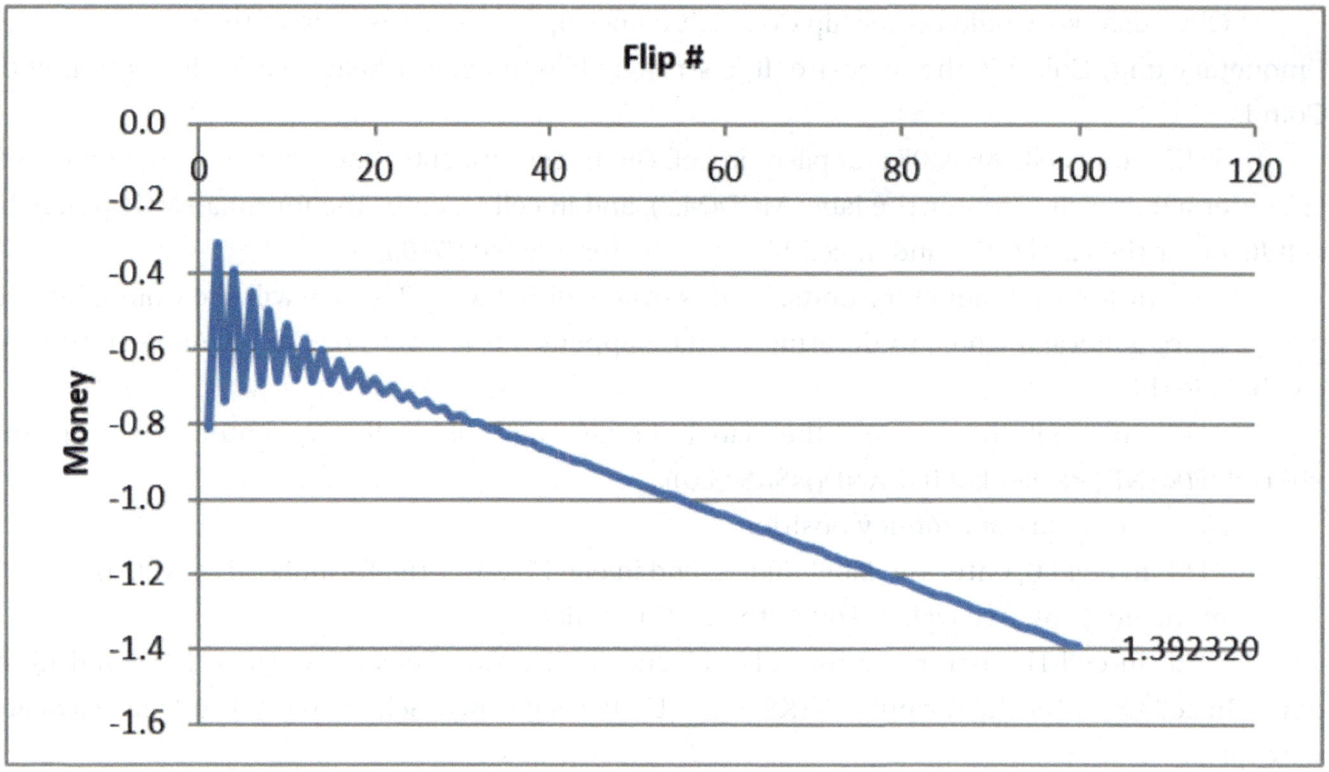

Figure 3.8: The exact evolution of Game B.

Your simulation results and Figure 3.8 show that Game B is a loser and a bigger loser than Game A. We can expect to lose about 1.4 monetary units playing Game B.

Mixing Two Losing Games

Having set up and run Games A and B separately, we are now ready to mix these two losing games. This will demonstrate Parrondo's Paradox because, somehow, mixing the losing games results in a winning game. In fact, there is an optimal mixing strategy, but we will randomly mix the two games by flipping a fair coin.

STEP In cell N1, enter the label *Random Mixing*. Copy cell range A6:A106, select cell N6, and paste. In cell O6, enter the label *Game*, and in cell O7, enter the formula =IF(RAND()<0.5,"A","B"). Fill it down.

Column O tells us which game we will play at each coin flip. It is easy to see by pressing F9 repeatedly that the letters A and B are bouncing around, indicating that we are mixing the games randomly.

We need to input Game B again (we cannot just use Game B in columns G:L) because it depends on the value of M to decide which coin to play.

STEP In cell P5, enter the label *If Game B is chosen*. Copy cell range H6:K7, select cell P6, and paste.

We need an IF statement to display the actual outcome of this game based on whether we play Game A or Game B. We take Game A from column B, since it does not depend on the amount of M we have, but we take Game B from column S.

STEP In cell T6, enter the label *Actual Result*, and in cell T7, enter the formula =IF(O7="A,"B7,S7).

Next, we determine our monetary position.

STEP In cell U6, enter the label *End* M, and in cell U7, enter the formula =IF(T7=1,1,-1).

We process the second flip and fill down to complete the implementation.

STEP In cell P8, enter the formula =U7. Fill it down. Select cell range Q7:T7 and fill it down. In cell U8, enter the formula =IF(T8=1,U7+1,U7-1). Fill it down. Select cell range U6:U106 and make a *Scatter* chart.

This completes the random mixing of two losing games. Cell U106 gives the final result of the game. Pressing F9 does not reveal much. We need to run a simulation.

STEP Select cell range U7:U106 and click MC*Sim* (in the *Add-ins* tab). Confirm that the *Record All Selected Cells* option is still checked and click *Proceed*.

We have the data to demonstrate Parrondo's Paradox, but we need to create an ensemble average chart.

STEP Return to the MC*Raw*5 sheet and copy row 1003. Go to the MC*Raw*7 sheet, select cell A1003, and paste. Make a chart of row 1003.

The results are absolutely stunning. Unlike our two previous charts, this one points upward, and the final value is positive! This is a winning game! Figure 3.9 shows the exact evolution of the randomly mixed games. The expected value of playing a random combination of Games A and B keeps rising the more you play. That is mind-boggling.

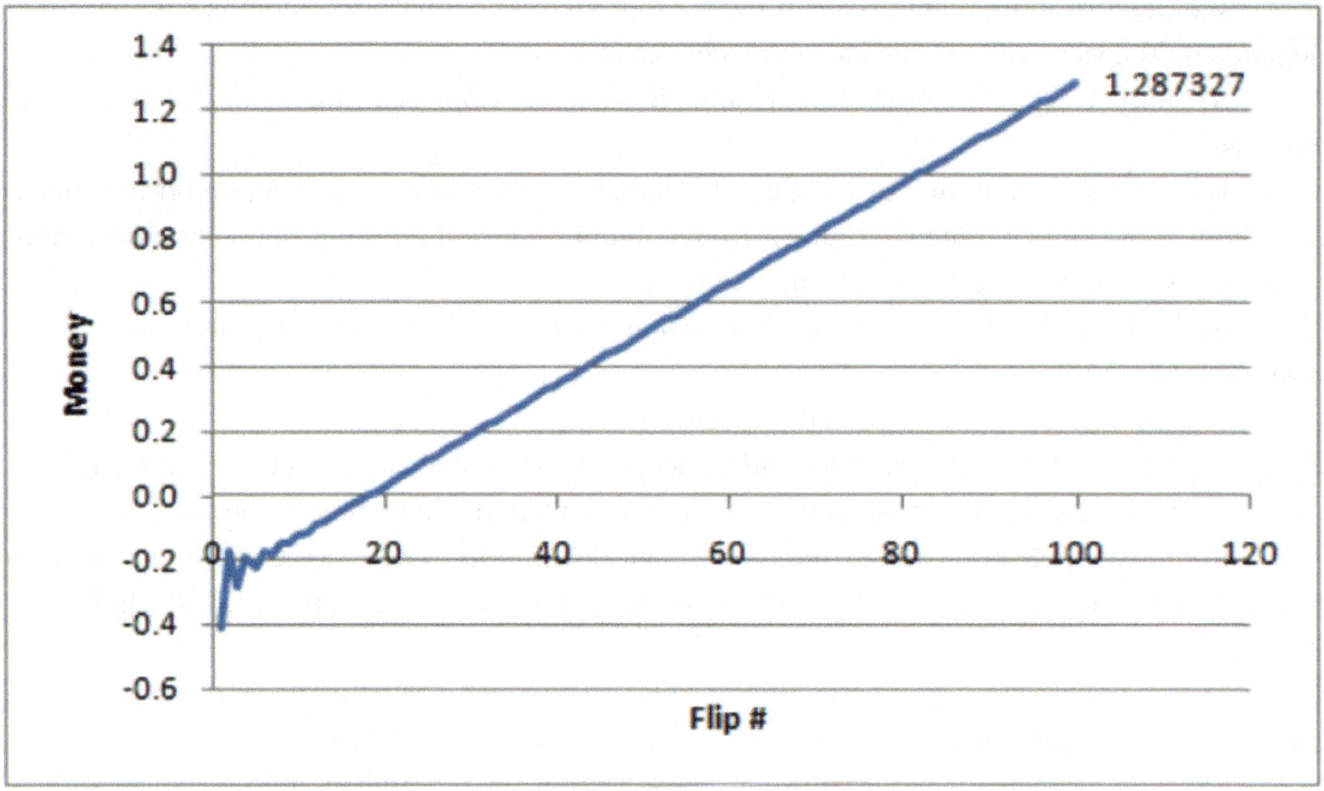

***Figure 3.9**: The exact evolution of randomly mixing A and B.*

By randomly mixing individually losing Games A and B, we can expect to win about 1.3 monetary units playing 100 times. This is Parrondo's Paradox.

What Is Going on Here?

Does this work show that you can walk into a casino and take turns playing blackjack and roulette and come out a winner? No.

Does it mean that you can combine two losing stocks and somehow make money? No.

Does it mean that I can take something poisonous and then drink another poison and the two will combine to heal me? No.

Parrondo's Paradox does not say that mixing *any* two losing games produces a winner. The two games and epsilon value were chosen carefully. Parrondo found a parameter value that generated the anomalous result. Think of a Cartesian plane with a coordinate that is like a black hole—all the other coordinates behave as expected, but this particular point is really weird. Parrondo found such a point by carefully picking the bias (epsilon) in Games A and B.

Applying this paradox to the real world is a challenge. Explaining the inspiration for Parrondo's discovery of the paradox will help us understand how the paradox emerges.

Parrondo is a physicist, and his discovery of an epsilon value that produced the paradox was influenced by something called the *flashing Brownian ratchet*. This is a process that alternates between two regimes in a sawtooth fashion.

STEP Watch this two-minute video to see the ratchet in action and how it applies to Parrondo's Paradox: vimeo.com/econexcel/parrondo. You can control the ratchet yourself here: dub.sh/ratchet.

It is true that Parrondo's Paradox requires a specific, and we might add rare, type of losing game to be mixed. The paradox would never emerge if the two losing games were like Game A. Mixing two Game As would produce a bigger negative outcome.

Game B, with its two coins, one of which is biased in our favor, holds the key to the paradox. Figure 3.8 tells us that for the first few flips, the expected value of Game B alternates. Mixing takes advantage of the positive parts of Game B in those first few flips.

Takeaways

Optical illusions and paradoxes are mind-bending. They violate what we expect to happen and force us to deal with something unbelievable.

STEP Watch a classic two-minute video of an optical illusion with an explanation of how it works: dub.sh/faceillusion.

Like an optical illusion, Parrondo's Paradox produces a shocking result: Loser plus loser equals winner. That should not happen.

At a magic show, we know a trick is involved, so the person was not really cut in half or made to disappear. There is a logical reason—we just do not know what it is unless it is explained to us.

Similarly, Parrondo's Paradox can be explained. The key lies in the ratchet, which trends down but in a sawtooth, herky-jerky motion. The video (dub.sh/ratchet) shows how it catches the ball at just the right time and pushes it upward, even as it is heading downward, producing an overall upward movement.

Parrondo's Paradox requires specific values for epsilon, the bias in coins being flipped, and Game B is actually a combination of two coins that are used based on whether the player's total amount of money is evenly divisible by 3.

It is Game B that has the ratchet that explains the paradox. Figure 3.8 shows that it is a losing game (heading downward), but look carefully at the beginning—the oscillations during the first few flips contain the explanation to the paradox.

STEP Listen to this 10-minute podcast at dub.sh/parrondo.

This podcast was generated by NotebookLM (a Google AI experiment in October of 2024 freely available at https://notebooklm.google.com/). In October of 2024, I was shocked by what this AI could do, and 18 months later, I remain quite impressed by Note-

We used simulation to explain Parrondo's Paradox, but it is not an integral part of the paradox. An analytical solution using Markov chains provides exact results. The analytical solution was used to create the exact evolution charts (Barreto, 2009).

Usually, we use simulation to represent a real-world process. We do not have to make it a perfect representation, but it must capture the essential elements.

We can go, however, in the other direction, from an artificial environment to the real world. Parrondo found something paradoxical, and now we are asking, "Is there something like this in reality?" Could it ever make sense to combine stocks or medicines or anything else in a way that reverses the negative result? The search is on.

Finally, random mixing produces a winning game with an expected value of about 1.3 monetary units at the 100th flip, but there is an optimal mix. Playing AB, then ABBABBABB repeatedly, produces an expected value of a little over 6 monetary units. Barreto (2009) explains the analytical solution and optimal mixing with Excel.

References

Barreto, H. (2009). "A Microsoft Excel Version of Parrondo's Paradox." SSRN *Working Paper.* Available at SSRN: https://ssrn.com/abstract=1431958 or http://dx.doi.org/10.2139/ssrn.1431958

Barreto, H. (2018, Sept. 28). *Ratchet effect.* [Video]. Vimeo. vimeo.com/econexcel/parrondo

Nicholls, E., Churches, O., and Loetscher, T. (2018). "Perception of an Ambiguous Figure Is Affected by Own-Age Social Biases." *Scientific Reports* 8, no. 12661. Open access: www.nature.com/articles/s41598-018-31129-7.

RayOman. (2009, August 17). *Charlie Chaplin Optic Illusion* [Video]. YouTube. https://www.youtube.com/watch?v=QbKw0_v2clo.

A Mathematica version: demonstrations.wolfram.com/TheParrondoParadox/.

A YouTube demonstration: www.youtube.com/watch?v=PpvboBJEozM.

For an entertaining read on paradoxes, try *Perplexing Paradoxes* by George Szpiro (2024).

3.3 Pooled Testing via Simulation

Those who lived through the COVID-19 pandemic are certain to remember it for a long time: masks, mandates, social distancing, vaccines, virtual meetings, and for many of us, losing loved ones. We will also remember testing for coronavirus with nasal swabs and at-home kits.

It never caught on in the United States during the COVID-19 pandemic, but pooled testing was considered because it could reduce the number of tests needed and save time (Mandavilli, 2020). Pooled testing was used successfully by the United States military during World War II to test men for syphilis (Dorfman, 1943).

The logic of pooled testing is straightforward. A university, for example, could take saliva or nasal swab samples from each student and test them individually, or it could combine a part of each sample from several people into a single group and test the pooled sample. If it is negative, then all the individuals in the combined pool are negative, and we have saved on testing every person in that group. If the pooled sample is positive, then individual tests would be performed on the reserved parts of each individual's sample to determine exactly who is infected.

This leads to a crucial question: *What is the optimal group size?* The bigger the group, the lower the number of groups tested but the higher the chances a group is positive, and then everyone in the group has to be tested (we ignore the possibility of subgroup testing, false positives or negatives, and other complications).

We solve this optimization problem by constructing an Excel spreadsheet and using Monte Carlo simulation. We proceed step by step and reveal Excel functions and tools as we create our model of pooled testing.

The Data Generation Process

The first thing we need to do is implement the random process by which some people get infected and others do not. We do this by drawing a random number and comparing it to a threshold value, so we get either a 0 (not infected) or a 1 (infected).

We make the simplifying assumption that everyone has the same likelihood of catching the virus—say, 5%. This is an *exogenous variable* (also called a *parameter*) in our model and it will serve as our threshold value for determining whether someone is infected.

STEP Enter 5% in cell A1 of a blank spreadsheet and label it as "infection rate" in cell B1. Save the Excel file (*PooledTesting.xlsx* is a good name).

Cell A1 displays 5%, which is the same as 0.05 in decimal notation. The number 0.05 is what the spreadsheet stores in its internal memory. It is worth remembering that what is displayed may be different from what is stored.

> **EXCEL TIP** Name cells, especially if you have many or complicated formulas. We have been using cell addresses, and we can, of course, refer to cell A1 in a formula, but cell addresses can be difficult to read. It is good practice to name a cell or a cell range so that formulas can use natural language to reference cells.

STEP Name cell A1 *InfectionRate* because this will make our future formulas easier to understand. If needed, search Excel's Help for "names in formulas."

Next, we incorporate randomness. As you know, Excel draws uniformly distributed random numbers in the interval from 0 to 1 with the RAND() function.

STEP In cell A3, enter the formula =RAND().

Just like the free throw shooting and coin-flipping examples, we use Excel's random number generator to determine whether or not a person gets COVID-19. We use an IF statement to group the RAND-generated values into two categories, 0 and 1.

STEP In cell A4, enter the formula =IF(A3<*InfectionRate*, 1, 0).

You probably see a 0 displayed in cell A4; if not, press F9 (you may have to use the *fn* key). Zero means the person is not infected.

STEP Press F9 repeatedly to recalculate the sheet until you see a 1 in cell A4. The chances are only 1 in 20, so be patient.

As you recalculated, cell A3 constantly changed, but cell A4 changed only if A3 switched from being above or below the infection rate. Cell A4 is a *binomial random variable* because it can take only the values 0 or 1.

Now that we know how to implement a random process that outputs whether or not an individual is infected, we can create an entire population of people, some who get infected with the virus and others who do not.

STEP In cell C1, enter the formula =IF(RAND()<*InfectionRate*,1,0).

Notice how we directly embedded the RAND() function in the cell formula. We do not know which random number was drawn, but we do know if it was less than 5% because then cell C1 would display "1."

STEP Fill down this formula all the way to cell C1000.

As you scroll back up to the top row, you will see a sprinkling of ones among many zeroes. With a 5% infection rate, roughly 1 in 20 cells will have random number draws less than 5% and therefore show the number one.

The fact that each cell in column C stands alone and does not depend on or influence other cells means we are assuming *independence*. In our model, one person with the virus does not affect the chances of anyone else being infected. This condition is surely violated in the real world. To improve our analysis, we should make the chances of infection depend on whether people with whom they come in contact have the virus.

However, since our focus here is on showing how pooled testing works, we will not model infection as dependent on people nearby. This would be a fun project where you would create clusters of cells, and if one got sick, the nearby cells would have a much higher chance of infection.

How many people in our population of 1,000 are infected?

STEP Enter the formula =SUM(C1:C1000) in cell D1 and the label *Number infected* in cell E1.

You will see a number around 50 in cell D1. The number of infected people is not always exactly 50 because chance is involved in who gets infected.

STEP Recalculate by pressing F9 a few times to get a sense of the variability in the number of infected people.

The total number of infected people can be less than 40 or more than 60, but that is not common. Usually, there are around 45 to 55 infected. There is no doubt that the number of infected people is a random number, since it is bouncing around when you recalculate the sheet. It makes common sense that adding binomial random variables will produce a random outcome.

We can make it easier to identify who is infected with a spreadsheet's conditional formatting capability. This offers the viewer visual cues that make data easier to understand.

STEP Select the entire column C and apply a formatting rule that highlights, with color, cells with a value of 1. Choose font and fill colors that you think emphasize being infected. If needed, search Excel's Help for "conditional formatting."

Now when you scroll down, it is easy to see who is infected. Recalculation changes who is infected—it is as if we rewound and replayed the world with each press of F9.

Having implemented the chance process for being infected or not, we turn to pooled testing. Instead of testing each person, we can group individuals and test their combined sample. If the pooled sample tests positive, then we know at least one person is infected; if not, we know no one is infected, and we do not have to test each individual in the group.

Instead of directly choosing the number of groups, it is more convenient to make group size the choice variable. Choosing group size determines how many groups we have, since:

$$\text{NumberofGroups} = \frac{\text{Population}}{\text{GroupSize}}$$

With our population of 1,000 people, a group size of 100 means we will have 10 groups. Intuitively, with an infection rate of 5%, 100 people in a group means that at least 1 person will be infected, and the group is probably going to test positive. We can make our intuition more convincing by computing the exact chances.

STEP Begin by entering 100 in cell D3 and the label *Group Size* next to it in cell E3. Enter the formula =1000/D3 in cell D4 and the label *Number of Groups* in cell E4.

An infection rate of 5% means each person has a 95% chance of not being infected. If there are 2 people (assuming the chances of infection are independent), then there is a 0.95 × 0.95 = 0.95^2 = 0.9025, or 90.25%, chance that neither is infected. This means there is a 100% − 90.25% = 9.75% chance that at least 1 of the 2 people is infected.

What are the chances that at least 1 person is infected in a group of 100 people? Remember, if even 1 person is infected in a group, we have to test everyone in the group to find out who is infected.

STEP In cell D6, enter the formula =(1–*InfectionRate*)^D3 and label *prob no one in the group infected* in cell E6. Format D6 as a percentage so that it displays 0.59%.

Next, we compute 100% minus the probability that no one in the group is infected to find the probability that at least 1 person is infected.

STEP In cell D7, enter the formula =1–D6 and label *prob at least one in the group infected* in cell E7. Format D7 as a percentage (if needed).

With an infection rate of 5%, doing pooled testing with a group size of 100 is wasteful. After all, it seems overwhelmingly likely (over 99%) that we will have to test everyone in each of the 10 groups, so we would end up doing 1,010 tests.

Can we make our spreadsheet show how many people are infected in each group and confirm the computations we just made? We can, but the approach we adopt uses a function that may be unfamiliar and advanced—the OFFSET reference function. Thus, we proceed slowly.

STEP In cell G1, enter the formula =OFFSET(E1,3,0).

Cell G1 computes the number of groups because the OFFSET function went to cell E1 (the first argument in the function), then went three rows down (the second argument). The third argument is 0, so it stayed in column E. If the movement arguments are a positive integer, we move down or right; negative integers move us up or left.

STEP Change the formula in cell G1 to =SUM(OFFSET(D1,0,0,3,1)).

Why does G1 display D1 plus 100? The two zeroes mean it did not move from the reference cell D1, but the fourth and fifth arguments control the height and width, respectively, of the cell range. Therefore, the formula says to add up the values in cells D1, D2 (which is blank), and D3 (100).

We want to add up the values in column C into 10 separate groups of 100 each. We can modify our OFFSET function to do the first group of 100.

STEP Change the formula in cell G1 to =SUM(OFFSET(C1,0,0,100,1)). To be clear, change the D1 to C1 and the 3 to 100.

The value reported in cell G1 is the sum of the first 100 people in the population. How can we get the second group of 100 people?

STEP Change the formula in cell G1 to =SUM(OFFSET($C$1,0,0,100,1)) and fill it down to cell G2.

Adding the dollar signs made C1 an absolute reference, so we kept our C1 starting point in cell G2, but we need to change the formula so it adds up the number of infected people in the second set of 100. We do that by changing the second argument because it controls how many rows to move from the reference cell.

STEP Change the formula in cell G2 to =SUM(OFFSET($C$1,100,0,100,1)).

EXCEL TIP Cell G2 reports how many people are infected in the second group of 100. We could fill down eight more cells and then change the second argument manually to 200, 300, and so on, but this is poor spreadsheet practice. *Never manually repeat* the same entry or an ordered sequence (e.g., numbers or dates). In addition, you want to *maximize flexibility*. Hard-coding numbers, like 100, in formulas is poor practice because you might want to change that number in the future.

In this case, we want our groupings to respond to changes in cell D3. If, for example, we have a group size of 50, we would then have 20 groups. We want the spreadsheet to automatically show how many people are infected in each of the 20 groups.

This task requires that we modify the second and fourth arguments. The fourth argument is the group size, which is simply cell D3. The second argument is more complicated. It is 0 for the first group, then increases by D3 for each group. One way to do this is to use the ROW function, which returns the row number of a cell.

STEP Replace the formula in cell G2 with =ROW(D6).

Cell G2 displays 6, the row number of cell D6. What happens if the ROW function does not have an argument?

STEP Change the formula in cell G2 to =ROW() and fill it down to G10.

Without an argument, the ROW function returns the row number of the cell that contains ROW() in the formula. We can use this to create a series that starts at 0 and increases by the amount in cell D3.

STEP Change the formula in cell G2 to =(ROW()–1)*$D$3 and fill it down to G10.

We can use our ROW function strategy in the OFFSET function's second argument to create a formula that gives us the number of infected people for any group size from 2 to 500 entered in D3. A "group" of 1 is simply individual testing, and with 1,000 people, a group size of 2 yields 500 groups. Choosing a group size of 500 gives us 2 groups.

We start with G1 (notice that ROW()-1 is zero for G1 so the second argument evaluates to zero) and fill down to G500 (since 500 is the maximum number of groups we can have).

STEP Change the formula in cell G1 to =SUM(OFFSET($C$1,(ROW()–1)*$D$3,0,$D$3,1)) and fill it down to G500.

Cells G1 to G10 now display the number of infected people in each of the 10 groups of 100 people.

STEP Click the letter C in column C to select the entire column, and then click the Format Painter button (in the *Home* tab in the *Ribbon*, or top menu). Now click the letter G in column G.

You applied the formatting in column C, including your conditional formatting to highlight the infected people, to column G. It (probably) shows all the groups highlighted, but it will soon come in handy when we lower the group size so that some groups have no infected people.

> **EXCEL TIP** It is good practice to *include checks* in your spreadsheets. In this case, an easy check is to see if the sum of infected people in the 10 groups equals the total number of infected people in the population in column C.

STEP In cell H1, enter the formula =SUM(G1:G500) and the label *check* in cell I1, then recalculate the sheet a few times.

It is easy to see that cells D1 and H1 are the same. If not, something is wrong, and you will have to go back to each step to find and fix the mistake.

STEP Change cell D3 to 200 and recalculate the sheet a few times.

Now only five cells in column G have nonzero values, representing the number of infected people in each of the five groups.

Group sizes of 100 and 200 are way too big to be the optimal size because we are extremely unlikely to get a group where everyone tests negative, so we almost always have to test everyone in the group. We need to try much smaller group sizes.

STEP Change cell D3 to 20 and recalculate the sheet a few times.

Now we are really getting somewhere. Column G is showing the number of infected people in each of 50 groups. You can see values of 0, 1, 2, 3, and less frequently, higher numbers. We love to see zeroes because they mean we do not have to test anyone in that group, so we saved 20 tests.

How many tests will we have to run in total? The COUNTIF function allows us to count the number of cells in a range that meet a specific condition.

STEP In cell H2, enter the formula =COUNTIF(G1:G500,"> 0") and the label *number of groups to test* in I2.

The COUNTIF function reports the number of cells in the range G1:G500 that have a value greater than zero. If we multiply this by the group size, we know how many individual tests we have to run. This is added to the number of group tests to give us our total number of tests.

STEP In cell H3, enter the formula =H2*D3 and the label *tests from infected groups* in I3. In cell H4, enter the formula =D4+H3 and the label *total tests* in I4.

Notice that once again, we did not hard-code numbers (like 20 for group size) into the formula. We want our spreadsheet to respond to changes in group size (cell D3) automatically.

Cell H4 is certainly giving us good news. "Total tests" is a random variable that is almost certainly less than 1,000. You are likely to see numbers around 690 tests, give or take 70 or so. This is about a 30% decrease in the number of tests from the 1,000 required by individual testing.

Finding the Optimal Group Size

In our spreadsheet, we have implemented a stochastic (or chance) process of getting infected and demonstrated the power of pooled testing. Grouping allows us to save on testing because when groups have no infected people, we do not have to test those individual samples.

Our spreadsheet shows that a group size of 20 is better than individual testing, but we do not want to do merely better than 1,000 tests. We want to perform the fewest number of tests. Our fundamental question is, *What is the optimal group size?*

There is a complication that we have to confront to answer our question: "Total tests" is a random variable. We cannot just look at a single outcome because we know there is chance involved. Suppose two dice are on a table, each showing 1, and I asked you to guess the sum of the next roll. You would not guess 2 because you know that is really unlikely.

We deal with the fact that "Total tests" is a random variable by focusing on the *expected value* of total tests. This is what we would typically observe. The best guess for the sum of two dice rolls is 7, the expected value. We need to find the expected value of total tests for a given group size so we can figure out which group size minimizes it.

There are mathematical rules for computing the expected value, but we will use Monte Carlo simulation. This approach is based on the idea that we can simply run the chance process (throwing two dice or hitting F9) many times and directly examine the results. We can compute the average of many repetitions (like rolling dice many times) to give us an approximation to the expected value.

So we seek the group size that minimizes the expected value of total tests, which we will approximate by simulation. We will run many repetitions (recalculating the sheet repeatedly) and keep track of the total number of tests to see how many total tests we can expect to run as we vary the group size.

While there are many simulation add-ins available for Excel, we can easily run a simulation using Excel's *Data Table* tool. It was designed not to run a simulation but to display multiple outcomes as inputs vary. To do this, it recalculates the sheet, which enables us to perform Monte Carlo analysis.

STEP In cell L1, enter the number 1, and enter 2 in cell L2. Select both cells and fill down to row 400 so that you have a series from 1 to 400 in column L.

Next, we provide the cell that we wish to track: total tests.

STEP In cell M1, enter the formula =H4.

We are now ready to create the Data Table.

STEP Select the cell range L1:M400, click the *Data* tab in the *Ribbon*, click *What-If Analysis* in the *Forecast* group, and select *Data Table . . .* A keyboard shortcut is *Alt-a-w-t*.

Excel pops up the *Data Table* input box.

STEP Click in the *column input cell* field, click on cell K1, and click OK.

Clicking on an empty cell would be meaningless if we were using the *Data Table* tool for its intended purpose, which is to show how an input cell affects a formula in another cell. All we want, however, is for Excel to recalculate the sheet and show us the total tests for that newly recalculated population in column C.

The display in column M shows 400 repetitions of hitting F9 and keeping track of total tests. This is exactly what we want because now we can take the average of the total tests' values to approximate the expected number of total tests when the group size is 20.

But before we do this, let's be clear about what a Data Table is actually doing. Be aware in the next step, however, that if you double-click on a cell in column M or click in the formula bar, you might get trapped in a cell. **If you get stuck, press the Esc (escape) key to get out.**

STEP Click on a few cells from M2 to M400 to see that they have an *array formula:* {=TABLE(,K1)}.

Excel has a friendly front end via *Data: What-If Analysis: Data Table . . .* to create an array formula (indicated by the curly brackets, {}) that can display multiple outputs. You cannot change or delete an individual cell in the range M2:M400. They are, in a sense, a single unit sharing the same formula.

You might also notice that the sheet is much slower as we enter formulas or press F9. This is due to the Data Table. Excel now has many more cells to recalculate and evaluate. We could do many more repetitions (usually simulations have tens of thousands of repetitions), but the delay in recalculation is not worth it. With 400 repetitions, the approximation is good enough for our purposes.

STEP In cell N1, enter the formula =AVERAGE(M1:M400) and the label *approximate expected value of total tests* in cell O1.

Cell N1 is our simulation's approximation to what we want to minimize. It gives us a handle on the center of the *sampling distribution* of the statistic "Total tests." A statistic is a recipe for what to do with observations (in this case, given by the formula in cell H4). If we make a *histogram* of the data in column M, we get an approximation to the sampling distribution of total tests.

Excel 2016 or greater is needed to make the histogram chart. This is not the *Histogram* option in the Data Analysis add-in (from the Analysis Tool-Pak). The histogram chart allows for dynamic updating and is a marked improvement over the histogram in the Data Analysis add-in.

STEP Select cell range M1:M400, click the *Insert* tab in the *Ribbon*, and select *Histogram* from the *Charts* group. It is in the *Statistic* chart group and, of course, in the collection of all charts (available by clicking the bottom-right corner square in the *Charts* group).

The default bin widths are a little too big, but they are easy to adjust.

STEP Double-click the chart's x-axis, and in the *Axis Options*, set the *Bin Width* to 20. Make the title "Approximate Sampling Distribution of Total Tests."

The chart is an approximation because it is based on only 400 repetitions. The exact sampling distribution of total tests would require an infinite number of repetitions. We can never get the exact sampling distribution or the exact expected value via simulation, but the more repetitions we do, the better the approximation.

Even with just 400 realizations of total tests, the graph looks a lot like the classic bell-shaped distribution of the normal (or Gaussian) curve. The center is the expected value of the total tests we will have with a group size of 20, and the dispersion in total tests is measured by its *standard error*.

STEP In cell N2, enter the formula =STDEV.P(M1:M400) and the label *approximate standard error of total tests* in cell O2.

The standard error of total tests tells us the variability in total tests. It is a measure of the size of the typical bounce in total tests.

STEP Press F9 a few times and watch cell H4.

Cell H4 is bouncing. It is centered around 690 and jumps by roughly plus or minus 70 total tests as you hit F9. You can also scroll up and down column M to see that the "Total tests" numbers are around 690 ± 70.

Simulation cannot give us the exact standard error, but the standard deviation of our 400 realizations of total tests is a good approximation of the standard error.

There are many ways to be confused here. One of them is to fixate on the computation of the standard deviation. We used STDEV.P (for population) instead of STDEV.S (for sample) because we are not using the standard deviation to estimate the population standard deviation, so we do not need to make a correction for degrees of freedom. Although the population standard deviation is correct, this makes almost no difference with 400 numbers.

STEP In cell N3, enter the formula =STDEV.S(M1:M400) and compare the result to cell N2.

The emphasis on population versus sample standard deviation in many Statistics courses is only relevant for small sample sizes—say, fewer than 30 observations. As the number of observations rises, the two grow ever closer.

To summarize, cells N1 and N2 tell us that we can expect to perform about 690 total tests, give or take roughly 70 tests. These are the numbers reported at the end of the previous section. This is for a group size of 20. Can we do better? We get to choose the group size, so we should explore how the expected number of total tests responds as we vary the group size.

STEP Change the group size (in cell D3) to 10 and press F9 a few times. Which specific cell should you focus on, and what do you conclude?

The cell we care about the most is cell N1 because it tells us (approximately) the expected number of tests we will have to run. Cell N1 is reporting good news. We can expect to perform about 500 ± 50 total tests. That beats the group size of 20 by almost 200 tests, on average, and is a large savings of a half versus 1,000 individual tests.

Why does a group size of 10 do better than 20? In various cells of the spreadsheet, there is evidence of what is happening. Lowering the group size from 20 to 10 increased the number of group tests from 50 to 100 (see cell D4), but the number of infected groups only went up a little bit (from roughly 32 to 40), and the groups are now much smaller. This is where the big savings are—instead of 32 × 20 = 640 tests, we only have to run, on average, 40 × 10 = 400 tests with a group size of 10.

STEP Confirm the claims about group size in the paragraph above by switching back and forth from 10 to 20 in cell D3. Notice how the other cells (especially H4) and the chart react to D3.

Spreadsheets are powerful because they can display a lot of information and dynamically update when you make changes. Your job is to make comparisons and process the information.

Can we do even better than a group size of 10?

STEP Change the group size (in cell D3) to 5.

Amazing! The number in cell N1 fell again. The expected number of total tests is now about 425 (426.22 is a more exact answer, found by analytical methods), give or take roughly 30 tests. That is a gain of almost 60% versus individual testing. Pooled testing saves a lot of tests compared to individual testing.

As before, the number of groups we have to test has risen (this time to 200), but many groups are found to be uninfected. Cell D6 reports a 77.4% chance that no one in a 5-person group will be infected. Thus, even though we test more groups, we more than make up for this because many groups test negative, saving us the need to test 5 people in the group.

The group size of 5 is, in fact, the optimal solution and answer to our question. Figure 3.10 reveals that we traveled down the expected number of total tests curve as we changed the group size from 20 to 10 and finally 5.

Figure 3.10 makes it easy to see that a group size of 5 is the minimum for the expected number of total tests curve, but it also reveals the trade-off involved. The two curves are added up to produce the top, total curve. At 10, we test 100 groups (the bottom curve) and we add that to 400 (the expected number of tests from positive groups), and this gives us 500 (the top curve).

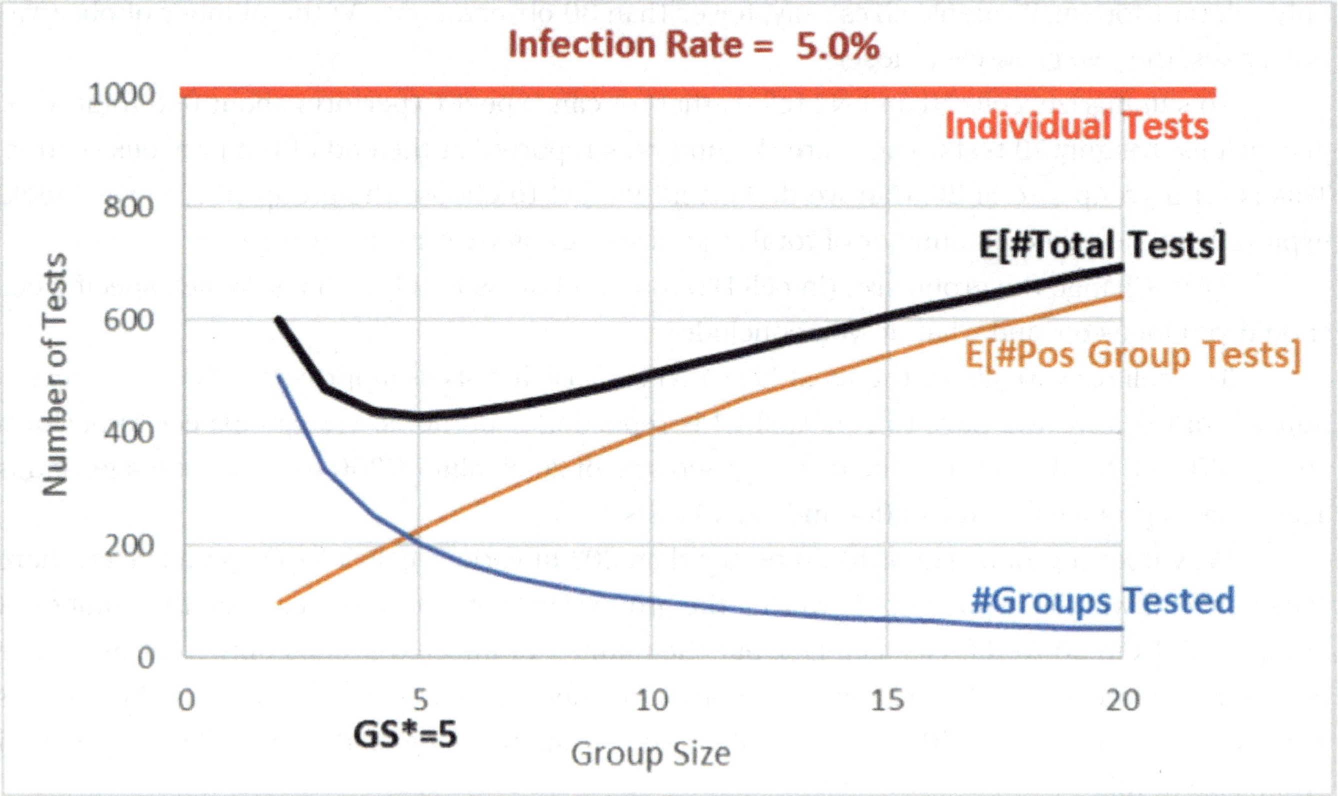

***Figure 3.10**: The expected number of tests as a function of group size.*

When we moved from 10 to 5, we added 100 tests (the bottom curve) but saved about 175 tests (the middle curve), lowering our expected total tests from 500 to 425. We cannot do any better than 425 total tests. Further reductions in group size will increase total tests.

Comparative Statics Analysis

We can ask another question that again shows off the power of spreadsheets: What happens if the infection rate changes—say, to 1%? What would be the optimal group size?

This kind of question is called *comparative statics analysis* because we want to know how our solution responds to a shock. We want to compare our initial optimal group size of five when the infection rate was 5%, to the new solution when the infection rate is 1%. This comparison reveals how the shock (changing the infection rate) affects the optimal response (group size).

STEP Change cell A1 to 1%, then use the spreadsheet to find the optimal group size. What group size would you recommend? Why?

You may have struggled with this because it turns out that the total tests curve is rather flat at its minimum. Thus, a simulation with 400 repetitions does not have the resolution to distinguish between group sizes in the range from 8 to 14 or so. Figure 3.11 makes this clear.

The exact answer for the optimal group size is, in fact, 11 groups. It has an expected number of total tests of 195.57 (again, using analytical methods). Choosing group sizes of 10 or 12 leads to a slightly higher number of total tests—although it is impossible to see this in Figure 3.11.

An infection rate of 1% shows simulation may not be an effective solution strategy for every problem. Of course, you could create a Data Table with more repetitions, but using simulation to distinguish between group sizes of 10 and 11 requires a Data Table so large that Excel would be unresponsive.

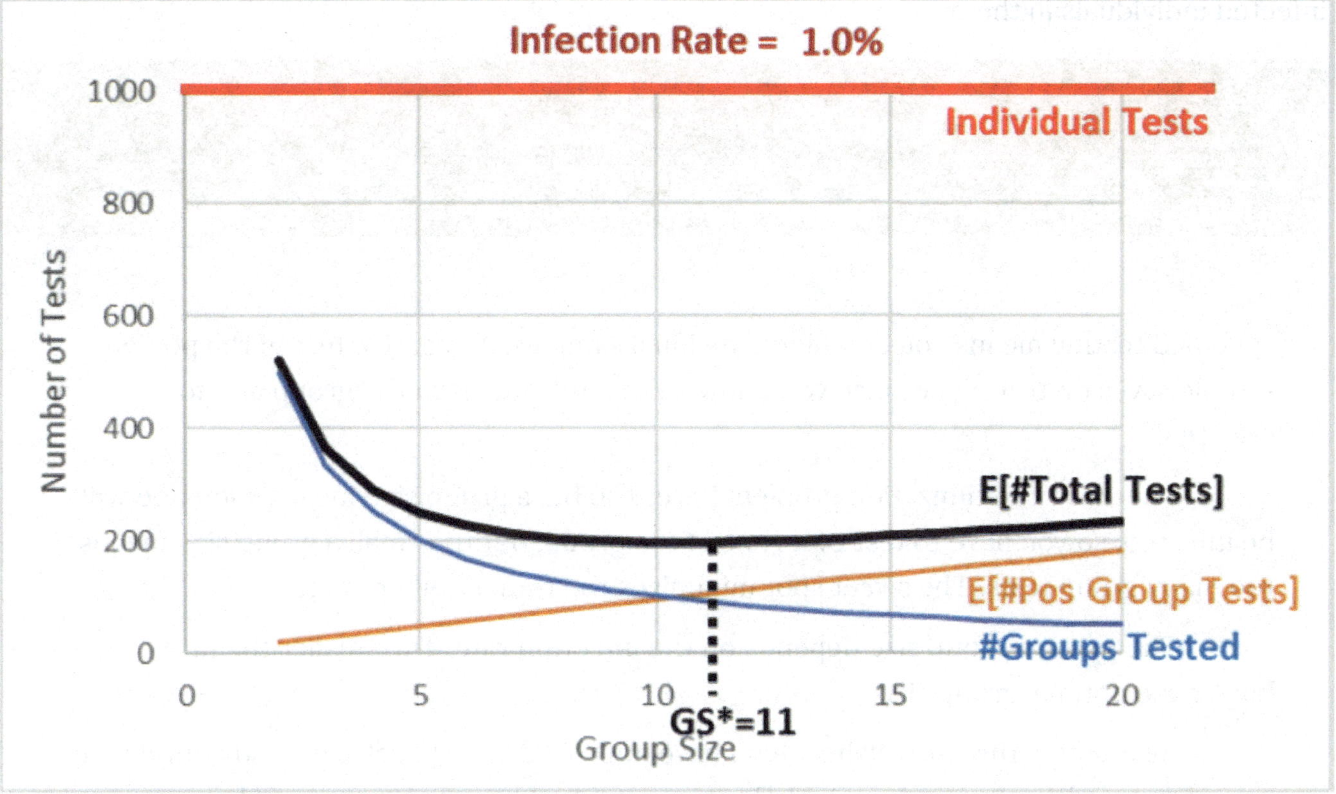

Figure 3.11: Optimal group size with a 1% infection rate.

As mentioned earlier, there are many Excel Monte Carlo simulation add-ins, and they can do millions of repetitions. We used MCSim in earlier work in section 3.2.. Even if we ran enough repetitions to see that 11 is the optimal solution, you should remember that simulation will never give you an exact result because it can never do an infinity of repetitions.

The good news is that any group size around 10 is going to be a little under 200, which is an 80% improvement over individual testing. There is no doubt about it—pooled testing can be a smart, effective way to reduce the number of total tests performed.

Our comparative statics analysis tells us that the lower the infection rate (from 5% to 1%), the bigger the optimal group size (from 5 to 11) and the greater the savings from pooled testing versus individual testing (from about 675 to 800 tests).

Finally, if you carefully compare Figures 3.10 and 3.11, you will see that the *#Groups Tested* curve (a rectangular hyperbola, since the numerator is constant at 1,000) stays the same in both graphs. Changing the infection rate shifts down the E[*#Pos Group Tests*] relationship, and this brings down and alters the shape of the E[*#Total Tests*] curve.

Comparative statics analysis shows that pooled testing is more effective when the infection rate falls. A lower infection rate means we can have bigger groups, yet they may still have no infected individuals in them.

Takeaways

Pooled testing means you combine individual samples. A negative test of the pooled sample saves on testing because you know all the individuals in the group are not infected.

There is an optimization problem here: Too big a group size means someone will be infected, so you have to test everyone in the group, but too small a group size means too many group tests. The sweet spot minimizes the total number of tests.

The optimal group size depends on the infection rate. The smaller the rate, the bigger the optimal group size.

By creating this spreadsheet, you have improved your Excel skills and confidence in using spreadsheets. You have added to your stock of knowledge that will help you next time you work with a spreadsheet.

The OFFSET function is really powerful, but it is difficult to understand and apply.

The Data Table is meant for what-if analysis, but it can be used as a simple Monte Carlo simulation tool. Each press of F9 recalculates the sheet and the Data Table.

You also learned or reinforced a great deal of statistical and economics concepts. Economics has a toolkit that gets used over and over again—look for similar concepts in future models and courses. Try to spot the patterns and repeated logic. Although it may not be explicitly stated, getting you to think like an economist is a fundamental goal of almost every Econ course.

Reference was made several times to the analytical solution. This was not shown because the math is somewhat advanced. To see it, download the *PooledTesting.xlsx* file from dub.sh/gbae and go to the *Analytical* sheet.

One methodology issue that is easy to forget but crucial is that we made many simplifying assumptions in our implementation of the data generation process. There may be other factors at play in the spread of COVID-19 or how tests actually work that affect the efficacy of pooling. Spatial connection was mentioned as something that would violate the independence assumed in our implementation. Another complication is that "a positive specimen can only get diluted so much before the coronavirus becomes undetectable. That means pooling will miss some people who harbor very low amounts of the virus" (Wu, 2020).

Our results apply to an imaginary, perfect world, not the real world. We need to be careful in moving from theory to reality. This requires both art and science.

The introduction cited Robert Dorfman as writing a paper on pooled testing back in 1943. It is a clever idea that you now understand can be used to greatly reduce the number of tests, which saves a lot of resources. Perhaps you will not be surprised to hear that Robert Dorfman was an economist.

References

Dorfman, R. (1943). "The Detection of Defective Members of Large Populations." *Ann. Math. Statist.* 14, no. 4, pp. 436–440, projecteuclid.org/euclid.aoms/1177731363.

Mandavilli, A. (2020). "Federal Officials Turn to a New Testing Strategy as Infections Surge." *The New York Times*, July 1, 2020, www.nytimes.com/2020/07/01/health/coronavirus-pooled-testing.html.

Wu, K. (2020). "Why Pooled Testing for the Coronavirus Isn't Working in America." *The New York Times*, August 18, 2020, www.nytimes.com/2020/08/18/health/coronavirus-pool-testing.html.

3.4 Search Theory Simulation

You want to buy something that many stores sell, but they charge different prices. Suppose that you cannot just google it to find the lowest price. Maybe you are at a huge farmer's market, and there are lots of vendors selling green beans. They are all the same, but the prices are different. How do you decide where to buy?

Believe it or not, this problem has been extensively studied. It is part of *search theory* and has produced several Nobel Prize winners in Economics. It also has a long history in mathematics, where it is known as an optimal stopping problem.

There are many different search scenarios and models. For example, you could be deciding which job to take. Once you pass on an offer, you cannot go back (this is called *sequential search*). Or you could be involved in some complicated game with asymmetric information, where one agent—say, the seller of a house—has more knowledge about the house than the potential buyers.

Fortunately, your green bean search problem is straightforward. The green beans are *homogeneous* (exactly alike), and you can gather as many prices as you want, then choose the cheapest one. The catch is that it is costly to search—*search* is just another way of saying "gather prices," but there are search costs.

If searches were costless, then the problem would be trivial—simply get all the prices and buy the cheapest one. The problem becomes interesting when collecting price information takes effort and time. In that case, you can search too little (so you would have found a much lower price with more searching) or search too much (so the slightly lower price you found was not worth it). You are facing an optimization problem!

We will set up and solve this optimization problem in Excel. We will use the Monte Carlo simulation add-in to explore how our total cost changes as we vary the amount we search. We will then do comparative statics analysis to see how the optimal solution responds when we shock the model.

Setting Up the Problem

First, we create a population of prices.

STEP Open a blank Excel workbook and name it *Search.xlsx*. Name the sheet *DGP* (for data generation process). In cell A1, enter the label *Price*. In cell A2, enter the formula =RAND(). Fill down to cell A101.

You now have 100 prices on your spreadsheet ranging from zero to one. Our target is the lowest price. We can easily find it with the MIN function.

STEP Enter the label *Minimum* in cell B1 and the formula =MIN(A2:A101) in cell B2. Scroll down until you find that lowest price. Press F9 to get a new set of prices and a new minimum. Each time you press F9, it is like a new day at the farmers market and the vendors have all changed their prices.

The cheapest price is close to zero (since RAND goes from zero to one), and it can be anywhere in the list of 100 numbers. As a buyer, you will not, however, do what you just did and simply enter a formula that yields the minimum price, because we assume that you cannot see the prices until you visit the store. You have to search to reveal each price.

Let's suppose that each search will cost you 0.04 monetary units. This is an exogenous variable. The 100 prices are also outside of your control. Your endogenous, or choice, variable is how many prices to reveal.

Your goal is to minimize the total cost of purchase, composed of the price you pay plus the search costs. The more you search, the lower the price you pay the vendor but the higher the costs of the search. You have to balance these two opposing forces.

Your spreadsheet is like a card game. Pressing F9 is like shuffling 100 cards. You want the lowest-numbered card in the deck. A search is like flipping a card over, but it costs you 0.04 for each card you reveal. What is the best number of cards to flip over? To answer this key question, we proceed slowly.

Suppose you decide to search just once. This has the advantage of the lowest search costs possible but the disadvantage that you will only get one price. How will you do if you adopt this strategy?

STEP In cell C1, enter a 1 (this represents how many prices you gather), and in cell C2, enter the formula =A2. In cell C3, enter 0.04 (this is the cost of your single search). In cell C4, we add the two cells above it together, so enter the formula =C2+C3. Press F9 a few times.

Each time you press F9, you get a new price in cell C2 (because the prices all change) and a new total cost in cell C4. Sometimes you do pretty well, close to 0, but sometimes you end up near 1, which is not good. But how can we know how you will usually do? How you do on average, not just in a single outcome, is how we evaluate the results of chance processes.

Monte Carlo simulation can tell us the typical result. We will use the MCSim add-in to run our simulation in Excel. If needed, download and install MCSim from dub.sh/addins.

STEP Run a simulation that tracks cell C4 with 10,000 repetitions by clicking *MCSim* in the *Add-ins* tab, entering C4 in the *Select a cell* input box, adding a 0 to the default 1,000 repetitions, and clicking *Proceed.*

Your results show an average around 0.54. This is what you can expect to usually pay, in total, for your green beans. This makes sense, since the average of RAND is 0.5 and you have to pay 0.04 for one search. Notice that the simulation values are not normally distributed, with a bell shape. Instead, you are equally likely to do really well (low total cost), badly (around 1), or somewhere in the middle (around 0.5).

The expected value of 0.54 is the number we use to convey the performance of the search-and-buy-at-one-store strategy. Of course, it does not matter if you pick the first store (in cell A2). You could pick any one of the 100 stores and get the same simulation results because each press of F9 puts up new random prices for all the stores, just like reshuffling a deck of cards.

STEP It is easy to confirm this by changing the formula in cell C2 to =A20 or =A54 or any other cell from A3 to A101 and tracking cell C4 in a new simulation. Your results are substantially (but not exactly) the same as the simulation with =A2 in cell C2.

Finding the Optimal Number of Searches

What happens to your total cost of buying green beans if we search more than once? Let's try 5 searches.

STEP In cell D1, enter a 5 (this represents gathering prices from 5 vendors), and in cell D2, enter the formula =MIN(A2:A6). This formula shows the lowest price in your sample from 5 stores, which is the one we would buy. As mentioned, you could pick any set of 5 stores, and you would get the same result. In cell D3, enter the formula =0.04*5 (0.2 is the cost of 5 searches). In cell D4, we add the two cells above it together, so enter the formula =D2+D3. Press F9 a few times.

Each press of F9 gives a single outcome, or realization, of the chance process. Sometimes you get lucky and get a low price, other times not. Notice that the total cost (in cell D4) is the sum of the lowest price and 0.2 (the cost of searching).

Do you think 5 searches are better than 1? We cannot answer this question by looking at cells C4 and D4 because they show just one realization. We need to compare the typical result of these two strategies. We know the expected value of the total cost of 1 search is 0.54. What is the typical result of 5 searches?

STEP Use the MCSim add-in to track cell D4. What do your results show?

Summary Statistics			Notes
Average	0.367		n = 5
SD	0.1411		
Max	1.052		
Min	0.200		

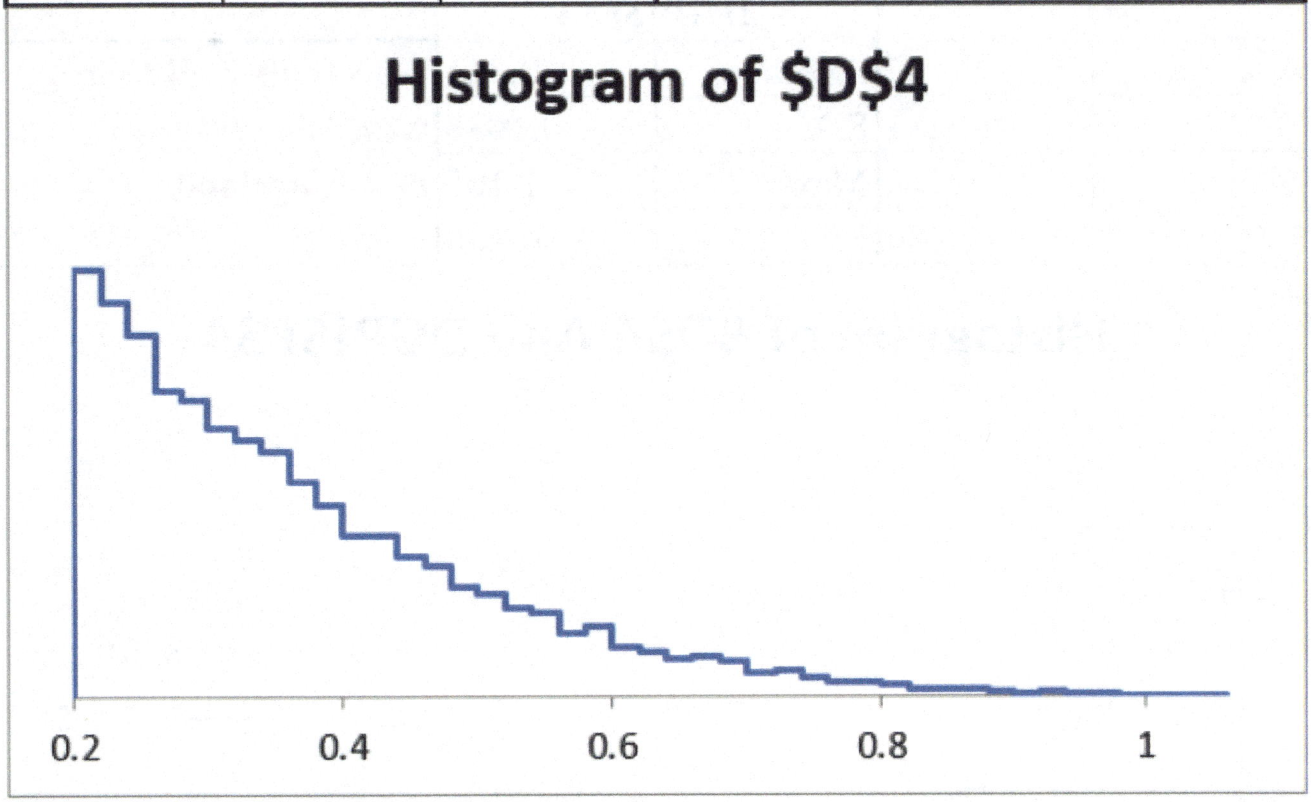

Figure 3.12: Total costs when gathering five prices.

Your results should be similar to Figure 3.12. These simulation results tell us that $n = 5$ is better than $n = 1$ because the typical result for 5 searches (approximated by the average of 10,000 repetitions) is around 0.37, which is much less than 0.54 (a roughly 30% decrease).

Maybe more searches are even better? How do 10 searches compare to 5?

STEP Run a simulation of 10 searches by setting up a 10-search scenario on the spreadsheet (in column E) and running a simulation. Try to figure it out first, but check the appendix, if needed, for more detailed help.

Your work shows that $n = 10$ is much worse than $n = 5$. How about $n = 4$?

STEP In cell F1, enter a 4, and in cell F2, enter the formula =MIN(A2:A5). In cell F3, enter the formula =0.04*4 (0.16 is the cost of 4 searches). In cell F4, we add the two cells above it together, so enter =F2+F3. Use the *MCSim* add-in to directly compare cells D4 and F4 by putting D4 in the *Select a cell* input box and F4 in the *Select a second cell* input box, then click *Proceed.*

Your results should show a close race. In fact, it is so close that we need to improve the resolution of the sim by increasing the number of repetitions.

STEP Track cells D4 and F4 again, but this time with 100,000 repetitions. This will take 10 times longer than the last sim.

$D$4		DGP!$F$4		Notes
Average	0.367	Average	0.361	n= 5 (pink) v 4 (blue)
SD	0.1414	SD	0.1638	with 100,000 reps
Max	1.110	Max	1.107	n=4 is optimal
Min	0.200	Min	0.160	

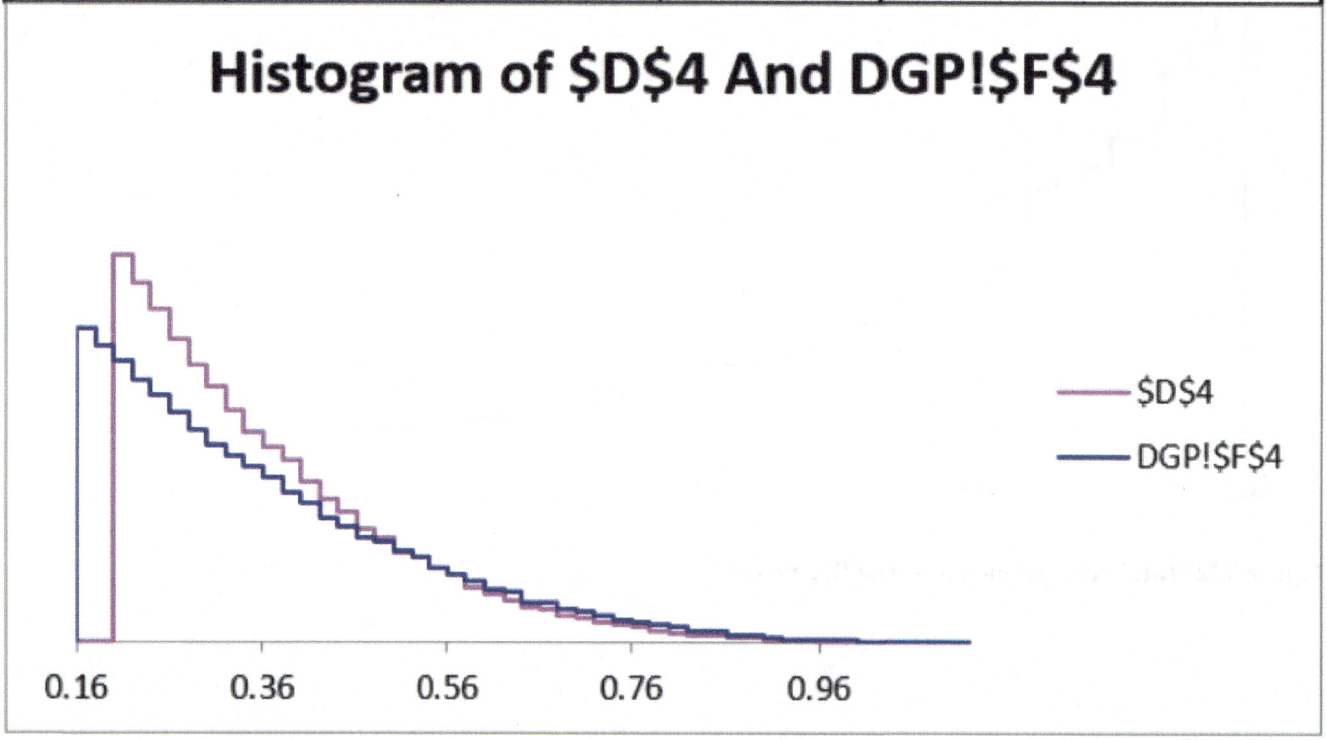

Figure 3.13: Four searches are slightly better than five.

It is still quite close, but as shown in Figure 3.13, you will get a slightly lower sim average of 0.361 or so with n = 4 than the sim average of about 0.367 with n = 5. In fact, it can be shown with analytical methods that n = 4 is the optimal solution. To see the math involved, download *Search.xlsx* from dub.sh/gbae.

Let's step back and think about what you have done. It took some work, but you used simulation to explore the U-shaped curve in Figure 3.14. It plots the exact expected value as the search increases from 1 to 10. The minimum, the answer to what you should do, is found at $n = 4$.

Prices U[0,1]
q=1 and c=0.04

Number of Searches	Expected Value of Price	Search Cost	Expected Value of Total Cost
1	0.500	0.04	0.540
2	0.333	0.08	0.413
3	0.250	0.12	0.370
4	*0.200*	*0.16*	*0.360*
5	0.167	0.2	0.367
6	0.143	0.24	0.383
7	0.125	0.28	0.405
8	0.111	0.32	0.431
9	0.100	0.36	0.460
10	0.091	0.4	0.491

Figure 3.14: Total costs are U-shaped with a minimum at n = 4.

Notice that 1 and 10 searches both yield high total costs, but for different reasons. With n = 1, you only pay 0.04 to search, but your usual purchase price is around 0.5. By searching 10 times, you lower the purchase price a lot (you are likely to find a seller with a low price, typically around 0.091), but you have to pay 0.4 in search costs.

Comparative Statics

An interesting shock to this model involves the cost of searching. What if something happened, like the internet, that lowered search costs? Instead of having to visit each store to find out the price, you can go to their web page and see the price. This makes searching much easier and cheaper. How would your search behavior respond to this shock?

Suppose the per-unit cost of searching fell from 0.04 to 0.01. What effect would that have on the optimal number of searches?

STEP Copy the DGP sheet and rename it *DGPLowerCost*. Change row 4 in columns C to F to reflect the new c = 0.01. Use the MC*Sim* add-in to find the new optimal number of searches. You can check your work (or get a few hints) using the discussion that follows, but try to do it yourself first.

The first thing to realize when search costs fall from 0.04 to 0.01 is that total costs are going to be lower for all search values. Instead of 0.54 for one search, the expected value of total costs is 0.51 when c = 0.01. For n = 4, the expected total cost falls from 0.36 to 0.24. Notice that costs fall by more the more you search.

If you actually tried to run simulations for different values of n, you might be confused by how close the results ended up being. Because of this, simulation is going to have trouble finding the exact answer. Figure 3.15 explains what is going on.

Prices U[0,1]
q=1 and c=0.04

Number of Searches	Expected Value of Price	Search Cost	Expected Value of Total Cost
1	0.500	0.01	0.510
2	0.333	0.02	0.353
3	0.250	0.03	0.280
4	0.200	0.04	0.240
5	0.167	0.05	0.217
6	0.143	0.06	0.203
7	0.125	0.07	0.195
8	0.111	0.08	0.191
9	***0.100***	***0.09***	***0.190***
10	0.091	0.1	0.191
11	0.083	0.11	0.193
12	0.077	0.12	0.197
13	0.071	0.13	0.201
14	0.067	0.14	0.207
15	0.063	0.15	0.213

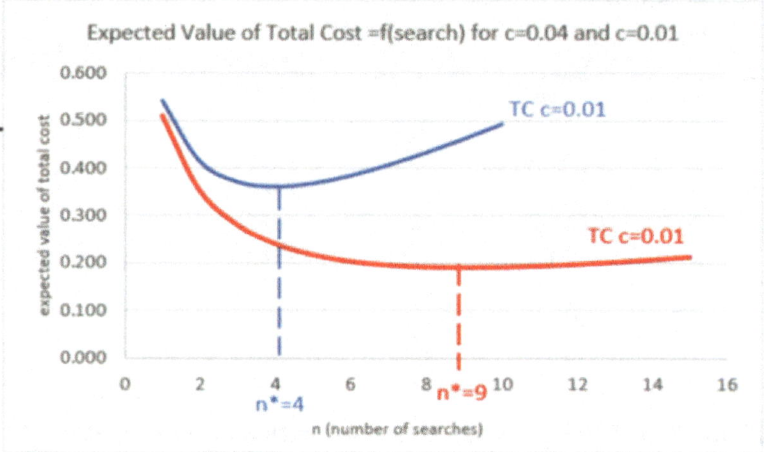

***Figure 3.15*: Comparative statics: Shocking the per-unit search cost.**

With $c = 0.01$, the expected value of the total cost curve has a minimum at $n = 9$, so this is the exactly correct answer, but notice how flat the curve is around that minimum. If your answer was 8 or 10, you missed by only 0.001.

Simulation struggles to get an exact answer because the total cost function is so shallow. You would have to run millions of repetitions to identify the exact minimum solution at $n = 9$.

However, simulation does give you the correct answer in the sense that the number of searches goes up as the cost of searching falls. This key result makes sense, since you will take advantage of cheaper search costs by searching more.

Simulation Versus Analytical Methods

Figures 3.14 and 3.15 show the exact expected value of the total cost. As mentioned earlier, if you are interested, you can download *Search.xlsx* from dub.sh/gbae to see how these analytical results were derived.

You might wonder why we used simulation when analytical methods give us an exact answer. There are two reasons. First, by implementing the problem in Excel, we get a deep, clear understanding of the role of randomness in this problem. It is one thing to say that prices are random, but seeing them bounce on the screen really conveys the data generation process.

Simulation is often helpful in understanding a problem because it requires building a model that reflects core components of a real-world scenario. This often enables a richer, fuller grasp of the forces at play.

The second reason for using simulation is that we have another independent method that is confirming the analytical solution. The averages in Figures 3.12 and 3.13 are very close to their expected values. We can be sure that we have found the right answer when both methods agree. And if they do not agree, we are alerted to a potential error in one of the methods.

Neither approach is foolproof. Simulation's main drawback is that it cannot give an exact answer. In addition, sometimes so many repetitions are needed to obtain a clear result that it is impractical.

But analytical methods using equations, algebra, and calculus are not perfect either. Sometimes, there is no way to derive the answer, and simulation is all we can do. Other times, the analytical method fails disastrously and gives us an incorrect answer. Simulation helps us avoid that trap.

Takeaways

Economists believe in the *law of one price*, the idea that competition makes prices converge. But this only applies in a frictionless world of perfect information. In our model, if c = 0, you simply get all the prices and pick the lowest one. In such a world, there would be no price dispersion, since everyone would go to the cheapest vendor, so all the sellers would have to match that price. The law of one price would hold.

In the real world, there are all sorts of frictions. An important one is incomplete information, so buyers do not know all the prices (and qualities) of goods and services. The real world has many different prices (just think of all the prices you see at gas stations as you are driving down the road), and buyers have to search to find low prices. Economists say that search is price discovery, which emphasizes how searching is a productive activity.

Consumers face a search optimization problem. The more they search, the lower the price they are likely to pay, but they have to spend resources—time and effort—to search. You can definitely oversearch, which means that the gain from the lower price you found was not worth the extra cost of searching. On the other hand, you cannot search enough—you saved on search costs, but you did not take advantage of the lower prices you would have found by searching more.

Consumers optimize and search an optimal amount like Goldilocks: not too little and not too much but just right. The fact that buyers will not choose to find every price explains why price dispersion exists. This is a key result. As Stigler (1961) famously said, "Price dispersion is a manifestation—and, indeed, it is the measure—of ignorance in the market."

We also showed that lowering search costs would increase the optimal number of searches, but we can point out a few interesting real-world implications of this result. For example, not all consumers face the same search costs. Suppose you are in a hurry (perhaps you have an important deadline at work), your search costs are high, and therefore it is optimal for you to search less. Different people in different situations have different optimal solutions.

Our comparative statics result that lower c leads to higher optimal n points to the fact that lower search costs reduce price dispersion. If the internet allows you to quickly scan gas stations in an area and go to the cheapest one, prices are going to come closer together. They will not all be exactly the same (as the law of one price says) because the search is not free, but they will not be as spread out.

Noneconomists sometimes demonize advertising. They see consumers as dupes, easily fooled and tricked by ads to buy things they do not need or want. But search theory shows advertising in a different light. It is a way to lower search costs. Sellers are trying to be noticed in a noisy, chaotic marketplace, so they provide consumers with information about prices and product characteristics.

Since we introduced the internet as a shock that lowered search costs, we close by pointing out that new online technologies have radically affected search theory. You know that every click is tracked, and the prices you see are personalized just for you. Optimal online searching is the subject of intense research today. Both buyers and sellers are faced with complicated, intertwined optimization problems.

References

Stigler, G. (1961). "The Economics of Information." *Journal of Political Economy* 69, no. 3, pp. 213–225, www.jstor.org/stable/1829263. This paper is recognized as the beginning of the economics of search. Stigler was recognized as the founder of information economics when he was awarded the Nobel Prize in Economics in 1982.

Appendix

For 10 searches, repeat the same procedure as for 5 searches, slightly changing the formula for the minimum price and costs of searching to account for 10, instead of 5, searches. It goes like this: In cell E1, enter a 10 (this represents gathering prices from 10 vendors), and in cell E2, enter the formula =MIN(A2:A11). This formula shows the lowest price in your sample from 10 stores, which is the one we would buy. In cell E3, enter the formula =0.04*10 (0.4 is the cost of 10 searches). In cell E4, we add the two cells above it together, so enter the formula =E2+E3. You are now ready to track cell E4 in a simulation to see the typical result for this search strategy.

You should find that 10 searches have an approximate expected value of around 0.49. This is higher than 5 searches and therefore is clearly not an optimal solution.

4. Growth

> The most powerful force in the universe is compound interest.
>
> Attributed to Albert Einstein

4.1 Growth Math

The learning objective is straightforward to state but difficult to accomplish: a deep appreciation of the power of compounding. You want to go beyond the simple mechanics of growth and truly grasp the nature of the force unleashed by exponential growth.

In addition, there are two subgoals:

1. Measuring growth via the CAGR, the compound annual growth rate
2. Understanding and using the Rule of 70

A Race

We are going to pit an arithmetic sequence against a geometric sequence (or progression). This is not a mystery, so we will reveal right now that the geometric sequence will win. Be on the lookout, however, for some surprising results.

An *arithmetic sequence* is a list of numbers with a common difference between each term. The sequence 4, 9, 14, 19, 24 is an arithmetic sequence with 5 as the difference.

Instead of a constant additive increase, a *geometric sequence* progresses by applying a multiplicative constant to each term. So 4, 8, 16, 32 is a geometric sequence with 2 as the multiplier. Notice that doubling is a 100% increase.

Starting from 4, it is easy to see that doubling beats adding 5 pretty quickly—by the third term. But what if we made it really uneven in choosing the additive and multiplicative constants?

Starting with $1, what if you got $1,000,000 more every day versus a 10% per day increase? We will use Excel to run this race.

Let's agree that the arithmetic sequence is going to jump out to a big lead. After two days, it has $2,000,001, while the geometric sequence will have $1.21. But what happens as time goes by?

STEP Save a blank Excel workbook as *Growth.xlsx* and enter the labels in row 2 as shown in Figure 4.1. In cells B1 and C1, enter the values $1000000 and 10% (including the $ and %) and name the cells *x* and *i* (for interest rate). Use Excel's Help or the web if needed to name the cells, and widen column B until the value is visible.

> **EXCEL TIP** Naming cells improves presentation and makes your implementation easier to follow. Using natural language text in formulas instead of cell addresses requires more setup time, but the improvement in readability of formulas is well worth the effort.

STEP Enter 0 and 1 in cells A3 and A4, respectively, then select both cells, click the bottom-right corner of cell A4, and drag down to cell A50. In cell B3, enter $1, and in cell B4, enter the formula =B3+*x*. Select cell B4 and double-click at the bottom-right corner to fill it down. Enter $1 in cell C3 and the formula =(1+i)*C3 in cell C4. Fill it down.

	A	B	C
1		$ 1,000,000	10%
2	Day	Amount	Amount
3	0	$ 1	$ 1
4	1	$ 1,000,001	$ 1.10
5	2	$ 2,000,001	$ 1.21
6	3	$ 3,000,001	$ 1.33
7	4	$ 4,000,001	$ 1.46

Figure 4.1: Setting up the race.

The formula in column C is produced by this algebraic simplification of the way the next term is produced in a geometric sequence:

$$x_{t+1} = x_t + ix_t$$

$$x_{t+1} = (1 + i)\, x_t$$

STEP Widen columns B and C to make sure the numbers are visible in row 50. It is obvious that \$1M per day is way ahead of 10% per day, but let's make a chart to show how far ahead the arithmetic sequence is: Select cell range A2:C50 and insert a *Scatter* chart. Give it a title (you can use *Racing Sequences*), label the x-axis (*Day* would work), and insert text boxes without fills or outlines to label the two series.

Your chart has a line with a slope of \$1M and what appears to be another line (the geometric sequence) on the x-axis. The values of the geometric sequence are so small, you cannot tell that they actually form a curve. What happens if we extend the sequence?

STEP Select cells A50:C50, click the bottom-right corner of cell C50, and drag down to row 153. Widen column C to see the values, and decrease the decimal places so only integer dollar values are displayed to make it easier to compare columns B and C.

After 150 days, the arithmetic sequence is still way ahead, roughly \$150M to \$1.6M, but we can see that the geometric sequence is starting to really gather momentum.

STEP Extend the sequences to row 253.

After 250 days, the geometric sequence is almost 100 times bigger—almost \$25 billion compared to \$250 million. When did the geometric sequence pass the arithmetic sequence?

STEP Scroll back up to the top of the sheet and enter the label *Difference* in cell D2 and the formula =C3–B3 in cell D3. Double-click the bottom-right corner of cell D3 to fill it down. Scroll down and widen column D as needed as you scroll.

You will see that the parentheses (indicating negative numbers) stop on day 201. That is the day the geometric sequence won the race, and its lead will grow wider, ever faster, from then on.

STEP Scroll back up and edit the SERIES formulas in the chart. Change the row numbers to 213 so that the formula for SERIES 1 looks like this: =SERIES(*Sheet1!*\$B\$2,*Sheet1!*\$A\$3:\$A\$213,*Sheet1!*\$B\$3:\$B\$213,1). Do the same for the second series.

Figure 4.2 shows what your chart should look like. Do not be misled into thinking that the geometric sequence was not growing at first and then started growing really fast around day 150. In fact, it grew at the same rate, 10%, every single day. Another mistake is to see every curve as having constant growth—do not fall into this trap.

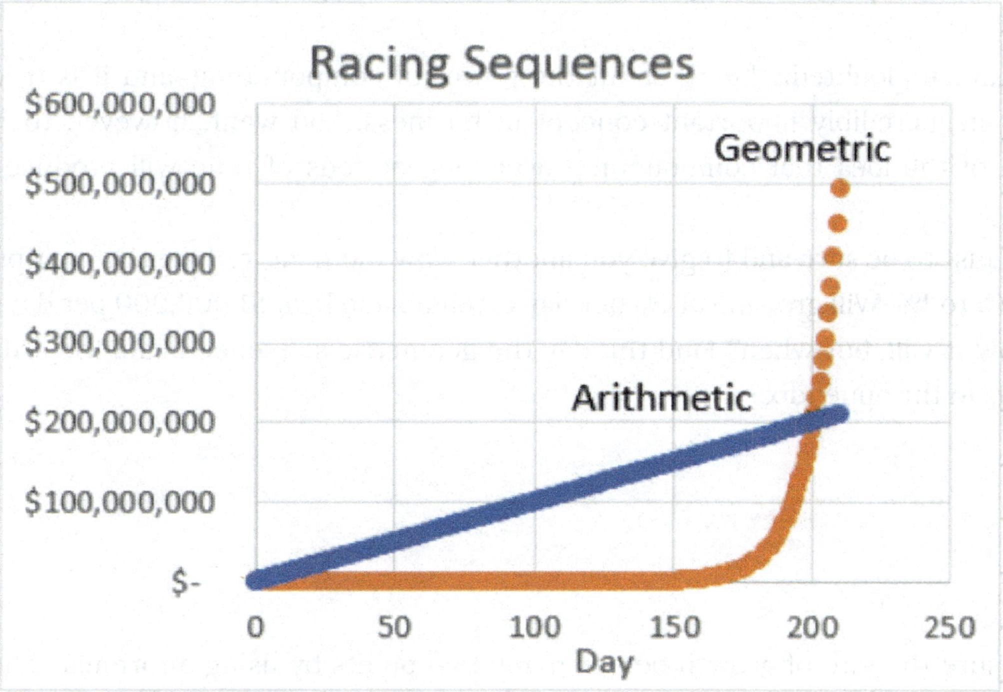

Figure 4.2: The geometric sequence wins!

One quick way to check if a curve is growing at a constant rate is to make the y-axis a log scale.

STEP Click on the y-axis (the $ values) and check the *Logarithmic scale* box in the *Axis Options* on the right of your screen.

The chart dramatically changes. The curve becomes a line and the line a curve. The fact that a log scale linearizes the curve means the curve is growing at a constant rate.

Now, you might think that we are at the surprising result mentioned at the beginning. After all, it is pretty impressive that 10% per day, after starting so incredibly far behind and falling even farther behind, overtakes $1M per day, but no, that is not it.

The big surprise is actually that no matter what (positive) numbers you pick for the constant difference and multiplicative factor, the geometric will *always* eventually beat the arithmetic sequence.

Let's be clear about this. You can make the constant difference as big as you want and the multiplicative factor as little as you want (as long as it is positive), and the geometric progression will eventually win the race. That is shocking and reveals the force embedded in compounding.

You could argue that this is expected because multiplication is more powerful than addition, and that is a true statement, but Figure 4.2 hints at another way to remember why geometric progressions are so powerful—they are curves instead of lines. Eventually, if they start from the same point and are both increasing, a curve will always pass a line.

You have undoubtedly heard about the power of compounding, and it is true that compounding is an incredibly important concept in business. You want, however, to have a deep appreciation of the idea that compounding over long periods of time will produce remarkable results.

STEP Just to be sure and to give you another wow moment, reduce the multiplicative constant in cell C1 to 1%. Will growing at 1% per day catch up and beat $1,000,000 per day? Amazingly, yes, you know it will, but when? Find the day the geometric sequence beats the arithmetic one. The answer is in the appendix.

CAGR

We can measure the rate of growth between any two points by using a formula called the *compound annual growth rate* (CAGR). The word *annual* is used because it is often applied to yearly data, but we can apply the CAGR to the daily frequency in the race we just ran. Instead of just stating the formula, it is worth seeing where it comes from.

We know that a geometric sequence is generated by adding a constant multiplicative factor (i) times the previous amount. Here are the first few terms, where x_0 is the initial value, x_1 is the next value, and so on.

$$x_1 = x_0 + ix_0 = (1+i)x_0$$

$$x_2 = x_1 + ix_1 = (1+i)x_1$$

$$x_3 = x_2 + ix_2 = (1+i)x_2$$

The subscript tells us the time period, with 0 meaning right now. The last equation above says the value of x in time period 3 equals the previous value of x plus the rate of growth times the previous value. The value of x in time period 3 also can be expressed as $(1 + i)$ times the value in time period 2.

We can rewrite x_2 by substituting in the formula for x_1 like this:

$$x_2 = (1+i)x_1 = (1+i)(1+i)x_0 = (1+i)^2 x_0$$

We can do the same for x_3:

$$x_3 = (1+i)x_2 = (1+i)(1+i)(1+i)x_0 = (1+i)^3 x_0$$

In fact, we could do this for any value in the sequence after the initial value:

$$x_t = (1+i)x_{t-1} = (1+i)^t x_0$$

The equation above says that starting from an initial value, x_0, the value of x at time t, x_t, will be $(1 + i)^t$ times the initial value. We do not have to know the previous value to get the next value. All we need is the initial value, the rate of growth, i, and the number of time periods.

Since this equation expresses where every point will be in the sequence, we can solve for i like this:

$$x_t = (1+i)^t x_0$$

$$\frac{x_t}{x_0} = (1+i)^t$$

$$\left[\frac{x_t}{x_0}\right]^{1/t} = 1+i$$

$$\left[\frac{x_t}{x_0}\right]^{1/t} - 1 = i$$

$$i = \left[\frac{x_t}{x_0}\right]^{1/t} - 1$$

The last equation is the CAGR. We can write it in a more user-friendly way:

$$i = \left(\frac{x_t}{x_0}\right)^{1/t} - 1$$

$$CAGR = \left(\frac{\text{Final Value}}{\text{Initial Value}}\right)^{1/\text{Number of Time Periods}} - 1$$

Given any two numbers and the number of time periods, the CAGR tells us what the rate of growth must be if the numbers are part of a geometric sequence. Let's put this formula to work.

STEP Label cell E1 as CAGR and enter the formula =(C9/C3)^(1/6)-1 in cell E2.

You calculated the rate of growth from the initial value of \$1 at $t = 0$ to the value in the sixth time period, and this will equal the rate of growth in cell C1.

Be careful with the number of time periods in the CAGR formula. From t = 0 to t = 6 and from cells C3 to C9, there are seven numbers, not six. The number of periods is always one less than the number of values in the sequence. The number of time periods, t, is the amount of time that has elapsed since the start. For a length of one unit of time, you need two numbers, the beginning and end.

STEP Modify your formula in cell E2 to compute the CAGR from time period 5 to 10. You will know you have it right if cell E2 equals cell C1.

Of course, we constructed the geometric sequence in column C, so we know the rate of growth. What if we did not know the rate of growth and had only beginning and ending values?

STEP Click on an empty cell and compute the CAGR from an initial value of 11.7 in t = 0 to 23.1652 in t = 14.

The correct formula is =(23.1652/11.7)^(1/14)-1, and Excel should be displaying 0.05. Notice that we do not need to know the numbers in the intervening time periods. If it is a geometric sequence—that is, growing at a constant rate—then we could compute the value at any time period using the generating equation, $x_t = (1 + i)^t x_0$.

Let's show that values between initial and final are irrelevant and introduce another measure of growth, the *average annual percentage change* (AAPC).

STEP Insert a new sheet and enter the formula =RAND()*1 in cell A1, =RAND()*2 in cell A2, and =RAND() times 3, 4, and 5 in cells A3, A4, and A5. Make a graph by selecting range A1:A5 and inserting a *Scatter* chart. Press F9 (you may have to use the *fn* key on your keyboard) a few times to recalculate the sheet.

Even though the values do not grow at a constant rate, we can compute the CAGR from A1 to A5.

STEP Label cell A6 CAGR, and in cell A7, enter the formula to compute it from A1 to A5.

The formula you entered (to be sure: =(A5/A1)^(1/4)-1) ignores the three points in between the first and last points. The CAGR assumes that a constant growth curve connects the first and last points.

There is another common measure of growth that does use all the points, the average annual percent change.

STEP In cell B2, enter the formula =(A2-A1)/A1 and fill it down.

Column B has the percentage changes from one year to the next. The average annual percent change takes the average of the percentage changes.

STEP Label cell B6 AAPC and enter the formula =AVERAGE(B2:B5) in cell B7. Press F9 a few times.

It is clear that the two measures are different. The CAGR answers a specific question: What is the constant rate of growth that would need to be applied to the initial value so that we end up at the final value? Unlike the CAGR, applying the AAPC growth rate to the first value will not produce the final value (unless the numbers are a geometric sequence). The AAPC is just an average of the annual percentage changes.

In fact, there are many more ways to measure growth than CAGR and AAPC, but these are the two most common ones. And there are many more averages than the usual one. There is one called the *geometric mean* (*mean* and *average* are synonyms). Instead of adding the values and dividing by *n* (the number of values), you multiply them and then take the $\frac{1}{n}th$ root.

STEP Enter the formula =A2/A1 in cell E2. Fill it down to E5. In cell E6, enter the formula =(E2*E3*E4*E5)^(1/4).

This is the geometric mean of the ratios in cells E2:E5. There is an easier way: Use Excel's GEOMEAN function.

STEP In cell E7, enter the formula =GEOMEAN(E2:E5). Confirm cells E6 and E7 are equal.

You probably have not noticed, but an important discovery is at hand.

STEP In cell E8, subtract 1 from the geometric mean in cell E6 or E7 (since they are the same).

Do you see it? Look carefully at cells A7 and E8—the CAGR and geometric mean of the ratios minus 1 are the same! That is striking.

The geometric mean has applications when the data generated come from a geometric sequence. For example, if an investment is growing at a constant percentage, we might use the geometric mean because, like the CAGR, applying the geometric mean growth rate to the first value will produce the last value.

The Rule of 70

The growth rate of a geometric sequence can be used to determine the time needed to double. We use the generating equation, but this time we know we want the initial value to double, and we want to solve for *t*:

$$x_t = (1+i)^t x_0$$

$$2x_0 = (1+i)^t x_0$$

$$2 = (1+i)^t$$

With t as an exponent, we face a challenge in solving for t. The path forward involves the logarithm, which is the inverse of exponentiation. We can take the natural log, *ln*, of both sides to solve for *t*:

$$2 = (1+i)^t$$

$$ln(2) = tln(1+i)$$

$$\frac{ln(2)}{ln(1+i)} = t$$

$$t = \frac{ln(2)}{ln(1+i)}$$

We can use this formula to find the exact time it will take a geometric sequence to double. If the growth rate is 10% per time period, we plug that into the formula and compute it.

STEP Return to *Sheet1* (where you raced the sequences) and set cell C1 to 10%. In cell G1, enter the label Exact Time to Double. In cell G2, enter the formula =LN(2)/LN(1+i).

You used Excel's natural log function, LN(), to compute that it will take a little over 7.2725 time periods for a geometric sequence growing at 10% to double.

Since the exact answer cannot be easily computed, an approximation is often used. It relies on the fact that $ln(1 + x) \approx x$.

STEP In cell G3, enter the formula =LN(1+i).

With i = 10%, $ln(1 + i)$ is almost 0.1, confirming the fact. In addition, $ln(2)$ is roughly 0.693 or, rounded to two decimal places, 0.70. This means we can approximate the exact answer like this:

$$t = \frac{ln(2)}{ln(1+i)}$$

$$t \approx \frac{0.7}{i}$$

We have derived the *Rule of* 70, an approximation we can write in a more friendly way like this:

$$\text{Time to Double} = \frac{70}{\text{Growth Rate (in Percentage)}}$$

If the growth rate is 10% per day, the Rule of 70 says it will take 70 divided by 10, or 7, time periods to double. This is not exactly true. The exact time to double is displayed by cell G2, but it is reasonably close.

STEP With cell C1 at 10%, notice that the initial value of $1 almost doubles by the 7th day and almost doubles again (to $4) by the 14th day.

We can try a different growth rate to see if the Rule of 70 works again. At 2% per day, the Rule of 70 says it will take about 35 days to double. Is this true?

STEP Change cell C1 to 2%. Did the Rule of 70 work?

Yes, cell G2 shows it will take just a little longer than 35 days to double at 2%. Also, the value in column C is $2 at t = 35, and if you scroll down, you will see that it is $4 at t = 70. It really does double almost every 35 days with a 2% per day growth rate.

STEP Set cell C1 to 70% and look at the values in column C.

The Rule of 70 is not doing well here. It is not true that we get doubling every year. This shows that the Rule of 70 works for "small" growth rates, and the smaller the growth rate, the better the approximation.

There is also the Rule of 72, which is a slightly worse approximation to $ln(2) \approx 0.693$ but has more divisors than the Rule of 70.

Growth Numeracy

Today's world population is roughly 8 billion, but humans started with small numbers and expanded. Galor (2022, p. 46) says,

> At the eve of the Neolithic Revolution [the birth of agriculture], in the year 10,000 BCE, an estimated 2.4 million human beings roamed the earth. Yet, by the year 1 CE, as the Roman Empire and the Mayan civilization approached their height, the world's population had multiplied seventy-eight fold and soared to 188 million.

Generative AI exploded in the public's consciousness in November 2022 when OpenAI released its latest version of ChatGPT. This was followed by many competitors. As part of my exploration and interaction with these new tools, I repeatedly tried to get various AIs to compute the CAGR for the increase in human population from 2.4 to 188 million over 10,000 years. Figure 4.3 shows one answer from ChatGPT 3.5 (free version) on June 7, 2023.

What is the growth rate for 2.4 to 188 for 10,000 years?

To calculate the growth rate from 2.4 to 188 over 10,000 years, we can use the compound annual growth rate (CAGR) formula. The CAGR formula is given by:

CAGR = (Ending Value / Beginning Value)^(1 / Number of Periods) – 1

In this case:
Beginning Value (BV) = 2.4
Ending Value (EV) = 188
Number of Periods (N) = 10,000 years

Let's calculate the growth rate:
CAGR = (188 / 2.4)^(1 / 10,000) – 1

Calculating this using a calculator or a spreadsheet, the growth rate (CAGR) from 2.4 to 188 over 10,000 years is approximately 3.23%.

Figure 4.3 – ChatGPT 3.5 computing CAGR.

The AIs always do a good job of explaining how to do the problem but sometimes give ridiculous answers. For example, the steps in Figure 4.3 are correct, but the final answer is nonsensical. At 3% per year, the Rule of 70 says there will be doubling around every 25 years. That would be 16 times in 100 years. We pass 78-fold before 200 years.

A moment's reflection shows that a 3% growth rate over such a long period of time is going to produce a huge number. How huge? Excel says 1.03 to the 10,000th power is 2×10^{128}. Today's world population of 8 billion is 8×10^9, so ChatGPT's answer is not in the ballpark.

STEP Use Excel to compute the CAGR for Galor's numbers: an initial value of 2.4 and a final value of 188 over 10,000 years. You can use ChatGPT's CAGR formula in Figure 4.3, since it did get that right.

In fact, the CAGR is tiny, about 0.000436. Rounding roughly to 0.0005, that is 0.05%, and the Rule of 70 would give doubling every 1,400 years. Now that CAGR makes sense.

Lesson: Never trust generative AI with a mathematical computation. More broadly, never trust any fact produced by an AI. Always check its claims.

ChatGPT 4 (the paid version in 2023) with a Mathematica plugin gets the CAGR computation right. But I still check every number it produces. AI will undoubtedly get better, but I will remain skeptical of any factual claim it makes. You should also.

As a final example, Poundstone (2016, p. 211) asked this survey question: Suppose you put $1,000 in a tax-free account that earns 7% per year on this investment. How many years will it take to double your original investment to $2,000?

1. Between 0 and 5 years
2. Between 5 and 15 years
3. Between 15 and 45 years
4. More than 45 years

Only 59% got it right. The Rule of 70 gives 10 years, so the correct answer is between 5 and 15 years. It cannot be 0 to 5, since 7% of $1,000 is $70. So it would be $1,070 next year and $1,147 in year 2, and there's no way it reaches $2,000 in 5 years. Likewise, 15 to 45 and more than 45 are obviously wrong, since $70 per year (ignoring compounding) times 30 years is over $2,000.

More importantly, those getting the correct answer "reported $32,000 more personal annual income, more than twice as much in savings, and rated themselves 15 percent happier" (Poundstone, 2016, p. 212). Maybe being numerate has its advantages.

Takeaways

In everyday English, *exponential* means "really fast." In math, it means an exponent is involved. Geometric sequences are exponential because they can be written with a generating equation like this: $x_t = (1 + i)^t x_0$.

Geometric sequences are much more powerful than arithmetic sequences, especially over a long time period. It is hard to believe, but true that a geometric sequence will always surpass an arithmetic sequence, no matter the positive constants used.

Mathematicians usually stress the multiplicative nature of geometric sequences to explain their power, but it is also true that starting from the same place and pointing up, a curve will always eventually pass a line.

We compute the compound annual growth rate with this formula:

$$CAGR = \left[\frac{\text{Final Value}}{\text{Initial Value}}\right]^{1/\text{Number of Time Periods}} - 1$$

The geometric mean (Excel function GEOMEAN()) is another way to compute the CAGR.

The Rule of 70 is mental math. You can quickly roughly compute how long it will take to double by dividing 70 by the growth rate. You can use the Rule of 70 to check a computed growth rate for reasonableness.

The mathematics of how things grow, CAGR, geometric mean, and the Rule of 70 are all part of being numerate. We apply these ideas to economic growth in the next section.

References

Searching the web reveals that it is pretty clear that he never said it, but the quote in the epigraph attributed to Albert Einstein certainly rings true. He is also supposed to have said something like "Compound interest is the Eighth Wonder of the World," but this is also doubtful. A good quote that the person actually said is from Charlie Munger

(Warren Buffett's partner): "The first rule of compounding is to never interrupt it unnecessarily."

Galor, O. (2022). *The Journey of Humanity* (Dutton).

Poundstone, W. (2016). *Head in the Cloud* (Little Brown and Company), archive.org/details/headincloudwhykn0000poun.

Appendix

A geometric sequence with a growth rate of 1% per day will pass an arithmetic sequence with a constant difference of $1M on day 2,161. Yes, that is roughly 10 times longer than it takes the geometric progression growing at 10% per day. And, yes, if you tried 0.1%, it would take 10 times longer. But no matter how small you make the growth rate or how big you make the constant difference, eventually, the geometric sequence wins!

4.2 Growth Data

We apply the CAGR and the Rule of 70 to long-run output data. The goal is to understand basic facts about economic growth around the world and over time.

Amazingly, economic growth is brand new. It is a mystery and the focus of intense research. Perhaps the biggest open problem in economics is why some countries grow and others do not. One result of uneven growth is that economic inequality across countries keeps getting bigger and bigger.

Data Source and Description

The data come from an economic historian named Angus Maddison. He spent his working life compiling and estimating a variety of economic and demographic variables around the world over very long periods of time. Briefly, Maddison's data are high quality, but they are noisier the farther back you go (Barreto, 2016). Visit www.theworldeconomy.org if you want to know more.

Annual gross domestic product (GDP) is the value of all final goods and services produced in a year. GDP is where we begin when we measure economic performance. There are three key adjustments that must be made to GDP when it is used to compare countries over time.

1. *Inflation*: GDP uses current prices to compute the value of output. If prices double but the number of units produced stays the same, nominal GDP doubles. That is not what we want. Our measure of economic performance needs to reflect only changes in output, not prices. Thus, we use real GDP because it holds prices constant over time and gives us a better measure of economic performance.
2. *Population*: If two countries have the same GDP but one has more people, we would say the smaller country is more productive in terms of output per person. We divide real GDP by the number of people to get real GDP per person (or per capita) to measure economic performance.
3. *Purchasing Power Parity*: To compare the GDP of countries with different monetary units, we need to convert currencies. For complicated reasons, the best way to do this involves a hypothetical "international Geary-Khamis dollar" (for more detail and an explanation, see www.google.com/search?q=geary-khamis). Adjusting real GDP for purchasing power parity by using international Geary-Khamis dollars gives us a better comparison of GDP across countries.

Real GDP per person adjusted for purchasing power parity is the key variable used to measure economic performance across countries over time. A lot of preparation and statistical adjustment is needed before we begin analyzing the data. Fortunately, Maddison has done this heavy lifting for us.

It is undoubtedly true that real GDP per person is a cornerstone of economic analysis, but it is far from perfect. Its biggest failing is that it says nothing about the distribution of output. We can divide an economy's GDP by the number of people, but it is not true that each person in that economy gets the same share of output. Measures of inequality in the distribution of output are an important aspect of economic performance that we will review later.

Accessing the Excel Workbook

STEP Go to dub.sh/gbae and click the Excel Workbooks link (top right). Click *LongRunGrowth.xlsm* to download it. Move the file from your download folder to a folder on your computer or network.

Notice that the file has an *.xlsm* extension. Regular Excel workbooks have an *xls* or *xlsx* extension. The *m* stands for *macro*. *LongRunGrowth.xlsm* is a macro-enabled Excel workbook. When you open it, you must enable macros to get full functionality from the file.

STEP Open *LongRunGrowth.xlsm*, read the *Intro* sheet, and be sure to click the Click to Test button. You may have to adjust your security settings as described in the *Intro* sheet.

Basic Geography

The workbook contains several sheets. The *IncomeGroups* sheet has World Bank classification of 217 countries and administrative regions by income. There are low-, lower-middle-, upper-middle-, and high-income groups.

STEP Go to the *IncomeGroups* sheet and scroll down to see the countries in each group. Look at a few rows and think about what you know about those four countries.

For example, row 25 has Niger, Ghana, Dominica, and Switzerland. You probably knew Switzerland is a rich country, but did you know Ghana is lower income but not as poor as Niger?

The countries are sorted alphabetically, so we cannot say anything about their order within a group. This sheet tells us nothing about Niger versus Somalia or Uganda other than they are all in the lowest income group.

The map in the sheet looks different from the usual world map. This is because it is doing an equal area projection. Unlike the usual Mercator map, which shows Greenland as huge, this map accurately reflects geographic size. It really is true that Africa is three times bigger than the United States.

The colors correspond to the income categories, as shown in the legend. While the map in the Excel workbook is informative, the online version is even better.

STEP Click on the map or copy and paste the link below it in a browser to explore the interactive version online. It displays name and category information as you hover over the country.

Data Sheets

Maddison provides three sets of numbers, organized in three sheets. The first is *Population*, the second GDP, and *PerCapita* GDP is the third.

STEP Click in each of the three sheets to see how the data are presented. Scroll down to see all the countries in column A (down to row 198).

The countries are organized by a combination of geography and cultural connection. Western Europe is followed by Western Offshoots: Australia, New Zealand, Canada, and the United States. Maddison also gives us groupings such as Latin America and East Asia.

As you scroll down, you will see labels that indicate how country borders have changed over time. For example, "Former Yugoslavia" includes the countries above it in the list (as of 2010, when these data were compiled), and row 65 has the label *Total former* USSR, with its countries above it.

Notice how the placement of the countries is the same in the three sheets. Maddison estimates population, then real GDP in 1990 Geary-Khamis (GK) dollars for each country or group.

The values in the *PerCapita GDP* sheet are simply real GDP divided by the number of people. We focus on the data in the *PerCapita GDP* sheet because this is real GDP per person adjusted for purchasing power parity—this is our measure of economic performance.

The *OnlyCountries* sheet removes all groups and headings from the *PerCapita GDP* sheet and displays an alphabetic listing of the countries. Sorting by real GDP per person in 2008 compares the economies of these countries at that time.

> **EXCEL TIP** Sorting is one of the most dangerous things you can do in a spreadsheet. It is remarkably easy to destroy a dataset by sorting only part of it. When you sort, be very, very careful.

STEP Select cell range A3:GR165 in the *OnlyCountries* sheet. The easiest way to do this is to click on cell A3, hold down the *Shift* key, and click on cell GR165. Click the *Data* tab in the *Ribbon* and click *Filter* (in the *Sort and Filter* group).

Excel has added downward-pointing arrows in the cells in row 3. Clicking one of these arrows pops up a menu and enables easy sorting of the data. You can remove the arrows by clicking the Filter button again.

STEP Click the down arrow in column GR and select *Sort Largest to Smallest*.

Excel obliges and now shows Hong Kong in row 4. It is the richest country in the Maddison dataset in 2008, the last available year. Today, Hong Kong is not a country but a special administrative region of China. It is still rich, but lists of richest countries today, using real GDP per person adjusted for purchasing power parity, usually show Luxembourg, Singapore, and Ireland as the richest countries.

STEP Scroll down slowly and look at the countries as they go by.

Switzerland is near the top, clearly in the high-income group. Dominica (not the Dominican Republic) is not included in Maddison's dataset (it is in the group of 21 small Caribbean countries). As you get near the bottom, you see Ghana (row 124), which is lower-middle income according to the World Bank. Niger, which is in the low-income group, is third from the bottom.

The data show that Ghana's real GDP per person of roughly GK$1,500 is 3× (three times) bigger than Niger. That is a lot, but it is nothing compared to the 50× difference between Switzerland and Niger. This staggering difference is evidence of an important lesson that we will explore again:

Lesson 1: Country real GDP per person is wildly uneven.

We can see the massive dispersion in economic performance by noting that the range in real GDP per person goes from a few hundred GK dollars in the poorest countries to 30,000 GK dollars in the richest countries. We can display this in a histogram.

STEP Select cell range GR3:GR165, click the *Insert* menu item in the *Ribbon*, and click the *Histogram* chart type. Click the *x*-axis and change the number of bins to 30.

Your histogram shows a tall rectangle at the left, indicating many poor countries, then a spread-out distribution gradually getting smaller and smaller as you go right (these are the richest countries).

Another way to see the big disparity in economic outcomes is by computing the standard deviation of real GDP per person for these countries.

STEP Enter the formula =STDEV.P(GR4:GR165) in cell GR2.

The SD displayed in cell GR2 says that the typical amount of dispersion around the average is about GK$8,000. That is a lot of dispersion, since the average is also around GK$8,000.

It has not always been this way. We will see when we start looking at long-run growth that countries used to be much closer in terms of economic performance, but we can also find evidence for this lesson in the short run.

STEP Copy cell GR2 and paste it in cell GJ2. Paste again in cell FZ2.

The earliest we can compute the SD for this set of countries is 1990 because the Soviet Union collapsed in 1989, and many countries in the set were part of the USSR. Even for this short period of time, the numbers are striking. The SD falls from GK$8,000 in 2008, to under GK$7,000 in 2000, and to GK$5,400 in 1990. This is evidence for the second lesson:

Lesson 2: The disparity in country real GDP per person is rising.

In fact, this part of the story is complicated. With free-flowing information and technology, we should see convergence in real GDP per person. There is some evidence that a subset of countries does converge (so the SD of real GDP per person would get smaller). Overall, however, as Maddison's set of countries shows, the spread in real GDP per person has been growing.

Growth over the Long Run

Now that we know how Maddison created and organized the data, we are ready to use the data to examine the historical record to learn about economic growth. Begin with a screencast that introduces the *Compare* sheet and emphasizes this lesson:

Lesson 3: Economic growth is brand new.

STEP Watch the video titled "Long Run Growth" at vimeo.com/econexcel/longrungrowth.

The screencast says that for millennia, every country was poor. Yes, there were a few rich individuals, mostly monarchs and rulers, but everyone else was living at a subsistence level. It is only in the last few hundred years that some countries have broken out of the poverty trap.

Why did growth suddenly (on a time scale of millennia) explode on the scene? Why did only some countries grow? Believe it or not, we do not actually know the specific mechanisms involved. It was not simply money or trading, since both have been around for a lot longer than the last few hundred years.

Economists point to the *market system* as the driver of growth. This loosely defined concept involves private property rights, rule of law, entrepreneurship, widespread individual striving for wealth, and celebration of financial success. This complicated, poorly understood cocktail of institutions and cultural norms has many names, such as capitalism and free enterprise.

We do not know exactly why, but growth emerged in Europe roughly a few hundred years ago, and then it evolved unevenly. Some countries grew and others did not. Some grew fast and others slowly. The *Compare* sheet can be used to display examples of this, as shown at the end of the "Long Run Growth" screencast.

STEP Use the *Compare* sheet from 1950 to 2008 to see if Maddison's data agree with the World Bank classification of Sudan as low income and Egypt as lower-middle income.

Your chart shows that these two countries, which share a border, were roughly equal in 1960 but are no longer so. Egypt has done much better than Sudan and now has double the real GDP per person.

STEP Choose an upper-middle-income country from the *IncomeGroups* sheet and add it to the chart.

Adding an upper-middle-income country changes the scale of the *y*-axis and places another series above Egypt and Sudan.

STEP Add a rich country from Europe to your chart.

The *y*-axis scale changes again, and the spread of the four countries is quite large. Sudan is pushed close to the *x*-axis, with Egypt slightly above it. Notice that the gap between the rich European country you added and your upper-middle-income country is big.

So far, we have been tracking the level of real GDP per person, but we are also interested in the growth rate of real GDP per person. The next screencast, "CAGR and AAPC for Norway," shows how we can use the Maddison dataset and *Compare* sheet to find the growth rate, and it makes this point:

Lesson 4: The magic growth number is 2% per year in real GDP per person.

STEP Watch the video titled "CAGR and AAPC for Norway" at vimeo.com/econexcel/cagr.

Joseph Schumpeter is well known for his theory of the entrepreneur as innovator, perhaps best captured in the oxymoron *creative destruction*. Schumpeter, like many others who have studied economic growth, was awed by the productive powers of the market system.

In *Capitalism, Socialism, and Democracy*, published in 1942, Schumpeter used data to describe the historical success of capitalism before pronouncing that it could not survive. The heroic entrepreneur would become obsolete as rational scientific thinking took hold. The demise of capitalism has not happened (yet).

Using noisy, imperfect measures of real GDP per person, Schumpeter found that the United States had enjoyed a spectacular run from after the Civil War to the Great Depression. He concluded that if this performance was repeated another 50 years, "this would do away with anything that according to present standards could be called poverty" (Schumpeter, 1942, p. 66).

Let's see if Maddison's data agree with Schumpeter as we explore the historical economic performance of the US economy.

STEP Use the Data Vertical button to get real GDP per person in the United States in a vertical column (as shown in the "CAGR and AAPC for Norway" screencast). Compute the CAGR in the United States from 1870 to 1929 and from 1950 to 2008 (as shown in the screencast). What would Schumpeter have said had he lived to see how the United States economy performed until 2008?

The United States actually did even better in the second half of the 20th century (2.06% per year) than during the Civil War to the Great Depression (1.77% per year). Schumpeter would have been shocked by this performance.

STEP Go to the *Compare* sheet and display US real GDP per person from 1870 to 2008. Click the Show Ann % button.

Your chart is a snapshot of US economic history. There are three periods:

1. Before the Civil War, the United States was underdeveloped, rural, and quite poor.
2. After the Civil War, Reconstruction and Western development created a truly national economy that grew rapidly.
3. The Great Depression was traumatic, as was World War II, but the US economy has done extremely well since the 1950s.

CAGRs of 1.86% per year from 1870 to 2008 and 2.06% per year since 1950 are excellent analytics for the US economy. The Rule of 70 tells us we will see doubling in real GDP per person every generation. But can we really count on this going forward? No, the fifth growth lesson says we cannot:

Lesson 5: Growth is not assured.

STEP Watch the video titled "Growth is not given" at vimeo.com/econexcel/growthnotassured.

There are many individual countries that could be used to support the lesson that growth is not assured, but perhaps Japan is the most surprising example.

STEP From the *Compare* sheet, display Japan's real GDP per person from 1950 to 2008. Click the Log button.

The log scale linearizes exponential curves and clearly shows the remarkable reversal in the Japanese economy. From 1950 to 1973, the Japanese economy grew at an incredible 8% per year. That is doubling every nine years!

But your chart shows that it suddenly leveled off in 1973. From 1973 to 1991, it grew at 3.3% per year. This is still excellent, and everyone thought Japan would take over the world (much like China is feared today).

And then suddenly, it all came to a screeching halt. From 1991 to 2008, Japanese CAGR fell to 1% per year. Look carefully at your log-scale chart to see how flat the line is starting around 1990.

Why did this happen? We do not know. Standard macroeconomic policies to stimulate the economy have not worked. Japan is an aging society with a rapidly falling birth rate, and it does not especially welcome immigrants, so demographic explanations abound. But this is typical of how economists study growth—we come up with stories after the fact. No one predicted the sudden reversal in economic performance in Japan.

Remember, however, the difference between levels and growth. Japan remains a rich country. If you visit, you will see all the markers of wealth, such as shopping malls and fancy restaurants. The Japanese enjoy long life expectancy and high education levels. The lack of growth, however, is a serious problem for the future.

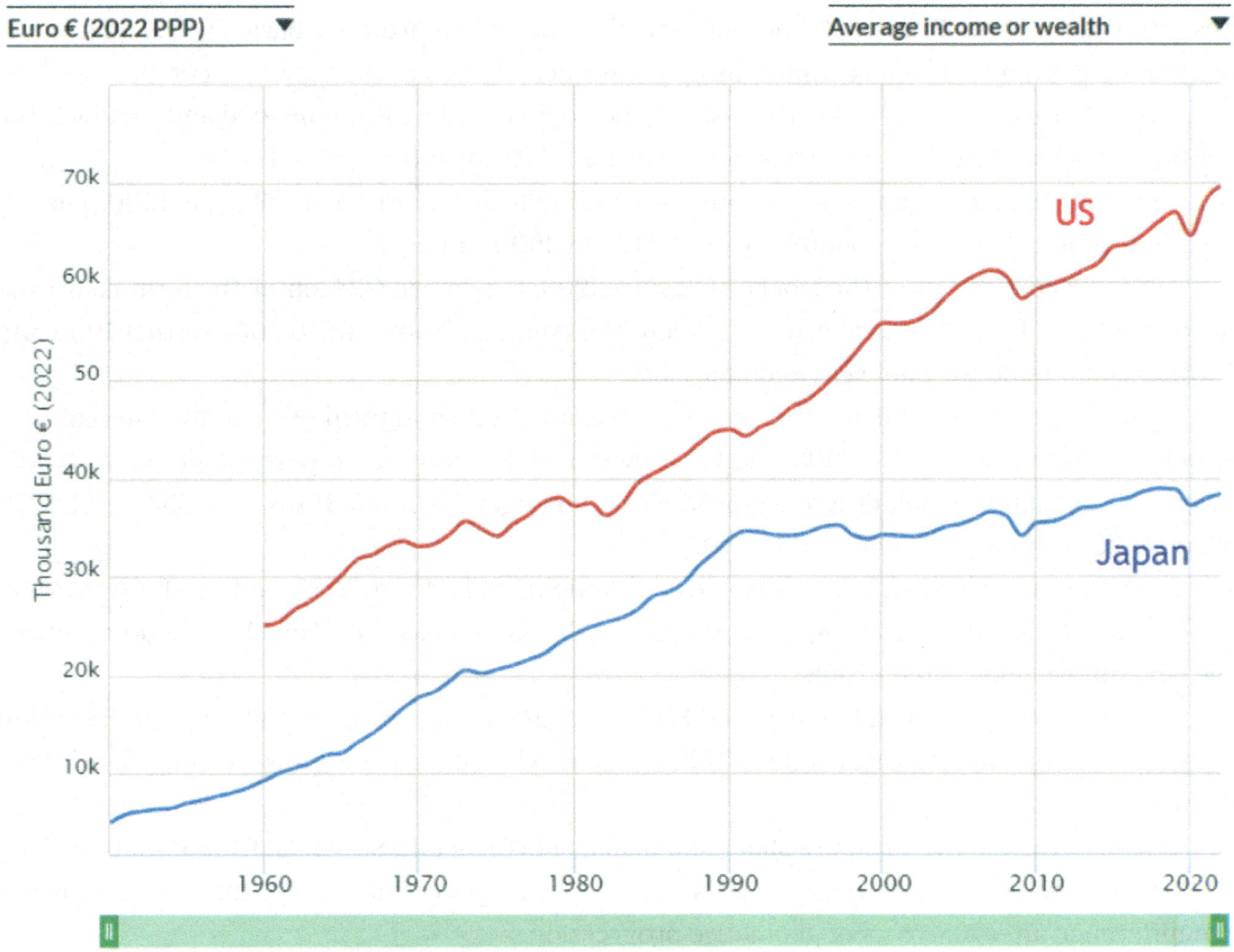

Figure 4.4: US and Japan, real GDP per person, 2022 Euro PPP.
Source: World Inequality Database / CC BY-NC-SA 4.0.

Maddison's data only go to 2008. What has happened to the United States and Japan since then? While there are many websites to choose from for country comparisons, an excellent one is wid.world. Figure 4.4 shows that Japan was growing incredibly fast until the early 1970s. It slowed down but did well until 1990. Since then, it has gone sideways. An economic juggernaut from 1950 to 1990 but suddenly stagnant the last few decades, Japan is a good example of the lesson that growth is not assured.

We conclude our whirlwind tour of economic growth across time and around the world with a final lesson:

Lesson 6: Seemingly small differences in CAGRs produce huge gaps in levels.

It is easy to think that there is little difference between percentage point changes in growth rates. After all, 0.01, 0.02, and 0.03 are all "small" numbers. So are they basically the same? No. Compounding is a powerful force, and this is why we need to be careful when we compare CAGRs.

STEP Return to the *OnlyCountries* sheet and copy it. Add a filter if needed and sort by 1900, largest to smallest. Delete all countries (rows) without data for 1900.

You should have a sample of 39 countries with real GDP per person values in 1900. The UK is the richest and China is the poorest when sorted by 1900 values.

STEP In cell GS3 enter the label CAGR *since* 1900, and in cell GS4, enter the formula for the CAGR, =(GR4/CN4)^(1/108)-1. Fill it down. Delete the columns from 1901 to 2007 so that 1900 and 2008 are side by side to enable easy comparison.

Compare New Zealand and the United States, in second and third place in 1900 in real GDP per person. From that time to 2008, the US growth rate is about half a percentage point (0.005) higher. This seemingly small difference produces a huge gap by 2008: 31,178 to 18,653 in 1990 GK dollars. A picture is worth a thousand words.

STEP In the *Compare* sheet, display the United States and New Zealand from 1900 to 2008.

That is astounding. Starting from essentially the same place, the "small" 0.5% point difference generates a huge gap by 2008.

Scroll down and look at Portugal and Sri Lanka. Again, they are essentially even in 1900 (and both poor), but in 2008 Portugal is three times richer. Why? Because it grew 1% point faster than Sri Lanka.

STEP Return to the *Compare* sheet and display Portugal and Sri Lanka from 1900 to 2008.

Again, the picture is striking. That seemingly small percentage point difference causes a huge difference after 108 years of geometric progression.

A mathematician would not be surprised. They might point out that the difference between 1% and 2% CAGR is a "small" one percentage point, but it is a "big" 100% difference. We have doubled the CAGR when we go from 1 to 2 percent per year.

This lesson applies to personal finance. An expense ratio for an Exchange Traded Fund (ETF) or mutual fund that is a "small" 0.5% will end up seriously decreasing the value of the investment over time. This is worth remembering.

Summary

There are many business applications of CAGR and the Rule of 70, but applying these tools to real GDP per person across countries is a great way to learn data analytics and the amazing story of economic growth.

Robert Lucas won a Nobel Prize in Economics, and he expressed the deep frustration of those who study development when he said,

> Is there some action a government of India could take that would lead the Indian economy to grow like Indonesia's or Egypt's? If so, what exactly? If not, what is it about the "nature of India" that makes it so? The consequences for human welfare involved in questions like these are simply staggering: once one starts to think about them, it is hard to think about anything else. (Lucas, 1988, p. 5)

The data show that economic growth exploded on the world stage just a few hundred years ago with the advent of the market system and simultaneous revolutions in science and industry. As a result, billions of people live healthier, richer lives. It is, of course, also true that billions remain poor, and we need to figure out exactly what it is about the market system that enables growth and development.

Solving the puzzle of economic growth is the biggest open problem in economics. The puzzle is incredibly challenging, and it is critically important that we figure it out.

If you do not believe this, consider Haiti and the Dominican Republic. Go to the *Compare* sheet and display real GDP per person for these two countries from 1950 to 2008.

It will only take a few seconds to do this (that is what is so powerful about this workbook), and the resulting chart is guaranteed to absolutely blow you away.

In "The Underlying Tragedy," an editorial in the October 15, 2010, edition of *The New York Times*, David Brooks communicates the frustration generated by our ignorance:

> Why is Haiti so poor? Well, it has a history of oppression, slavery and colonialism. But so does Barbados, and Barbados is doing pretty well. Haiti has endured ruthless dictators, corruption and foreign invasions. But so has the Dominican Republic, and the D.R. is in much better shape. Haiti and the Dominican Republic share the same island and the same basic environment, yet the border between the two societies offers one of the starkest contrasts on earth—with trees and progress on one side, and deforestation and poverty and early death on the other.

Lucas was right; once you start thinking about economic growth and are aware of the tremendous variability in outcomes, it is hard to think about anything else.

Adam Smith's *An Inquiry into the Nature and Causes of the Wealth of Nations* was first published in 1776, at the dawn of the British Industrial Revolution. Smith had no data on real GDP per person, but he knew something really weird was going on. He asked a fundamental and enduring question, "Why are some countries rich and others poor?"

We still do not know the answer.

Takeaways

Angus Maddison spent his life compiling estimates of output per person stretching all the way back to AD 1. Maddison's data enable us to see long-run economic growth.

A generation is roughly 30 years, so growth of a little over 2% per year will produce doubling every generation. That is considered really good for rich countries.

Poor countries often grow faster than 2% when they first adopt the market system. This is called catch-up growth.

It is easy to fall into the trap of thinking that real GDP per person is a perfect measure. It is not. It has several weaknesses, but perhaps its biggest problem is that it says nothing about the distribution of output.

Here are the six lessons in one place:

Lesson 1: Country real GDP per person is wildly uneven.
Lesson 2: The disparity in country real GDP per person is rising.
Lesson 3: Economic growth is brand new.
Lesson 4: The magic growth number is 2% per year in real GDP per person.
Lesson 5: Growth is not assured.
Lesson 6: Seemingly small differences in CAGRs produce huge gaps in levels.

References

Barreto, H. (2023, August 11). *CAGR and AAPC for Norway* [Video]. Vimeo. vimeo.com/econexcel/cagr.

Barreto, H. (2023, August 12). *Long run growth* [Video]. Vimeo. vimeo.com/econexcel/longrungrowth.

Barreto, H. (2023, August 12). *Growth is not given* [Video]. Vimeo. vimeo.com/econexcel/growthnotassured.

Lucas, R. (1988). "On the Mechanics of Economic Development." *Journal of Monetary Economics* 22, pp. 3–42.

Schumpeter, J. (1942). *Capitalism, Socialism, and Democracy* (George Allen & Unwin Ltd.).

4.3 PV and IRR

You are teaching a child about money. You lay out three US nickels, worth 5 cents each, in a row and then two dimes, each worth 10 cents, below the nickels, as in Figure 4.5.

Figure 4.5: Three nickels and two dimes: Which is worth more?

You ask the child if the nickels or the dimes are worth more. The child says the nickels because there are more of them. Yes, more is better, you say, but nickels and dimes are not equivalent. How would you explain that two dimes are worth more than three nickels?

You could replace each dime with two nickels, and now you have four nickels in the bottom row. With everything in nickels, we would easily see that the bottom row has more nickels, and so it is worth more.

Or if you have a bunch of pennies lying around, you could replace each nickel with a stack of five pennies and each dime with a stack of 10 pennies. With everything in pennies, we can use the child's "more is better" logic: 20 pennies is more than 15 pennies.

Both approaches rely on *standardizing* the two options so that we are comparing apples to apples. You have no problem knowing that two dimes are worth more than three nickels because you are instantly converting the coins to cents. You are standardizing without even knowing it.

If you think this is obvious, then you will have no problem with present value. It does the same thing, translating money in the future to money now so that we can correctly determine worth. Let's see how it works.

Present Value (PV)

Whenever you are faced with a decision involving money over time, there is a complication because of the fact that money has a time dimension. The confusing part is that we often ignore the time unit on money, but it is definitely there.

Everyone knows that $1,000 right now is worth way more than $1,000 fifty years from now. Both are denominated in dollars, but both also have a differing time unit, so they are not equivalent.

Just like you cannot treat nickels and dimes as equivalent coins, you cannot directly compare numerical values of money at different points in time. You also would not say "I have 3 cars and 4 pencils, so I have 7 carpencils" because cars and pencils are different things, and "carpencils" is meaningless. The same is true of money at different points in time.

If you had a portfolio of $1,000 in cash and a promise (that you could rely on with certainty) of $1,000 fifty years from now, you could not say that this portfolio is worth $2,000. Although less obvious, this is the same as saying "I have 7 carpencils."

There is, however, a way to value your portfolio—convert the future money into present value. This is exactly the same as the strategy we used for the nickels and dimes problem in Figure 4.5.

The common time period chosen is usually the present, and this is why it is called present value. Alternatively, future value uses a common time period in the future. We often use *present-value* as a verb. For example, we present-valued $1,000 two years from now at 10%, and it is $826.45.

Suppose we want to know the present value of $10,000 five years from now with a 9% discount rate (dr). We are looking for the number that, if allowed to grow at 9%, would be $10,000 five years from now.

STEP Open a blank Excel workbook and save it as *PVIRR.xlsx*. Enter the text *You get* in cell A1, and in cell B1, enter $10000 (using the $ automatically formats the cell as $). In cell C1, enter the text *in year* and enter the 5 in cell D1. In cell E1, enter the text *and dr is* and 9% in cell F1 (again, using % correctly formats the cell). Name cell F1 *dr* (the easiest way is by selecting cell F1 and then clicking in the *Name* Box and entering *dr*).

To be clear, present value is the amount needed right now (the present) so that it will grow into a given target value (in the future). Present value answers the question, "How much is a future amount of money worth today?"

STEP In cell A2, enter the label *Year*, and in cell B2, enter the label *Value*. In cell A3, enter the number 5, followed by 4 in cell A4, 3 in cell A5, and so on down to 0 in cell A8. Enter the formula =B1 in cell B3.

Now, what is the formula in cell B4? In previous work, we saw that the next number (t + 1) in a geometric sequence was given by:

$$x_{t+1} = x_t + ix_t$$

$$x_{t+1} = (1+i)\,x_t$$

Here we are doing the reverse of that. Instead of the next number (which we know), we want the *previous* number that produced it:

$$x_{t+1} = (1+i)\,x_t$$

$$x_t = \frac{{}_{t+1}}{1+i}$$

Instead of *i*, by convention, we use the phrase *discount rate* (*dr*) for the constant growth rate when we compute present value. We are discounting, or lowering, the number when we compute its present value. The % growth rate used is also sometimes abbreviated with the letter *r*. No matter what symbol you use, what you are doing is computing what the previous number in the sequence would be if it grew at that constant growth rate.

STEP In cell B4, enter the formula =B3/(1+*dr*), assuming you named cell F1 *dr*. Format cell B4 as $.

Excel shows $9,174.31. If you had that amount of money, it would grow to $10,000 in a year with a growth rate of 9% per year.

STEP Select cell B4 and fill it down to cell B8.

You are showing the present value of $10,000 five years from now with a 9% discount rate. In other words, if you had $6,499.31 right now, in five years it would become $10K by growing at 9% per year.

There is, of course, a faster way. We can bring a number for any future time period, *t*, back to the present, t = 0, with the *Present Value Equation:*

The present value, x_0, depends on three inputs:

1. The amount in the future
2. The discount rate (which is the growth rate)
3. The number of time periods in the future

STEP In cell C8, enter the formula =B1/(1+*dr*)^5.

The equivalence of cells B8 and C8 confirms that the one-step version of the present value computation works.

The Present Value Equation makes clear that the farther in the future, the lower the present value, since you would divide by a bigger number as t rises. Similarly, the higher the discount rate, the lower the present value.

STEP Change the discount rate in cell F1 to values higher and lower than 9% and keep track of the PV in cells B8 and C8.

If you set the discount rate to zero, then the present value is the same as the future amount. Without any growth rate, to reach the target future amount, you have to start with that future amount.

The Lottery Decision

The biggest lottery jackpot as of this writing was on November 8, 2022, to one Powerball ticket in California for $2.08 billion! Lotteries always advertise their jackpot as the total payout even though it is distributed over time.

As usual, the winner took the immediate cash alternative, which was $997.6 million—a little less than half of what they would have received in 30 payments over 29 years. There are many ways to think about how to decide between taking a single amount now versus a stream of payments. One way is to compute the present value of the stream of payments and compare it to the cash alternative.

Real-world lotteries have complicated payout schemes with rising amounts over time, so we will consider a simple hypothetical lottery with a constant payout. Let's suppose that the jackpot is $1.5 million, which is paid out in 30 payments of $50,000 each year. The immediate cash alternative is $750,000.

So which one would you take and why? We agree that saying, "Give me the $1.5 million because it is more than $750,000" is exactly equivalent to the child saying, "I like 3 nickels more than 2 dimes because there are more of them." We have to do the present value math. If you are leaning toward the lump sum now, present-valuing might change your mind.

STEP Insert a new sheet in your *PVIRR.xlsx* workbook. Enter the label *Year* in cell A1 and the label *Amount* in cell B1. In cell A2, enter a 0 followed by a 1 in cell A3. Select cells A2 and A3 and then fill down to cell A31. It should show a value of 29. Enter $50000 in cell B2 and the formula =B2 in cell B3. Fill it down. This way we can easily change the payment stream. Finally, sum the $50,000 payments in cell B32.

Of course, cell B32 should show $1.5 million. Less obvious is the fact that in a real sense, this is an illegal sum. The payments of $50,000 come at different times, so they are not equivalent. Excel (and the lottery people) do not care about the time dimension of money, but ignoring the time unit does not make it go away.

We can compute the sum correctly if we present-value all of the payments. That way, we will be adding dollars that have the same time unit—the present.

STEP In cell C1, enter the label PV, and in cell D1, enter 5%. Name cell D1 *IRR* (explained in the following section). In cell C2, enter the formula =B2/(1+IRR)^A2 and fill it down.

Cell C2 is the same as B2 because the present value of any amount right now is that amount. The zero in the exponent for time makes the denominator 1. But look at the other values in column C. They are getting smaller and smaller as you look down. That is because it takes less money now (present value) to grow to $50,000 the farther in the future we get the $50,000.

STEP Copy cell B32 and paste it in cell C32.

You are looking at the correct way to sum the stream of payments. We have a single number, $807,054, to represent its value. The "simple" addition of the 30 payments of $50,000 is a gross misrepresentation of the true value of the stream of payments. It is amazing to people who understand the time value of money that lottery jackpots are allowed to be advertised as the sum of payments over time.

We would never compare the $1.5 million to the immediate cash payout, but we can directly compare the present value to the immediate cash payout. With 5% per year, the present value of the stream of payments is greater than the immediate payout, so we would take the stream of payments.

There is one problem, however; the present value depends on the discount rate used.

STEP Change cell D1 to 10%, and scroll down to see the present value of the stream of payments.

The future amounts are all smaller (since the growth rate is bigger), and the sum of the present values for each payment is $518,480. Since this is less than the immediate cash payout of $750,000, we should take the cash amount in this case.

This shows that there is no one-size-fits-all answer to deciding the question of cash or a stream of payments. It depends on the discount rate used. If you had the ability to invest the immediate cash payout at 10% per year, the cash payout is worth more to you. If, however, the best you can do is 5% per year, then you would take the stream of payments.

Internal Rate of Return (IRR)

We can use the fact that the present value depends on the discount rate to explain the internal rate of return. We begin by computing the IRR (also known as the ROR, or rate of return) for our hypothetical lottery question of how to take our winnings.

STEP In cell F1, enter the label *Amount*, and in cell F2, enter $750000. Enter $0 in cell F3 and then fill it down to cell F31.

Columns B and F now have two alternative streams. One is $50,000 from now until year 29, and the other is $750,000 now and nothing until year 29. We subtract column F from B to create a single series that captures two streams.

STEP In cell H1, enter the label *Net Amount*, and in cell H2, enter the formula =B2-F2. Fill it down to cell H31.

Column H makes clear that we can frame the question of how to take our lottery winnings as an investment project. Cell H2 shows negative $700,000 (the parentheses and red text signal that the dollar amount is less than zero), so this is what we are committing to this project. In return, we get the stream of $50,000 payments in the future.

We need to present-value the amounts in column H in order to make them have the same time unit, the present.

STEP In cell I1, enter the label NPV, and in cell I2, enter the formula =H2/(1+IRR)^A2. Fill it down to I31. Copy cell C32 and paste it in cell I32.

Cell I32 shows the net present value for a given discount rate. If this number is positive, then the investment project ($50,000 over 29 years) is worthwhile; if it is negative, it is not. At 5%, the project is worthwhile (take the stream of payments); at 10% it is not (take the immediate cash payout).

This work leads us to an interesting question: What is the break-even discount rate? In other words, what is the percentage growth rate that would make the net present value zero?

STEP In cell K1, enter the label IRR, and in cell K2, enter the formula =IRR(H2:H31). You do not need to provide a *guess* parameter.

The Excel function IRR computes the internal rate of return, which is the 5.72% displayed in cell K2. The IRR function is solving for the value of IRR in this equation:

$$0 = \frac{x_0}{(1+IRR)^0} + \frac{x1}{(1+IRR)^1} + \frac{x_2}{(1+IRR)^2} + \ldots + \frac{x_{29}}{(1+IRR)^{29}}$$

There is no analytical solution for finding the value of IRR in the equation above, so Excel uses an iterative algorithm. The guess parameter helps the function find a solution in more complicated investment projects. In fact, for really complicated projects with costs and returns appearing over time, the IRR method can fail. Such projects require use of the NPV method.

STEP Copy cell K2, select cell D1, click the down arrow on the *Paste* item in the *Ribbon* (in the *Home* tab), and paste *Values*.

Cell I32 is now displaying a value that is almost zero. “E-10” means 10 to the minus 10 power, so it has 10 zeroes after the decimal point. This demonstrates that Excel’s IRR function correctly computed the IRR, the value of the discount rate that sets the net present value to zero.

The IRR tells us the quality of the investment project. The higher the IRR, the better the project.

We can compare the IRR of different projects. Suppose you have an investment opportunity that earns you 10%. Then you would take the immediate cash payout. However, if your best investment option yields only 5%, then the IRR of this project is higher, and you would take the stream of payments.

Notice that we get the same answer to which option to take if we use the discount rate to compute the present value of the stream or compare that same discount rate to the IRR.

Takeaways

Suppose someone asked you if you’d prefer 100 US dollars or 840 Tajikistani somoni (yes, that is the currency of Tajikistan). Which would you choose? You certainly would not say, “840 is more than 100, so I will take the somoni.”

You cannot answer until you use the exchange rate to convert the 840 somoni to dollars or 100 dollars to somoni. Once they are in the same units, you can compare the values.

Just as you need an exchange rate to compare money denominated in different currencies, you need to convert money paid or received at different points in time to a common denominator so that you can make the right comparison.

We say “The present value is $100” to express the value of a future amount today.

We also use *present-value* as a verb: “to present-value” means to do the computation of dividing the future amount by $(1 + dr)^t$.

The *Present Value Equation* is

$$x_0 = \frac{x_t}{(1 + dr)^t}$$

Choosing the discount rate can be complicated and is beyond the scope of this book. It depends on the riskiness of the investment and other factors.

Especially for projects with long time horizons, present value can be extremely sensitive to the chosen discount rate.

Inflation affects present value, but the concept of present value does not depend on rising price levels. Even with zero inflation (constant prices), we would see positive discount rates and, therefore, discounting of money in the future. It is true, however, that higher inflation leads to higher interest rates and, therefore, lowers present value.

The IRR is the discount rate that sets the NPV = 0.

The IRR is a number that can be used to judge an investment project. If *IRR > hurdlerate* (the market interest rate or cost of funds), then the project is worth pursuing.

The IRR only works for simple investment projects with upfront costs and future returns. For more complicated projects, the NPV method should be used.

The NPV method uses the decision-maker's discount rate (the market interest rate or cost of funds) to present-value the net stream. If NPV > 0, then the project is worth pursuing.

The NPV and IRR methods will give the same answer. Thus, using both methods is a good check on the computations and final decision.

Lottery jackpots are misleading because they do not advertise the immediate cash option. They announce total dollars over time, which is like saying that the winner gets 7 carpencils.

There is no way a lottery would be allowed to state the jackpot as the sum of dollars over time if it was a financial product. Lotteries, however, are run by state agencies and are exempt from truth-in-advertising laws.

Lotteries falsely advertise the jackpot because eye-popping numbers are great for the lottery business. More people are attracted to buy tickets as the jackpot rises, and huge sums can trigger lottery mania, where many new customers buy tickets.

Most winners choose the immediate cash payout, but this decision should include consideration of the time value of money. Even without considering the tax implications, the lump sum option is usually the wrong decision on strictly financial terms.

4.4 College IRR

Almost everyone thinks a college education today is expensive, but they still underestimate how much it really costs. The tuition, fees, and books are tens of thousands of dollars, but that is just the out-of-pocket cost.

Even more costly is foregone income. Instead of going to college, you could be working and earning money. Adding opportunity cost to out-of-pocket cost yields a total cost of hundreds of thousands of dollars over four years.

There is no doubt about it—college is really expensive!

If it is so expensive, why do people go to college? Because there is a strong positive relationship between education and earnings—the more educated you are, the more money you make on average.

But exactly how much more do college grads earn? Figure 4.6 shows the college wage premium (as a percentage over high school wage) is about 75%.

Notice that Figure 4.6 shows a great deal of variation in the college wage premium for different demographic groups. Asians have the highest excess returns for college.

Figure 4.6 also shows that after the COVID-19 pandemic, the college wage premium has fallen. This is due to higher wages for workers without a college degree after the pandemic.

One thing the chart does not show is the college wage premium by major. College graduates with degrees in quantitative fields such as business analytics earn higher incomes, on average, than nonquant majors.

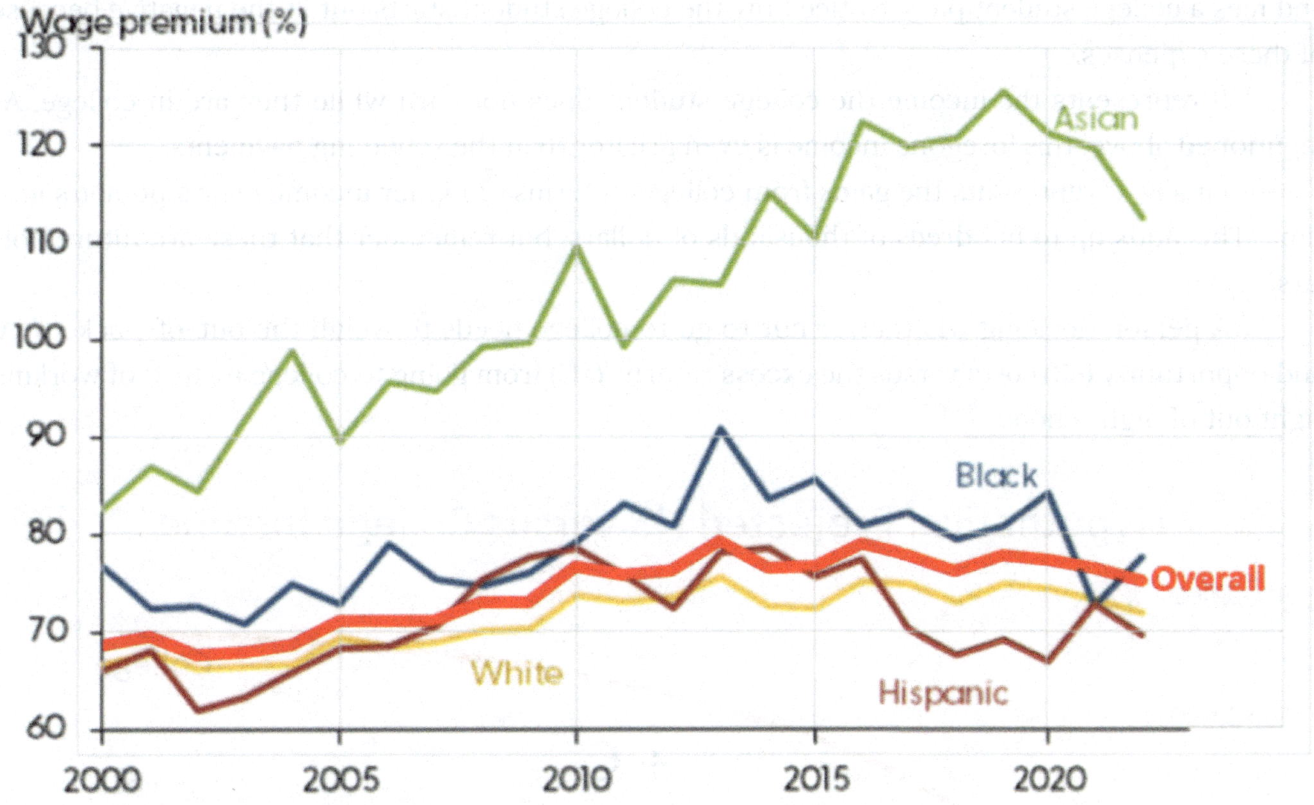

Figure 4.6*: *The college wage premium over time.
Source: Bengali et. al, 2023 / Used with permission.

The college wage premium chart is focused solely on the higher incomes earned by college graduates. It does not capture any of the other benefits of a college education: access to more and better jobs, lower unemployment and poverty rates, longer and healthier lives, higher savings rates for retirement, and better-educated children.

We will ignore these other benefits and consider only the higher incomes earned by college graduates. This is weighed against the cost of college, which we know is high and has been rising rapidly. So is college still worth it? We will compute the college IRR to answer this question.

Visualizing the College Decision

Figure 4.7 is a stylized graph (it accurately represents a relationship without actual data) that displays the costs and benefits of college. It shows that college grads make more over their lifetimes. It also captures that both paths grow, but college grows faster.

The three letters in Figure 4.7 label three areas in the chart. A represents the tuition, books, and fees a college student pays. Notice how the college student starts out in the negative because of these expenses.

B represents the income the college student does not earn while they are in college. As mentioned above, this foregone income is even greater than the schooling payments.

Finally, C represents the gains from college in terms of higher income over a person's lifetime. This adds up to hundreds of thousands of dollars, but remember that these are future dollars.

A person deciding whether or not to go to college needs to weigh the out-of-pocket (-A) and opportunity (-B) costs versus the excess returns (+C) from going to college instead of working right out of high school.

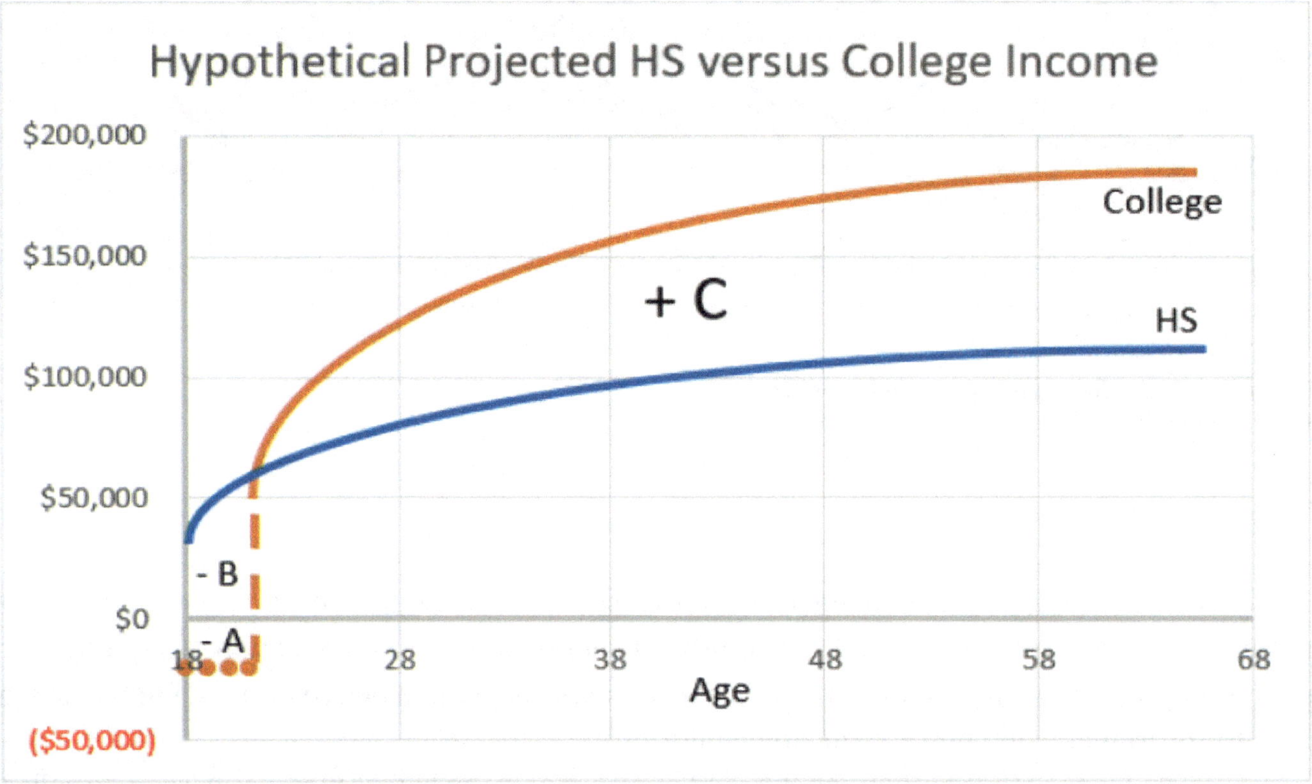

***Figure 4.7:* A stylized graph of the decision to attend college: A = out-of-pocket costs; B = opportunity costs; C = excess returns.**

Figure 4.7 also makes clear that time is an important part of the problem. You cannot simply look at the graph and conclude that the area of the excess returns (C) is much bigger than the costs (A and B), so college is a good investment. The excess returns are in the future, so we cannot directly compare them to the costs. In fact, every year on the *Age* axis is a dollar amount with different units.

To solve this problem correctly, we have to apply the concepts of present value and internal rate of return. We do so with a simplified version of the problem.

A Toy Model

STEP Insert a sheet in your *PVIRR.xlsx* workbook. Enter the labels *Age*, *HS*, and *College* in cells A1, B1, and C1, respectively. In cell A2, enter 18, and in cell A3, enter 19. Select the cells and fill down to age 64 (row 48). In cell B2, enter $40000, and in cell B3, enter the formula =B2. Fill it down. In cell C2, enter -$20000 (this is the out-of-pocket cost), and in cell C3, enter the formula =C2. Fill it down to cell C5 (representing four years of college). In cell C6, enter $70,000, and in cell C7, enter the formula =C6. Fill it down.

You have created a simplified version of the decision to attend college. Figure 4.8 is a chart of the data in columns A, B, and C. It does not display the subtlety of increasing income over time, but it does have the essential nature of the decision—the college path has an investment up front and starts out in the negative, but you are compensated for this by higher future earnings.

Notice also that our simplified problem's college income of $70,000 per year is 75% more than the high school graduate's $40,000—this reflects the real-world college wage premium of 75%.

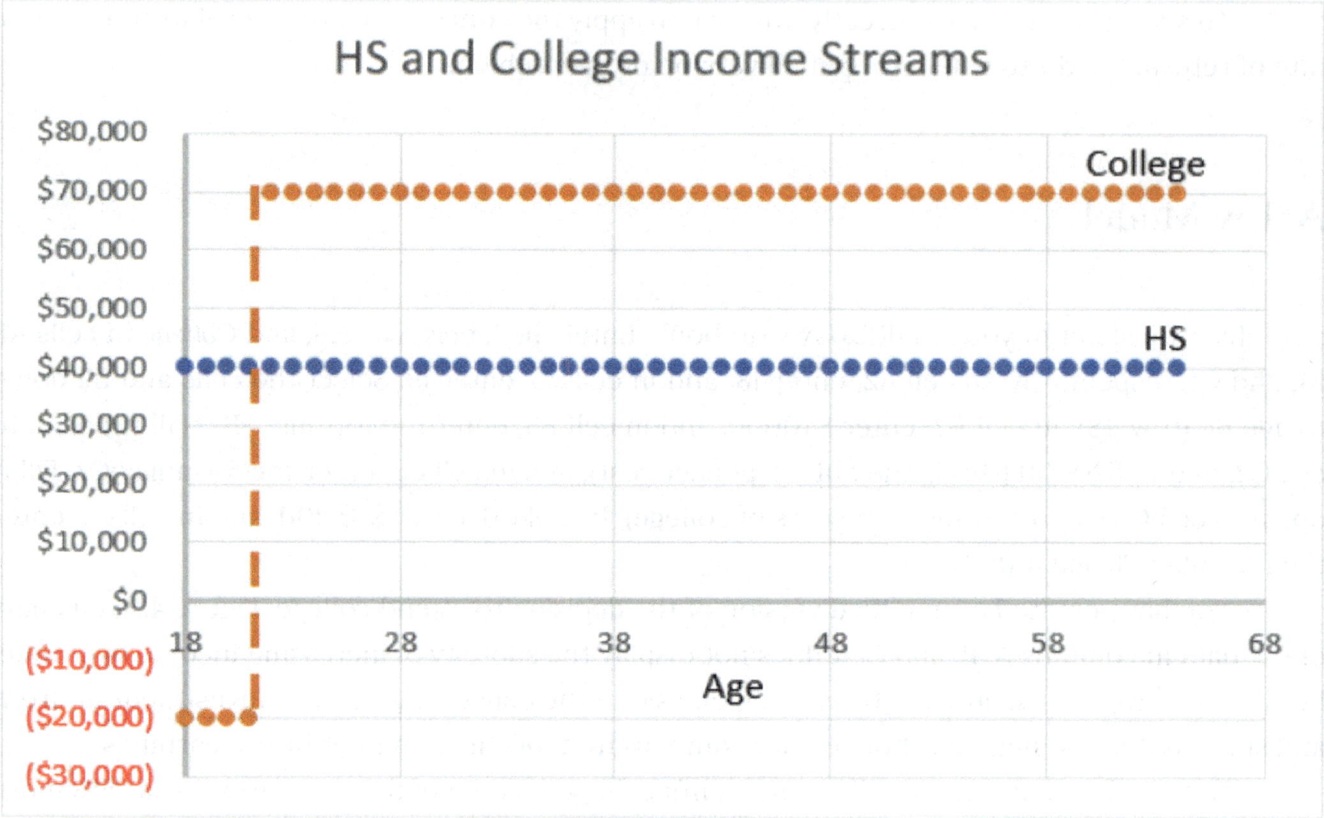

Figure 4.8: *A simplified version of the decision to attend college.*

But how can we determine if the investment in a college education is actually worth it?

STEP Enter the label *College Project* in cell E1 followed by the formula =C2-B2 in cell E2. Fill it down to cell E48.

Now we clearly see the nature of the investment project. You invest $60,000 each year for four years ($20,000 out of pocket and $40,000 in opportunity costs), and in return you get $30,000 each year until you retire.

How can we determine the quality of this project? That is easy with Excel.

STEP Enter the label *IRR* in cell G1, and in cell G2, enter the formula =IRR(E2:E48).

A rate of return of 10.5% per year is pretty good. It is likely that you cannot do better than this with another project, so you would make the human capital investment and go to college.

The problem can also be solved by computing the net present value. Using any discount rate less than the IRR will give a positive NPV and result in the same decision to go to college.

STEP Enter the label *dr* in cell I1 and the value 6% in cell I2. Enter the labels PV HS and PV *College* in cells J1 and K1, respectively. In cell J2, enter the formula =B2/(1+$I$2)^(A2-18) and fill it down to cell J48. In cell K2, enter the formula =C2/(1+$I$2)^(A2-18) and fill it down to cell K48.

The dollars in columns J and K can be added because they all have the same time dimension—age 18 dollars.

STEP Enter the label *sum of* PV HS in cell L1 and compute the sum of the present-valued high school dollars in cell L2. Enter the label *sum of* PV *College* in cell M1 and compute the sum of the present-valued college dollars in cell M2.

With a discount rate of 6%, the college income stream is worth 826,135 present value (age 18) dollars, which is more than the $660,975 produced by the high school option. Thus, you would go to college.

Figure 4.9 offers a good way of understanding and remembering what present value is all about. Present value operates like scrunching an accordion, compacting the x-axis values back to the origin. Present value brings the dollars at different ages back to age 18 so that they can be compared.

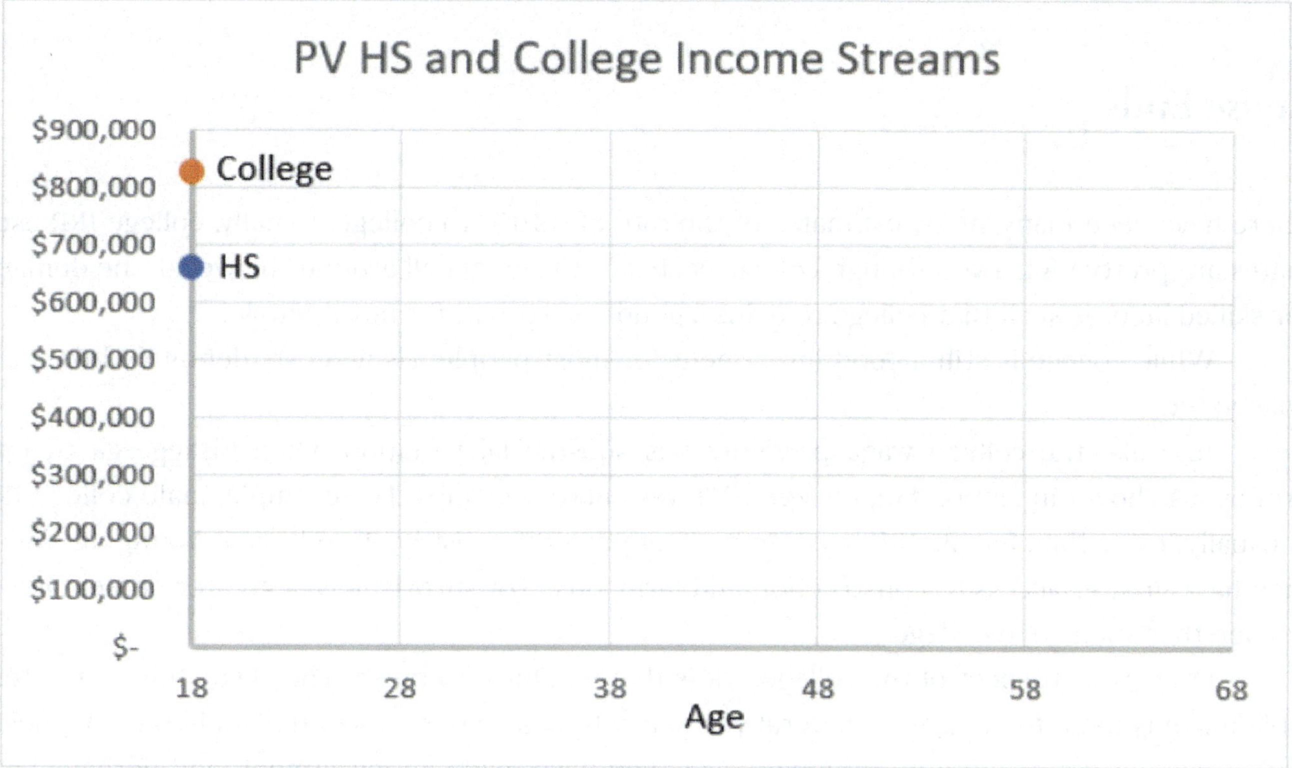

***Figure 4.9**: Visualizing present value.*

Unlike Figures 4.7 and 4.8, which show dollar values over time, Figure 4.9 removes the time element from the graph. It adds up the present value at each year and shows the sum as a single dot at Age=18.

Notice how the PV and IRR methods agree. With a discount rate of 6%, both green-light college: PV because the PV of the college stream at 6% is greater than the PV of the high school stream and IRR because 10.5% is greater than 6%.

STEP Change the discount rate in cell I2 to 11.5%. What is the optimal decision now?

PV says not to go to college because the present value of the college stream is less than the high school stream. IRR is also flashing a red light, since the IRR of 10.5% is less than the discount rate of 11.5%.

STEP Enter the formula =G2 in cell I2. What happens?

You just showed that Excel's IRR function is working as advertised. The sum of the present values of the two streams is identical when the discount rate is 10.5%, so this is the IRR. PV says it is an absolute tie, so flip a coin on going to college, and IRR says the same thing because IRR = discount rate.

Did you notice that we never added the dollars in columns B and C? That would be a silly thing to do, right?

Loose Ends

There have been many, many estimates of the rate of return to college. Usually, college IRR estimates are pretty high. Even though college costs are rising fast all around the world, the demand for skilled labor is such that college remains a good investment for most people.

While college is still a good investment for most people, rising costs definitely lower the college IRR.

Just like the college wage premium has substantial variation when disaggregated into groups (as shown in Figure 4.6), college IRRs vary across groups. For example, male college IRR is usually lower than female IRR because male opportunity cost is often higher. Young, unskilled men have greater access to construction and farm jobs. Not surprisingly, a greater percentage of women than men go to college.

One critical aspect of the college IRR is that you have to finish. The absolutely worst possible move is to go to college for several years, pay tens of thousands of dollars in out-of-pocket and opportunity costs, and not graduate. Now you have made an investment (and perhaps have student debt), and the return is really low because college only pays off with higher wages if you have a college degree.

The risk of going to college and not graduating is a serious issue. Correctly modeling the college IRR to include the riskiness of the investment in college is the focus of much research.

Takeaways

People with college degrees earn more, on average, than those without. This makes sense because very few people would go to college if they did not get a return on their investment.

College is an investment, it is called human capital, and it has an IRR. In fact, it is usually quite high, and going to college for many people is a sound financial decision.

PV and IRR are two ways to make a decision about an investment with costs and returns over time. They yield the same answer.

The present value method brings all the expenses and returns over time to the present. If the net present value is greater than zero, the investment is a winner at that given discount rate. Choosing the discount rate can be complicated.

The internal rate of return is the discount rate that sets the NPV = 0. The IRR is a measure of the quality of an investment. If the IRR is greater than the discount rate, the investment is a winner.

Everything said here about college also applies to graduate school. Getting an MBA, law or medical training, or any graduate degree has a rate of return. Finishing a graduate program is as critical as completing your college education.

References

Bengali, L., Sander, M., Valleta, R., and Zhao, C. (2023). "Falling College Wage Premiums by Race and Ethnicity." *FRBSF Economic Letter* 2023-22 (August 28), www.frbsf.org/research-and-insights/publications/economic-letter/2023/08/falling-college-wage-premiums-by-race-and-ethnicity/. The opinions expressed in this article do not necessarily reflect the views of the Federal Reserve Bank of San Francisco or the Federal Reserve System.

5. Unemployment

> The outstanding faults of the economic society in which we live are its failure to provide for full employment and its arbitrary and inequitable distribution of wealth and incomes.
>
> John Maynard Keynes

5.1 Unemployment via the FRED Excel Add-In

FRED, the Federal Reserve Economic Data archive, compiles information from many sources. It is freely available online at fred.stlouisfed.org/, but we will access it through the FRED Excel add-in. This saves a lot of time and effort in getting the data in Excel for further analysis.

The latest FRED Add-In for Microsoft Excel is available from fred.stlouisfed.org/fred-addin/

. This chapter refers to an archived legacy FRED add-in file that is reliable and easy to use, but is no longer supported by FRED.

STEP Download *FRED.xlam* from dub.sh/addins. Use the Add-ins Manager (keyboard shortcut *Alt, t, i*) to install it.

We will use the FRED add-in to get and work with unemployment data, but an important goal is to demonstrate the remarkable power of this open-access software. It opens the door to a huge trove of data.

To set the stage for our work on unemployment, recall that an economy's long-run performance is measured by the growth rate of real GDP per person. The magic number for rich countries is 2% per year. This gives a doubling of output per person roughly every generation.

When we focus on the short run, or the business cycle, we cannot use GDP because it takes too long to compile the data and publish the results. GDP is computed quarterly with a few months of lag and is often revised after initial release.

We need something at this moment that tells us how the economy is doing right now. New work is being done on this problem using internet activity, but the traditional approach to measuring the current state of the economy relies on a monthly labor market survey.

Each month, the Bureau of Labor Statistics (BLS) releases the results of its Current Population Survey (CPS). Tens of thousands of households around the United States are interviewed, and people are asked about their jobs, earnings, and other details.

In the third week of each month, the BLS releases a report on the number of workers, jobs, and perhaps most importantly, the unemployment rate for the previous month. You can see that we are already a month behind in our quest to read the economy, but this is much better than GDP.

The unemployment rate is a key indicator of short-run economic performance. When it is high, the economy is doing poorly, and when it is low (but not too low), the economy is doing well. The magic number for the overall unemployment rate is around 4% to 5%.

STEP Use your favorite browser to search for the "current unemployment rate."

You interpret the unemployment rate by seeing if it is around 4% and by its change from the previous month.

Our goal is to understand how the unemployment rate is computed and what it tells us. We proceed by explaining how unemployment is defined and measured. Along the way, we will learn about other labor statistics and seasonal adjustment. In the next section, we examine subgroups of people—unemployment is not the same for everyone. We will see that the overall unemployment rate masks substantial variation across demographic groups and geographic areas.

Defining and Measuring Unemployment

Labor market statistics are based on a series of mutually exclusive categories. We place people in groups, or buckets, and then compute ratios. We begin with the total population.

STEP Open a blank Excel workbook and save as *Unemployment.xlsx*. Enter *pop* (or POP, as case does not matter) in cell A1, click on the FRED tab in the *Ribbon*, and click the Get FRED Data button in the top-left corner.

You just used Excel to connect to the St. Louis Fed and downloaded the total population in the United States from the FRED website! Notice the blue link in cell A5. If you click it, you go to the FRED web page for this variable, and it has more documentation.

As you just saw, the FRED Excel add-in is easy to use, but you do need to know how it works. You control what you get by providing four inputs:

1. Series ID
2. Data manipulation (can be blank)
3. Frequency (can be blank)
4. Start Date (can be blank)

The FRED add-in works by taking the information you input in the first four rows of a spreadsheet and then outputting the results in two columns starting in row 5. The only thing required is the *Series ID*; it fills in default choices if the other three items are not given.

STEP Change cell A3 from M to A (it can be lowercase *a*) and click the Get FRED Data button. You can also use the Frequency Aggregation button in the FRED menu, but typing the letter *a* is easier.

You now have the total population in the United States on an annual (yearly) basis. Taking into account the units of the variable in cell B1, we can see the US population was about 335 million people in 2023.

Notice that cell B3 continues to display "Monthly" because that is the original frequency of the variable. By entering an A, you directed FRED to report the variable on a yearly basis.

To get to the unemployment rate, we walk through a series of separations, as depicted in Figure 5.1. Each step down splits the category above into two mutually exclusive parts.

From a total population of 335 million people, we remove everyone who is in the military, a prison, or a hospital. There are several million people in this category. The United States has one of the highest incarceration rates in the category. The United States has one of the highest incarceration rates in the world (see www.sentencingproject.org/research) and a large standing army, so the civilian, noninstitutional population is about 330 million people.

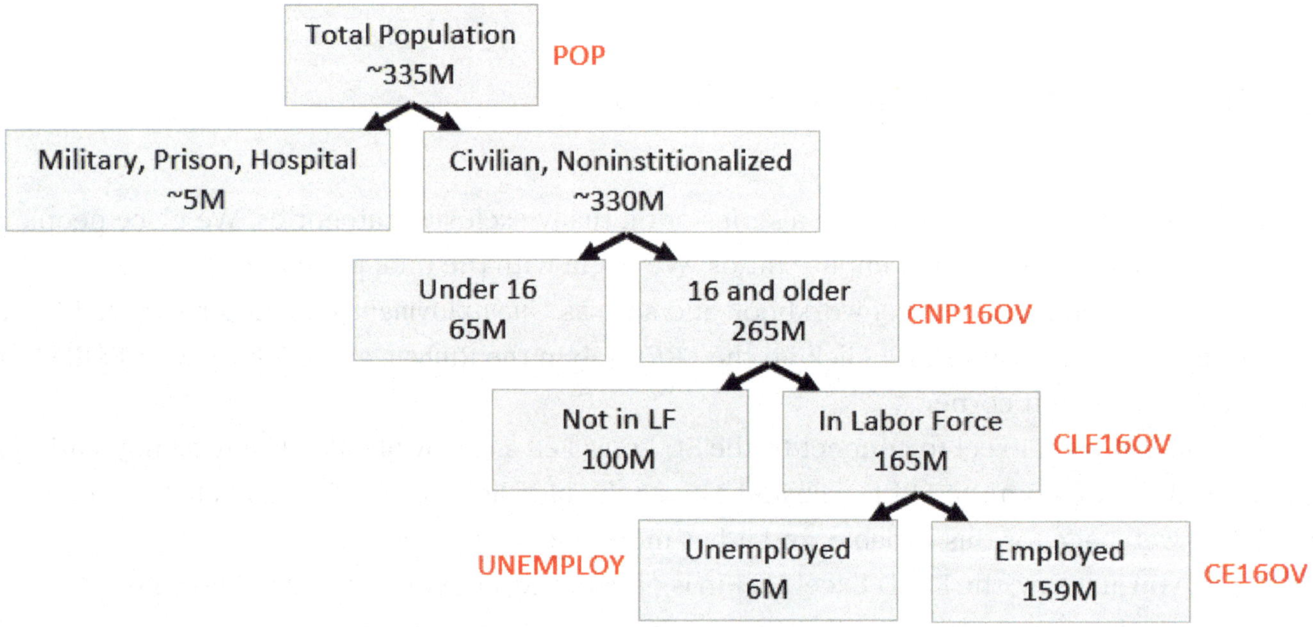

Figure 5.1: Labor market survey flow chart with FRED Series IDs.

Next, we split the civilian, noninstitutional population into children, those under 16 years old, and working-age people, those 16 and over. The United States today, like most rich countries, is rather old, with only about a fifth of the population under 16 years old.

The next step is crucial. We separate the 265 million working-age people into two groups: those who want to work and those who do not. Those who work or want to work are said to be in the labor force. Those who do not (for example, they are in school, retired, or taking care of children) are out of the labor force.

Finally, the last split in Figure 5.1 separates the labor force into two parts: those with a job (employed) and those without a job (unemployed). In August 2023, the number of unemployed people was quite low relative to the total number of people in the labor force.

The numbers in Figure 5.1 are much more volatile at the bottom than at the top. The number of unemployed people fluctuates quite a bit, while the population numbers at the top change much more slowly and predictably.

Figure 5.1 also reveals that not having a job does not guarantee that you are unemployed. After all, you might not have a job, but you might not want one. Then you are not unemployed but out of the labor force. To be defined as unemployed, you must not have a job *and want to work*.

Now that we have the major labor market categories, we can compute two important labor statistics:

$$UnemploymentRate = \frac{Unemployed}{LaborForce}$$

$$LaborForceParticipationRate(LFPR) = \frac{LaborForce}{CivNonInstPop16+}$$

The *unemployment rate* is the percentage of the labor force that is unemployed. The LFPR is the percentage of the civilian, noninstitutional, working-age population that is in the labor force.

Unemployment Data

We can apply the framework in Figure 5.1 to practice our FRED skills, confirm the numbers in each category, and replicate the unemployment rate and LFPR statistics reported by the BLS.

STEP In cell C1, enter CNP16OV (civilian, noninstitutional population aged 16 and over, so the penultimate character is the uppercase letter O, not the number 0). Click the Get FRED Data button.

Notice that the dates are not aligned. We need to fix that.

STEP Enter 1/1/1952 (the latest of the dates for the two series) in cells A4 and C4. Click the Get FRED Data button.

We can make a chart of the two series with FRED's built-in graphing tool.

STEP Click the Build Graph button and select *Create Multiple Series Graph.* Click *Series* 1 and select *pop.* Click *Series* 2 and *select* CNP16OV. Click the Build Graph button in the bottom left corner.

You created a chart in the signature FRED style, with a blue border and source information at the bottom. Multiple series charts do not include titles. You can add a title and other enhancements via the usual chart options—it is an Excel chart that can be edited and manipulated like any Excel chart.

We continue on our whirlwind tour of labor market statistics and FRED by confirming that the labor force is the sum of employed and unemployed people and showing how the unemployment rate and LFPR are computed.

STEP Insert a new sheet in your workbook. Using the *Series IDs* in Figure 5.1, get data on the civilian, noninstitutional population 16 and over, in the labor force, employed, and unemployed from 1/1/1952. See the appendix if you have trouble.

Notice that in row 5, with the clickable link that takes you to the FRED website, the word *Level* is used. This is standard macroeconomics terminology for the value of a variable or indicator at a point in time. Often, we take the levels and perform other computations, such as the percentage change.

The number of employed in January 1952 is 60,460 (in cell F8). Does this mean there were 60,460 people working in the United States at that time? No, that is simply too small a number. Cell F2 tells us that the data are in thousands, so the employment level was 60,460,000 at that time.

STEP In cell I7, enter the label *Emp+Unemp=LF Check.* In cell I8, enter a formula to confirm that this is true. See the appendix if you need help.

Having confirmed that the labor force is the number of people working plus the number of people unemployed, we can use the data to compute the unemployment rate and LFPR.

STEP In cell J7, enter the label UNRATE. In cell J8, enter a formula that computes the unemployment rate. Format the unemployment rate as a percentage with one decimal point. See the appendix if you need help.

How can we check our work? That is easy. We use the FRED add-in to download the unemployment rate and see if we got the same numbers.

But we have a problem—we do not know the *Series ID* for the unemployment rate. Fortunately, FRED has a search tool that we can use to find the *Series ID.*

STEP Click the Data Search button (with the magnifying glass) in the FRED menu. Enter the search text *unemployment rate* and click the Search button.

FRED displays a lot of hits, but the top two look promising. If you scroll right in the search window, you will see the *Series IDs* and other information. The only difference between the two is that one is SA and the other is NSA. This means *seasonally adjusted* and *not seasonally adjusted*.

We seasonally adjust variables that vary systematically over the year. For example, construction employment falls in the winter and rises in the summer. Seasonal adjustment would tweak the construction employment numbers higher in the winter and lower in the summer so we can remove the seasonal component and make a better comparison across months.

STEP Click the SA (topmost) unemployment rate to select it as shown in Figure 5.2. Click the Add Series ID button at the bottom of the search window and click *Close*.

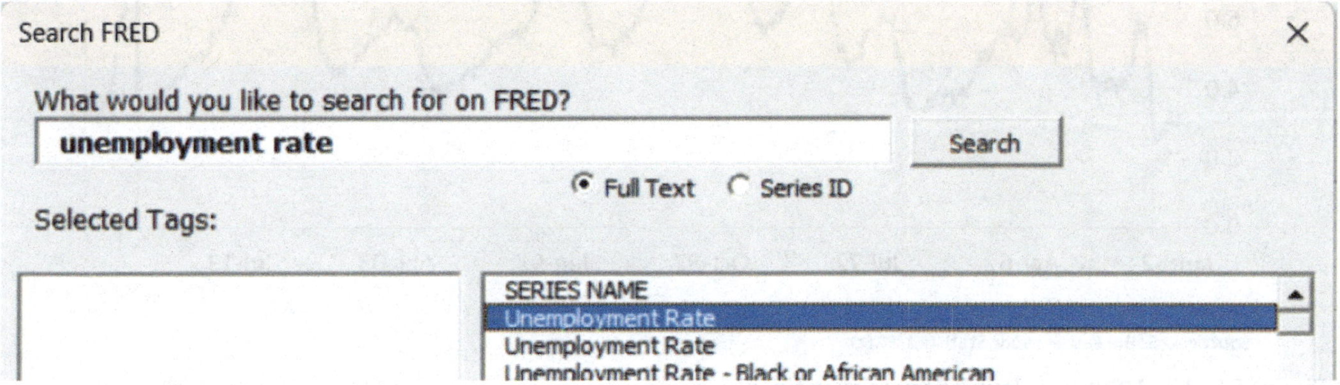

Figure 5.2: FRED's Data Search window.
Source: Screenshot of Excel interface, © Microsoft Corporation. Add-in by Federal Reserve Bank of St. Louis (FRED).

FRED places information in cells I1:I4. We need to move it so that FRED does not download data on top of our work in columns I and J.

STEP Move cell range I1:I4 to cells K1:K4. Replace the start date with 1/1/1952. Click the Get FRED Data button.

It is immediately obvious that our computed version of the unemployment rate matches the *Series ID* UNRATE.

STEP Replicate Figure 5.3 by clicking the Build Graph button and selecting *Create Graph(s)*. Select the UNRATE series and check the option *Include U.S. Recession Shading*. Finally, click the Build Graph(s) button.

Figure 5.3: The US unemployment rate over time.
Source: USBLS via FRED, Public Domain Data / FRED Terms.

The gray bars mean the economy was in a recession. Increases in the unemployment rate are strongly associated with recessionary periods.

The most recent spike was during the COVID-19 pandemic. The data in your spreadsheet show the highest unemployment rate was 14.7% in April 2020 (cell L827). Fortunately, it rapidly came back down.

STEP Apply the same steps used for the unemployment rate to the LFPR. Find the *Series ID*, download the data, and compare it to your own computed version to confirm they are the same. Create a chart of the LFPR with recession shading to replicate Figure 5.4. See the appendix if you need help.

***Figure 5.4*: The US LFPR (Series ID CIVPART) over time.**
Source: USBLS via FRED, Public Domain Data / FRED Terms.

Unlike the unemployment rate, which bounces around a lot, the LFPR saw a steady increase until the early 2000s, when the labor force was about two-thirds of the civilian, noninstitutional population 16 and older.

The LFPR fell dramatically during the COVID-19 pandemic, down to about 60% before recovering a bit. As of this writing in 2025, it was still lower than its peak. This means working-age people are not as interested in working as they used to be before the pandemic.

Takeaways

The FRED Excel add-in is a powerful tool that instantly downloads data from FRED into Excel.

It works by taking input from the first four rows of a sheet. Only the first row, with the *Series ID*, is required.

If you do not know the *Series ID*, search for it with the *Data Search* tool.

The charts created by the FRED add-in have a signature blue border and source information. FRED uses Excel's *Line* chart type, and this requires the same dates for all series.

Unemployment statistics are generated by the results from the monthly Current Population Survey.

The questions are designed to create mutually exclusive categories, such as younger than 16 years old or 16 and over.

To be unemployed, you have to be without a job but want to work. If you do not want to work (you are in school or retired or any other reason), you are out of the labor force. See Figure 5.1.

The unemployment rate is the ratio of the number of people unemployed to the number of people in the labor force.

The magic number (like batting .300) for the unemployment rate is 4% to 5%. In the long run, we want real GDP per person growth of 2% per year, and the higher the better. High unemployment is bad, of course, but the UNRATE can be so low that the economy overheats and prices rise too fast.

Because the unemployment rate is estimated every month, it is used as a predictor of short-run economic performance.

The LFPR (labor force participation rate) is another important labor market statistic. It is the ratio of the number of people in the labor force to the number of civilians 16 and over who are not institutionalized (in prison or a medical facility).

References

The epigraph is from the opening sentence of the last chapter of Keynes, J. M. (1936). *The General Theory of Employment, Interest and Money*. Full text online at http://www.marxists.org/reference/subject/economics/keynes/general-theory. This book led to the reorganization of economics into micro- and macroeconomics. It also radically changed the way economists thought about the role of government. Instead of passive onlookers, after Keynes, the Fed and other government actors saw themselves as responsible for actively managing the economy.

U.S. Bureau of Labor Statistics, *Labor Force Participation Rate* [CIVPART], retrieved from FRED, Federal Reserve Bank of St. Louis; https://fred.stlouisfed.org/series/CIVPART.

U.S. Bureau of Labor Statistics, *Unemployment Rate* [UNRATE], retrieved from FRED, Federal Reserve Bank of St. Louis; https://fred.stlouisfed.org/series/UNRATE.

Appendix

Download Four Series

To download the civilian, noninstitutional population 16 and over, labor force, employed, and unemployed from 1/1/1952, enter the *Series IDs* in row 1: CNP16OV in cell A1, CLF16OV in cell C1, CE16OV in cell E1, and UNEMPLOY in cell G1.

In row 4 of columns A, C, E, and G, enter 1/1/1952.

Click the Get FRED Data button from the FRED menu.

In a few moments (depending on the speed of your internet connection and how much data it needs to download), the spreadsheet fills with data for the four variables you requested, beginning with labels in row 7, followed by numbers.

Emp+Unemp=LF Check

In cell I8, enter the formula =D8-F8-H8 and fill it down.

The many zeroes confirm that the sum of *Employed* and *Unemployed* equals the *Labor Force*. The few ones are rounding errors. It is definitely true that the labor force is the number of people 16 and over who have or want a job.

Compute UNRATE

In cell J8, enter the formula =H8/D8. Click the % (Percent Style) button in the *Home* tab in the *Ribbon* and add a decimal place (using the Increase Decimal button near the % button). Fill it down.

LFPR

The first hit in a search of *labor force participation rate* is CIVPART. Selecting it and clicking the Add Series ID button puts the information on the sheet, but you have to move it to cell M1:N4.

Do not forget to change the date to 1/1/1952. If you do forget, then change the date and download the data again.

With CIVPART downloaded in columns M and N, enter the label LFPR in cell O7 and the formula =D8/B8 in cell O8. Format it as % with one decimal place. Fill it down.

It is easy to see that your LFPR in column O replicates CIVPART in column N.

To make the chart, simply click the Build Graph button and select CIVPART.

5.2 Unemployment by Subgroups

The headline unemployment rate number (with FRED *Series ID* UNRATE) is widely reported and discussed. Every month, the CPS asks about 60,000 households a series of questions, and their answers are used to take the pulse of the economy.

We are pleased when we hear the unemployment rate is around 4% or that it has fallen from the previous month if it is above 4%.

We know, however, that a single number cannot possibly tell us everything about something as complicated as an entire economy. The overall unemployment rate is an aggregate, high-level view of the economy. By zooming in and breaking it into its constituent parts, we can learn more about how the economy is really doing.

Male and Female

As of this writing, the CPS gives people the option of answering that they are either male or female.

We can download unemployment rates for these two groups and compare them to the overall unemployment rate.

There is a better way to get the needed *Series IDs* than searching for them, but you need the older, more stable version of the FRED Excel add-in available at dub.sh/addins. If you installed it in the previous section, it should be available, but use the Add-in Manager (*Alt, t, i*) to access it if needed.

STEP Insert a sheet in your *Unemployment.xlsx* workbook and click the FRED tab on the *Ribbon*. Click Browse Popular Data Releases and select *Household Survey*. Move your cursor over *Unemployment Rate* (16yrs+) and select it, as shown in Figure 5.5.

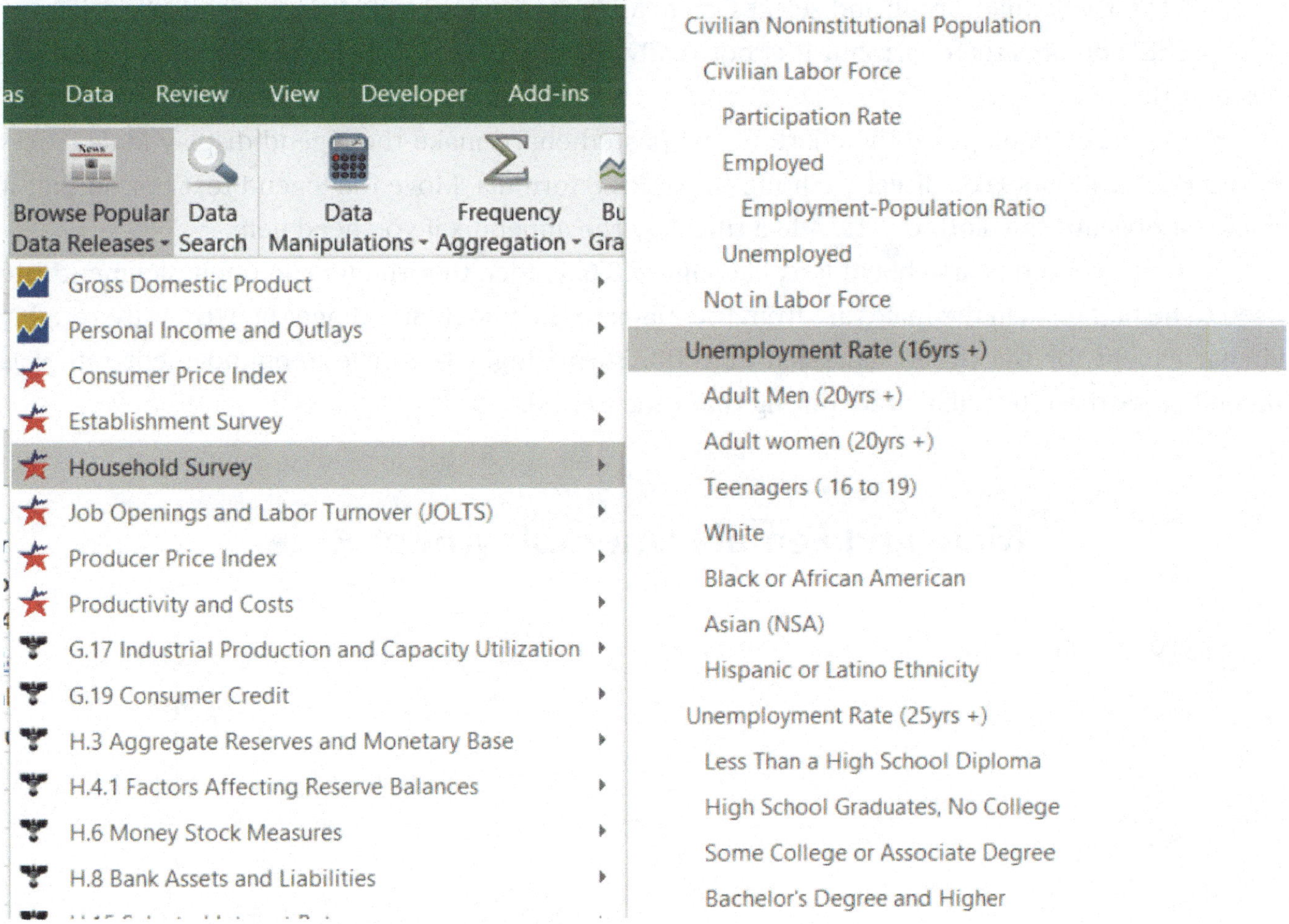

Figure 5.5: FRED Popular Data Releases options.
Source: Screenshot of Excel interface, © Microsoft Corporation. Add-in by Federal Reserve Bank of St. Louis (FRED).

FRED puts UNRATE in cell A1. This is certainly a fast and easy way to get a *Series ID*! Of course, it only works for variables that are popular and often downloaded.

We repeat this process to get male and female unemployment rates. As you do it, be sure to look at the other variables available in the household survey (which is the CPS). Notice how some of them are indented, capturing the logic of the survey.

STEP Click Browse Popular Data Releases and select *Household Survey* again, but this time select *Adult Men (20yrs +)*. Repeat this one more time, but select *Adult Women (20yrs +)*.

FRED places the *Series IDs* for male and female unemployment rates in cells C1 and E1. With this information, we are ready to download the data.

STEP Click Get FRED Data.

With the data downloaded, we can proceed to create a chart that compares male and female unemployment.

STEP Click Build Graph and select *Create Multiple Series Graph*. Select both LNS series.

FRED creates the chart, but it is not ready for prime time. The legend needs work, and it has no title.

STEP Copy and paste the chart. In the pasted chart, make the legend display *Male (20yrs +)* and *Female (20yrs +)* by directly editing the SERIES formula. Move the legend text box so that it does not obscure the plotted data. Add a title. See the appendix if you need help.

Your finished chart should look like Figure 5.6. Notice that the female unemployment rate used to be higher than the male rate from the 1950s to the mid-1980s. Since then, they are roughly similar except for the Great Recession of 2008. Surprisingly, the male unemployment rate was much higher than the female rate during that time period.

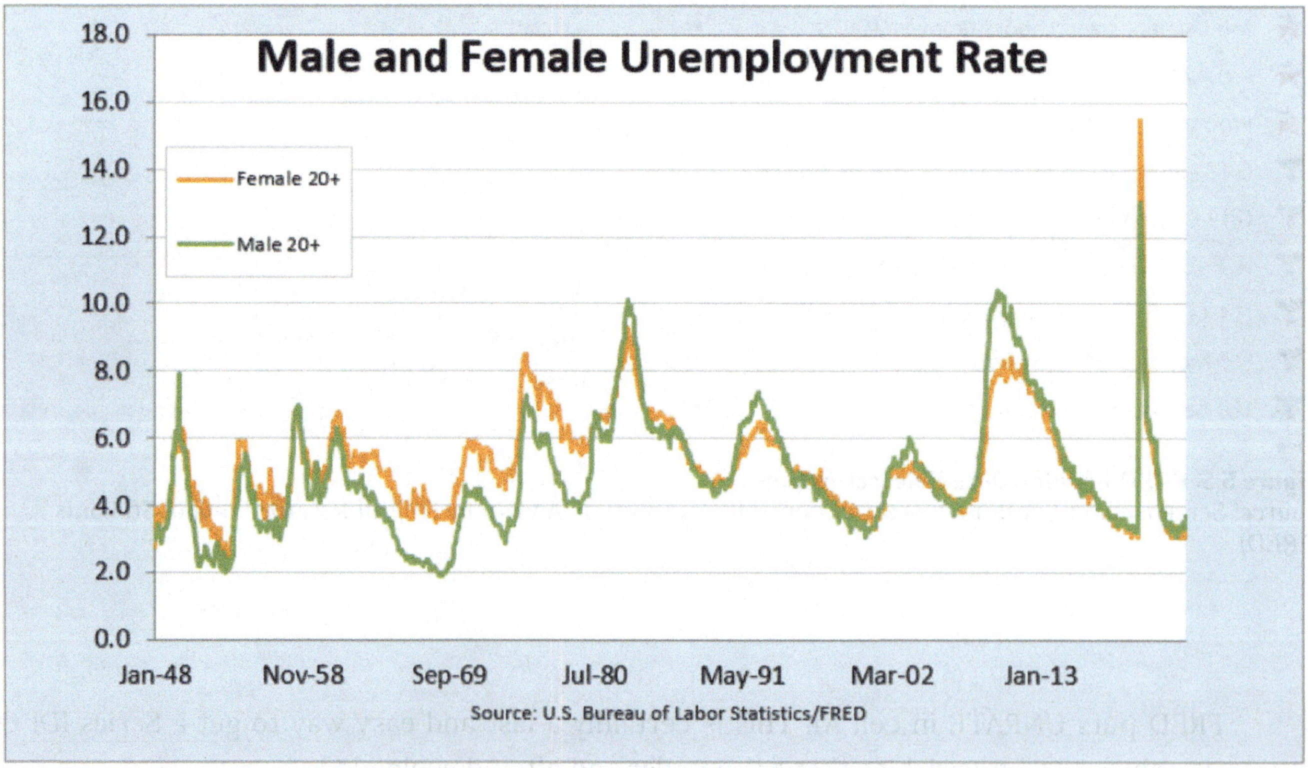

Figure 5.6: A FRED chart of historical male and female unemployment rates.
Source: USBLS via FRED, Public Domain Data / FRED Terms.

Teenage Unemployment

STEP Insert a new sheet in your workbook and download the overall unemployment rate and the teenage unemployment rate. Create a chart of these two series with a descriptive legend and title. Follow the same steps as before.

Figure 5.7 shows that the teenage unemployment rate is always much higher than the overall unemployment rate. The reason is not simply because many teenagers do not work. Remember, many teenagers in high school or college will say they are not looking for work, so they are not counted as unemployed.

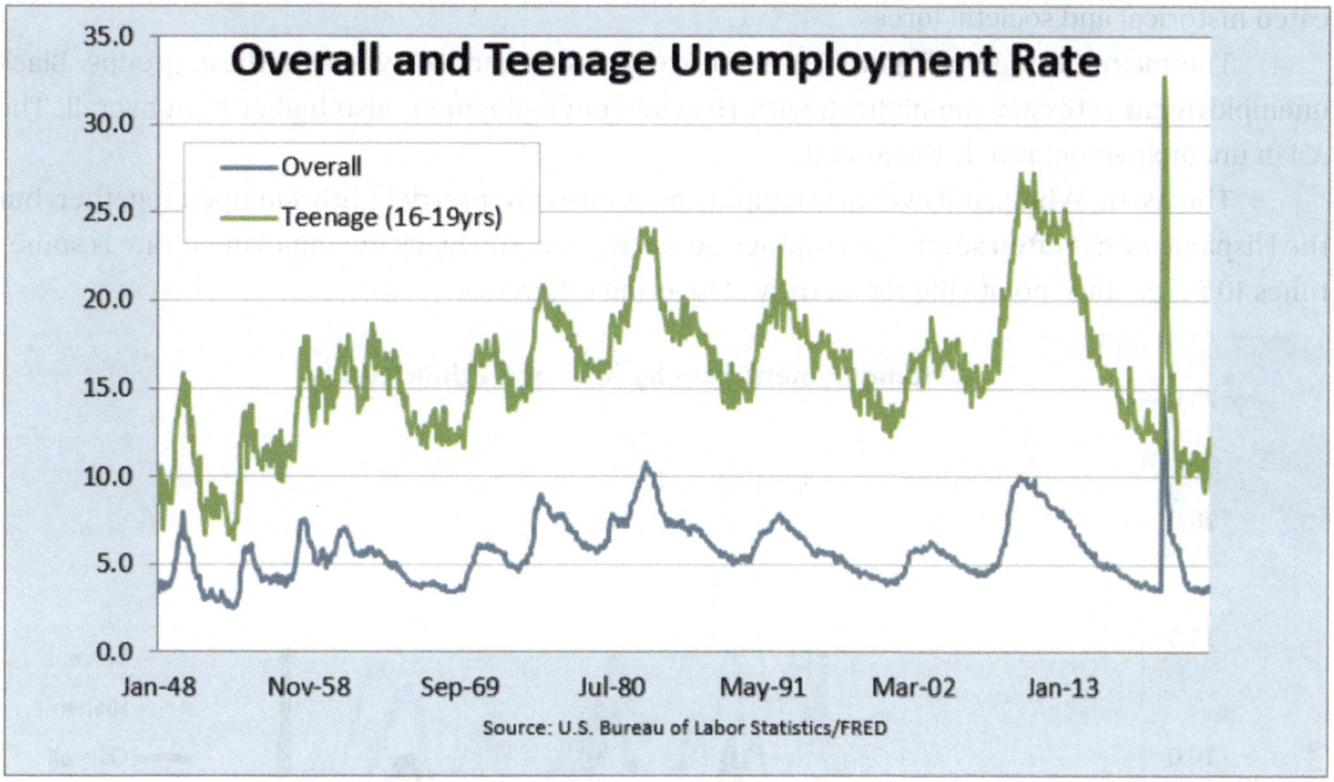

Figure 5.7: Teenage unemployment is always higher than overall.
Source: USBLS via FRED, Public Domain Data / FRED Terms.

Teenage unemployment is always so high because teenagers who are looking for work are unskilled and have relatively few potential job opportunities. Thus, teenagers who want to work have a difficult time finding a job.

Teenagers are especially vulnerable during recessions, when their already high unemployment rate goes even higher. Figure 5.7 shows that the pandemic was especially hard on teenagers, as their unemployment rate was over 30%.

Unemployment by Race and Ethnicity

We can use Browse Popular Data Releases to select the unemployment rate for the available racial and ethnic groups. We download data for the overall, White, Black, Asian, and Hispanic groups, with Series IDs of UNRATE, LNS14000003, LNS14000006, LNS14032183, and LNS14000009, respectively. Then we make a chart using the *Scatter* type as described below. Figure 5.8 shows the result of this work.

Figure 5.8 can lead to confusion and misunderstanding. The differences observed between these groups are not necessarily indicative of their abilities but rather a consequence of complicated historical and societal forces.

The main message of Figure 5.8 is the tremendous variability across these groups. Black unemployment rates are the highest, with Hispanic unemployment also higher than overall. The Asian unemployment rate is the lowest.

The Asian, White, and overall unemployment rates are pretty tightly clumped together, but the Hispanic rate is often several percentage points higher. The Black unemployment rate is sometimes 10 percentage points higher—a truly staggering difference.

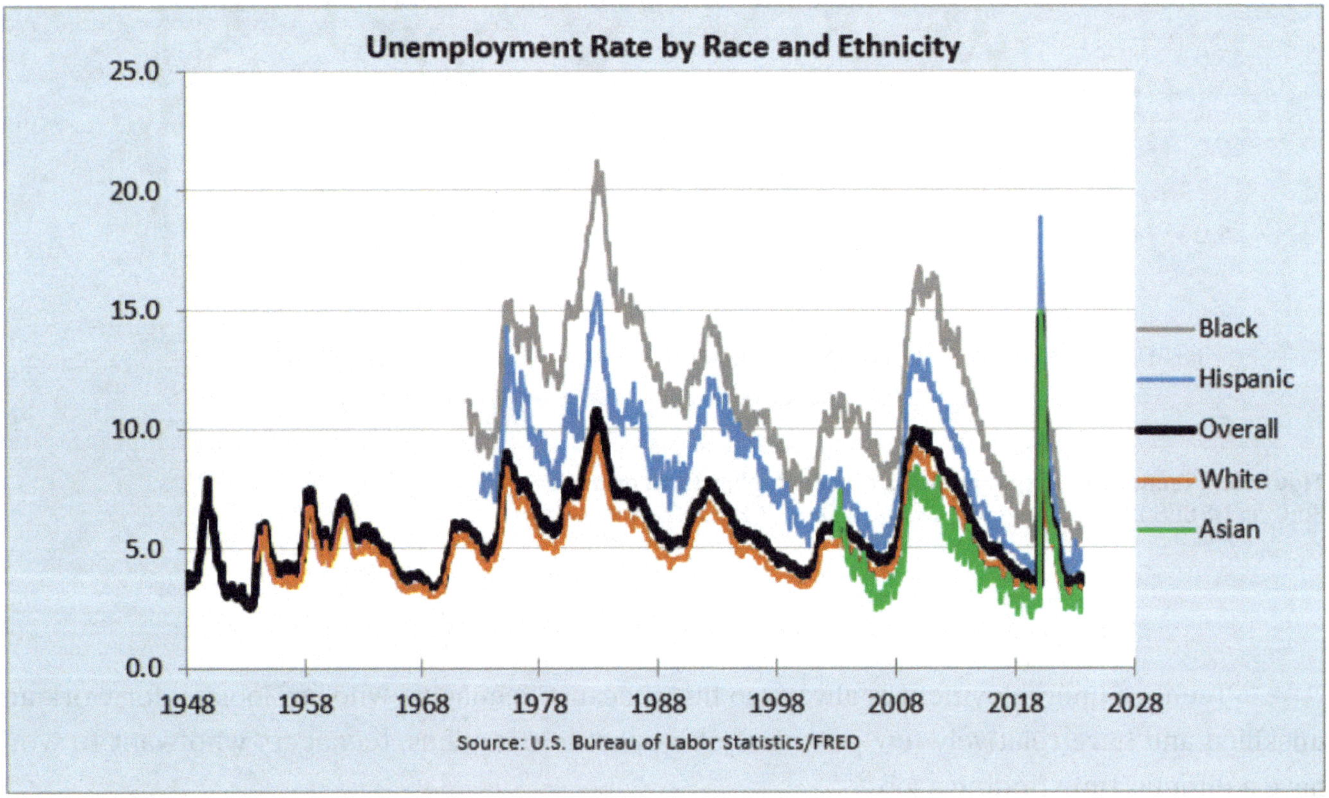

Figure 5.8: High variability in unemployment rate by race and ethnicity.
Source: USBLS via FRED, Public Domain Data / FRED Terms.

While FRED's Build Graph tool allows selection of only three series, we created Figure 5.8 by adding more series by copying and pasting the SERIES formula and editing it.

We also had to change the chart type from *Line* to *Scatter* to get around the fact that the variables have different start dates.

Excel stores dates as a number, the number of days since January 1, 1900. Confusingly, Mac Excel 2008 and earlier used a date system based on 1/1/1904. Many mistakes were made when a workbook was shared across Windows and Mac Excel, but today's workbooks avoid this complication.

STEP Select cell A8 and click the down arrow on the Format button in the *Home* tab. Select the *Format Cells* option at the bottom of the list, then select *General* as shown in Figure 5.9 and click OK.

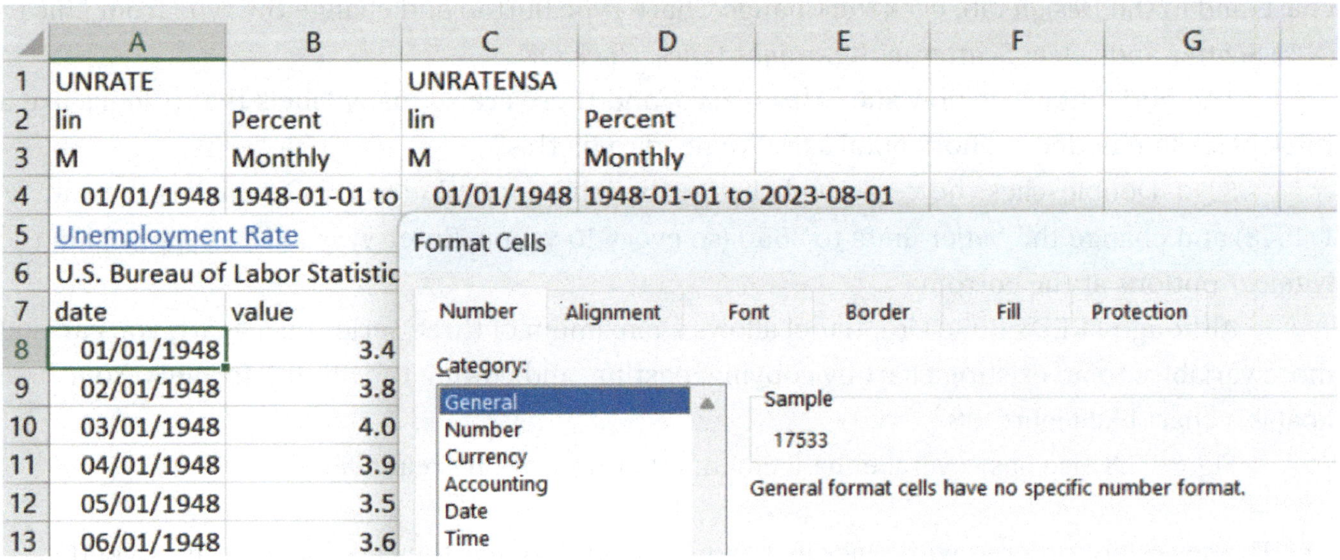

Figure 5.9: Formatting date values.
Source: Screenshot of Excel interface, © Microsoft Corporation.

Excel shows 17533 in cell A8. This is the number Excel has for that cell. If you format it as a date, it can be displayed in a variety of date formats.

EXCEL TIP Dates in Excel are numbers. This means they can be manipulated by mathematical operations like addition and multiplication. The exact same date value can be displayed in many ways, such as 3/14, 14-Mar, and so on.

To make sure you truly understand how dates are handled in Excel, try this quick example.

STEP Enter the dates 1/1/1899, 1/1/1900, and 1/1/1901 in three separate cells. Format the cells as *General*.

Excel displays 1/1/1900 as 1 and 1/1/1901 as 367 (1900 was a leap year, so it had 366 days). Nothing, however, happens to 1/1/1899 because it is not a number; it is text (notice the left-justification). You can subtract 1/1/1900 from 1/1/1901 and get 366, but you cannot use 1/1/1899 (or any date before 1/1/1900) in an arithmetic operation. This is worth remembering if you ever work with dates older than 1/1/1900.

Now that you really understand that dates are numbers, it is easy to see that we can make a *Scatter* chart using dates as the *x*-axis variable.

STEP Create a chart of the UNRATE series alone using the Build Graph tool. Click on the chart, and in the *Design* tab, click the Change Chart Type button and change the type from *Line* to (X Y) *Scatter* and select *Scatter with Straight Lines*. Click OK.

The horizontal axis now starts from zero, and there are so many labels that it looks like a thick black line under the horizontal axis. We need to fix this.

STEP Double-click the *x*-axis and change the minimum value to 17533 (which is the date 1/1/1948) and change the *Major* units to 3650 (so every 10 years). Enter *yyyy* in the *Type* field in the *Number* options at the bottom.

Although FRED's Build Graph tool allows a maximum of three series on a chart, you can add more variables to an existing chart by copying, pasting, and editing the SERIES formula. Your final goal is a chart like Figure 5.8.

Figure 5.8 also has several enhancements that improve its readability:

1. The series are ordered with Black as 1 and Asian as 5 so that they are listed in the legend in that order. This makes it easier for the reader to understand that Black unemployment is highest and Asian is lowest.
2. The dates on the *x*-axis are formatted in years.
3. The overall series is thicker and colored black to help it stand out.

The legend text order can be difficult to control. Microsoft support says, "Under Chart Tools, on the Design tab, in the Data group, click Select Data. In the Select Data Source dialog box, in the Legend Entries (Series) box, click the data series that you want to change the order of. Click the Move Up or Move Down arrows to move the data series to the position that you want."

Unemployment by Education

The final set of subgroups available in the Browse Popular Data Releases is education. Like race and ethnic groups, there is great variation in unemployment rates by education level.

STEP Click Browse Popular Data Releases and get the unemployment rate for people aged 25 years and older, along with the four subgroups below it. Create a chart that clearly displays the unemployment rate of these groups.

Takeaways

The Browse Popular Data Releases button is another way to use FRED. While we focused on the household survey (CPS) and unemployment rates, it is easy to see that there are many other popular data series that are a click away.

While UNRATE, the overall unemployment rate for the United States, is undoubtedly the main indicator of economic performance, it is also true that it suppresses a great deal of variability.

Different subgroups experience wildly different levels of unemployment. Especially during recessions, teenagers, Black and Hispanic people, and less-educated people suffer disproportionately higher unemployment.

Disaggregating the unemployment rate to reveal differences among subgroups is an example of a general strategy. Like an average hides dispersion in a list of numbers, UNRATE never tells the whole story.

References

U.S. Bureau of Labor Statistics, *Unemployment Rate – Asian* [LNS14032183], retrieved from FRED, Federal Reserve Bank of St. Louis; https://fred.stlouisfed.org/series/LNS14032183.

U.S. Bureau of Labor Statistics, *Unemployment Rate – Black or African American* [LNS14000006], retrieved from FRED, Federal Reserve Bank of St. Louis; https://fred.stlouisfed.org/series/LNS14000006.

U.S. Bureau of Labor Statistics, *Unemployment Rate – Hispanic or Latino* [LNS14000009], retrieved from FRED, Federal Reserve Bank of St. Louis; https://fred.stlouisfed.org/series/LNS14000009.

U.S. Bureau of Labor Statistics, *Unemployment Rate – Men* [LNS14000001],retrieved from FRED, Federal Reserve Bank of St. Louis; https://fred.stlouisfed.org/series/LNS14000001.

U.S. Bureau of Labor Statistics, *Unemployment Rate – White* [LNS14000003], retrieved from FRED, Federal Reserve Bank of St. Louis; https://fred.stlouisfed.org/series/LNS14000003.

U.S. Bureau of Labor Statistics, *Unemployment Rate – Women* [LNS14000002], retrieved from FRED, Federal Reserve Bank of St. Louis; https://fred.stlouisfed.org/series/LNS14000002.

U.S. Bureau of Labor Statistics, *Unemployment Rate for Teenagers in the United States* (DISCONTINUED) [USAURTNAA], retrieved from FRED, Federal Reserve Bank of St. Louis; https://fred.stlouisfed.org/series/USAURTNAA

Appendix: Editing the Legend Text

STEP Click the male unemployment series so you see its formula in the formula bar: =SERIES("LNS14000025",MF!$C$8:$C$915,MF!$D$8:$D$915,1). Replace LNS14000025 with *Male (20yrs +)*. Press *Enter*.

Repeat this procedure for the female unemployment rate.

5.3 Seasonal Adjustment

Data are smoothed when they exhibit a strong seasonal pattern. Seasonal adjustment enables better comparison by removing the seasonal trend.

Many statistics are routinely seasonally adjusted. We use the unemployment rate as an example of what seasonal adjustment does and how it works.

We use a powerful Excel tool called a *PivotTable* (notice that Microsoft does not use a space between the two words). Introduced in 1994 in Excel 5.0, Microsoft's Help says that PivotTables are "an interactive way to quickly summarize large amounts of data."

An Example

We begin by getting seasonally adjusted (SA) and not seasonally adjusted (NSA) versions of the unemployment rate.

STEP In a blank sheet, search FRED for *unemployment rate* and select the two top hits. Click *Add Series ID* and close the search box.

Excel enters UNRATE and UNRATENSA in the top row of your spreadsheet. These are both measures of the unemployment rate, but one is seasonally adjusted, and the other is not. How do they compare?

STEP Download data for both series and make two separate charts.

It is easy to see that the UNRATENSA chart is much more jagged than the UNRATE chart. The raw, unadjusted unemployment rate is always higher in the winter and summer and falls quite a bit in the last quarter as retail sales increase.

We can see this seasonal pattern more clearly by looking at the unemployment rate for each month. To do this, we need to prepare the data and then make a PivotTable.

Our strategy is to use Excel's TEXT function to extract the month from each date. Recall from the previous section that Excel stores dates as numbers. You see 1/1/1948, but Excel has 17533 (the number of days since January 1, 1900) in its memory. We can apply many different date formats to display this number as a date, such as just the year (yyyy) or the month-year (mmm-yy).

Excel's TEXT function converts numbers to text, and this allows us to display the month in each date value. We use mmm as the format code.

STEP In cell E7, enter the label *Month*, and in cell E8, enter the formula =TEXT(A8, "*mmm*"). Fill it down.

Excel displays the months for each date value in column A. Notice that it does this to cell A8 also, which is in its raw number form.

We use the same strategy to extract the year.

STEP In cell F7, enter the label *Year*, and in cell F8, enter the formula =TEXT(A8, "*yyyy*"). Fill it down.

Similar to the previous step, Excel displays the year for each date value in column A. As before, it does this to the number in cell A8 also.

STEP Change cell B7 to SA and D7 to NSA.

We are now ready to compute the average unemployment rate for each month. We could use formulas to do this, but a PivotTable does it in seconds.

STEP Go to the *Insert* tab in the *Ribbon*. Click the PivotTable button in the top left.

Excel displays the *Create PivotTable* dialog box. It may have prepopulated the Table/Range field, but this is probably wrong.

STEP In the Table/Range field, select the cell range from A7 to column F and the bottom row of your downloaded data. The range should look like this: Sheet1!$A$7:$F$915 (although your bottom row may be bigger).

STEP Click the *New Worksheet* radio button and click OK.

Excel inserts a new sheet in your workbook. On the right is a context-sensitive area that pops up whenever you are in a PivotTable and an empty PivotTable in columns A, B, and C.

Different versions of Excel have different PivotTable interfaces, so you may need to adjust the instructions that follow. Do not be passive—search the internet or use generative AI (such as ChatGPT) to figure out how to work with PivotTables on your version of Excel.

STEP You may be able to just click the *Month* variable listed on the right of your screen, or you may have to click and drag down to the *Rows* area below the listed variables.

Excel adds the *Month* variable to the PivotTable, creating a list of months in column A.

STEP Click NSA or click and drag NSA into the *Values* area.

Excel adds the NSA variable, but we do not want the sum (which is the default). We want the average for each month.

STEP Click on the *Sum of* NSA in the *Values* area (bottom left of your screen) and select *Value Field Settings*. In the dialog box that pops up, select the *Average* (instead of the default *Sum*) and click OK.

The average unadjusted unemployment rate (UNRATENSA) for each month is now displayed. This is a one-dimensional cross tabulation (crosstab).

Notice that the values are higher in the winter months, they fall, then they go up again in June and July before falling again at the end of the year. This is happening because of seasonality in the unemployment rate.

STEP Repeat this procedure for SA. In other words, add SA to the table and then change it from *Sum* to *Average* via the *Value Field Settings*.

Notice that the SA column (the seasonally adjusted unemployment rate) is much more stable across the months. It has had the seasonal component removed, and the data are smoothed.

A chart will make this crystal clear.

STEP Select the PivotTable data and insert a *Line* chart (since the *x*-axis is text, this is an appropriate chart) to reproduce Figure 5.10.

The nearly horizontal line shows how the unemployment rate has been smoothed. The squiggly line shows the persistent pattern inherent in the raw, unadjusted data. The unemployment rate is usually high in the winter, then falls, then pops up again in the summer before falling again the rest of the year.

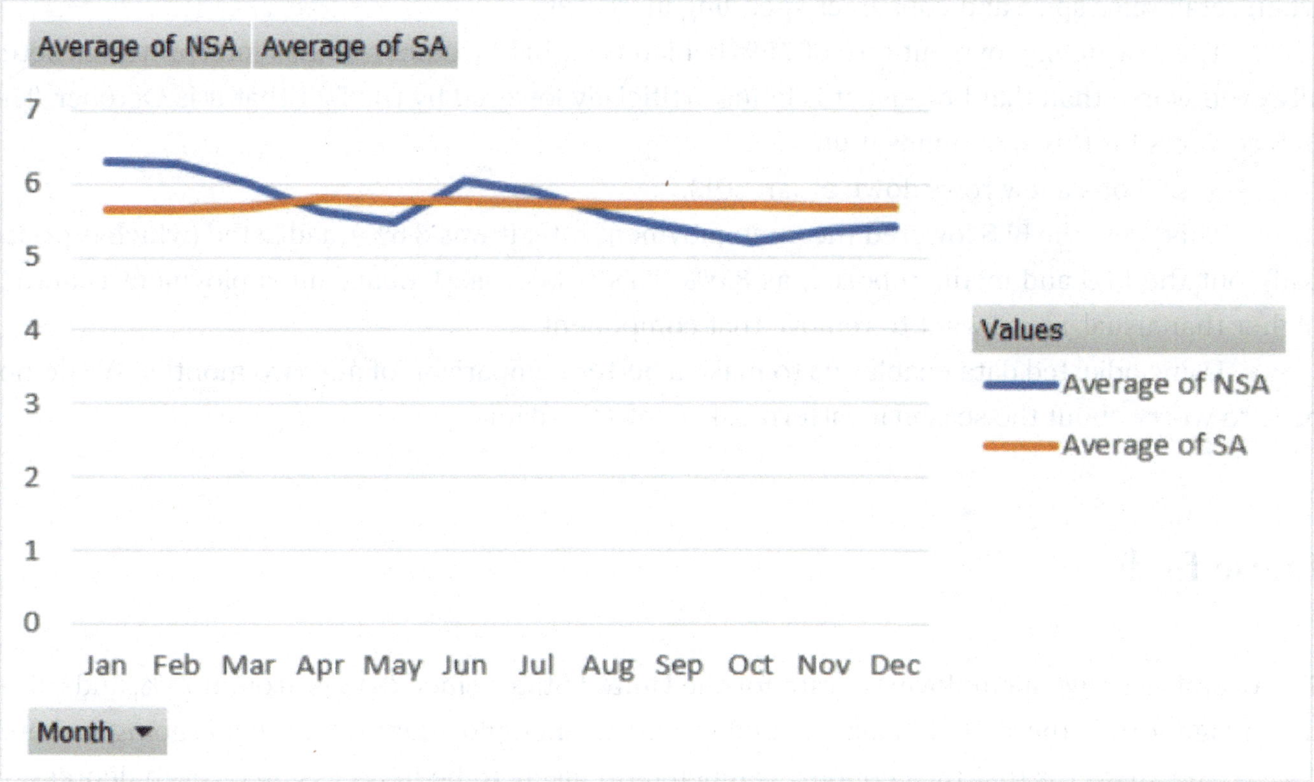

***Figure 5.10*: Unadjusted and seasonally adjusted monthly average UNRATE.**
Source: Source: USBLS via FRED, Public Domain Data / FRED Terms.

The Meaning of Seasonal Adjustment

Suppose we used the unadjusted unemployment rate, and it was 6.2%, but the month was unknown. We would have a problem correctly interpreting this number. If it was for January, then it seems typical, but if it was for October, we would conclude the economy was struggling because it is higher than usual for October.

Seasonal adjustment solves this problem. If the unemployment rate is seasonally adjusted, we can use it to make a decision for any month. A 6.2% seasonally adjusted rate is not good, no matter the month.

Another way to understand what seasonal adjustment does is to look at the data and compare the two series.

STEP Return to your data sheet and go to row 785. Look at the Oct, Nov, and Dec values in column B versus D.

The BLS has literally inflated (revised upward) the values in column D to create the values in column B for those months. This is because historically, unemployment is lower in the fall months when retail sales spike and consumer spending increases.

The raw unemployment rate of 7.5% (which is high) in October 2012 is interpreted as actually even worse than that because it is being artificially lowered by the fact that it is October. The BLS corrects for this and bumps it up.

STEP Look a few rows down at Jan 2013.

This time, the BLS lowered the unemployment rate. It was 8.5% unadjusted (which is pretty bad), but the BLS and media report it as 8.0%. This is because January unemployment is always higher than usual, so we want to remove that component.

Using adjusted data enables us to make a better comparison of any two months. We do not have to worry about the seasonal pattern baked into the data.

Loose Ends

The overall average unemployment rate for the United States since 1948 is around 7.1%, and this is much higher than the 4% to 5% magic number for the unemployment rate. What is going on here?

The answer is that the economy is much more likely to be in recession or even depression with high unemployment than it is to be overheated with extremely low unemployment rates.

It is also true that the few times the unemployment rate is too low, it can only go down a few percentage points below 4%. On the other hand, when the economy crashes, the unemployment rate can and has soared into the double-digit territory.

Another issue that you might be wondering about is exactly how the BLS does the seasonal adjustment. This is an advanced topic beyond the scope of this book. The procedure involves a complicated model. The BLS is transparent about the methodology, which it calls the X-13ARIMA-SEATS Seasonal Adjustment Method, on its website at bls.gov. It would be a challenging and perhaps fun project to replicate the reported adjusted values.

There are many ways to seasonally adjust, and different statistical agencies do different things. They are all looking to remove seasonality from data collected at intervals throughout the year.

Discovery

Along with the unemployment rate, labor market experts closely follow the labor force participation rate. Seasonal adjustment is also routinely applied to the LFPR, but do you think it operates the same way? Let's find out.

STEP Your task is to apply the same steps used for the unemployment example described above to the LFPR to make a chart like Figure 5.10. You will download both the SA and NSA versions of the LFPR, extract the month (using Excel's TEXT function), and make a PivotTable of the average LFPR for each month (for both SA and NSA). Finally, you will make a *Line* chart of the two series.

What did you discover—is the seasonal adjustment for LFPR the same as or different from the unemployment rate? In what specific ways are they the same or different?

Takeaways

We seasonally adjust variables that vary systematically over the year. For example, construction employment falls in the winter and rises in the summer. Seasonal adjustment would tweak the construction employment numbers higher in the winter and lower in the summer so that we can remove the seasonal component and make a better comparison across months.

Seasonal adjustment involves removing the cyclical component of a variable, so we get a better reading of what is really going on.

When you hear an unemployment rate in the media, it is almost certainly a seasonally adjusted unemployment rate.

Using seasonally adjusted variables enables better comparison and interpretation.

An Excel PivotTable is a powerful summary tool that enables data exploration and display of relationships in the data.

PivotTables can produce static cross tabs, but they are also a great way to dynamically visualize data. Moving variables around can quickly provide different views of the data.

6. Constrained Optimization

Edgeworth's simplification was this assumption: *every man [person] is a pleasure machine.*

Robert Heilbroner

6.1 Maximizing Utility

Figure 6.1: Computer-generated image of cigars and brandies.
Source: Stable Diffusion, 2023/ License.

Figure 6.1 shows two things, cigars and brandies, that we will pretend that you enjoy. Economists model the satisfaction and happiness provided by consumption of goods and services by using a *utility function.*

Your utility function is given by this equation:

$$U = 18B - 3B^2 + 20C - C^2$$

Your job is to choose the number of brandies (B) and cigars (C) that maximize your utility (U).

This optimization problem can be solved analytically, with calculus and algebra, but we will use Excel's Solver instead. As you recall, Solver is a numerical approach to finding the optimal solution.

We need to recast the problem in a way that Excel can understand it, then run Solver to find the optimal values of B and C.

The work that follows assumes that you have done the lifeguard problem (in chapter 2) and remember some of it. If you have not or do not remember it, you can continue working, but you will learn more if you review the lifeguard problem before you begin this material.

Implementing the Problem in Excel

Optimization problems always have three parts:

1. Goal (objective function)
2. Endogenous variables
3. Exogenous variables

We know we want to maximize the utility function, so that is our goal. It has to be a formula in a cell that depends on other cells in the spreadsheet.

Your endogenous, or choice, variables are B and C. We implement this part of the problem with cells that Solver will use for trial solutions. In the *Solver* dialog box, these are called the *changing cells.*

Finally, the exogenous variables are things the decision-maker cannot change. They are part of the environment. In this problem, your exogenous variables are the coefficients (18, −3, 20, and −1) and exponents in the utility function. We could set up cells for these exogenous variables, but we will keep things simple and just enter the utility function as is.

STEP Open a blank Excel workbook and save it as *UtilityMax.xlsx*. In cell A1, enter a 1, and in cell B1, enter the label *Brandies*. In cell A2, enter a 1, and in cell B2, enter the label *Cigars*. In cell A4, enter the formula =18*A1-3*A1^2+20*A2-A2^2 and press the *Enter* key.

Excel displays 34 in cell A4 because if you smoke one cigar and sip one brandy, your utility function says that you get 34 utils of satisfaction. Now, there is no such thing as a util, but we will ignore this inconvenient truth, and utils will be the units of measurement of satisfaction.

STEP Change cell A1 to 2.

Your utility rises to 43 utils. This is an improvement in your happiness, but you do not want to simply improve; you want to maximize utility. What are the best values of B and C, the ones that make utility the largest number possible?

Solving the Problem in Excel

Once we have implemented the problem in Excel, with a formula for the objective function that depends on other cells, we can utilize Solver. It will explore the objective function, trying many solutions. It follows an algorithm, or recipe, when deciding where to move next.

There are many different optimization algorithms. Sometimes, one fails, but another works. Some are good for several different kinds of problems and others are only useful for specific applications. There is no single algorithm that is better than the others.

STEP Open the *Solver* dialog box by clicking the *Data* tab and clicking *Solver*. If it is not there, use the keyboard shortcut *Alt, t, i* to bring up the *Add-ins Manager* and install it. Click in the objective function field, click on cell A4, click in the *Changing Variable Cells* field, and select both A1 and A2. Click *Solve*. Click OK when Excel displays a dialog box reporting that it has found a solution.

Solver's answer is really close to the exact solution, which is to drink 3 brandies and smoke 10 cigars. This yields a utility of 127. You may not believe it, but you will see that it is impossible to get utility higher than 127.

Remember that Solver is hunting and pecking, plugging and chugging through many trial solutions. It changes direction when it does worse and continues forward when it is doing better. It stops when it does not improve by very much. Hence, it sometimes gets the exact right answer, but mostly it just gets very close.

STEP Let's make sure it is clear that Solver's answer is not exactly right by widening column A and displaying more decimal points until you see a few zeroes (click the Increase decimal button repeatedly in the *Number* group in the *Home* tab).

Your screen should look similar to Figure 6.2. We would never report all those digits because they are meaningless and exhibit false precision. We interpret Solver's answer as $B^* = 3$ and $C^* = 10$ and $U^* = 127$, which is the correct answer.

	A	B
1	3.00000071	Brandies
2	9.999996396	Cigars
3		
4	126.9999999999850000	Utility

Figure 6.2: Solver results.

Displaying the Optimal Solution

To visualize the optimal solution, we first use a 3D Surface chart. In the next section, we will create a 2D graph, since economists and mathematicians often use contour plots to display two-variable optimization problems.

To create a chart in Excel, we need data. The 3D chart requires a specific layout, with the x-axis in a row, the y-axis in a column, and the z-axis (vertical) in the interior of the table.

STEP In cells D2 to D12, enter 0 to 10 by 1. In cells, E1 to Y1, enter 0 to 20 by 1. These are the two horizontal axes in our 3D plot. In cell E2, enter the formula =18*$D2-3*$D2^2+20*E$1-E$1^2.

Notice how the $ is being used. We are going to fill this formula down and then right. When we fill it down, it will change the row number for the brandies and continue to use row 1 for the cigars part of the utility function.

STEP Fill your formula in E2 down and then examine the formulas in cells E3 and E12 to confirm that the row number is changing for column D but stays constant at 1 for column E.

STEP Select cells E2 to E12, then fill right. Examine the formulas in cells Y3 and Y12 to confirm that column D stays constant but the cigars part of the utility function has changing columns.

Our clever use of the $ has enabled us to create a table that shows how utility varies with changing amounts of brandies (in column D) and cigars (in row 1). The interior of the table displays values of utility.

It is easy to see that the maximum utility value is in cell O5. It is surrounded by lower values. Solver reached the top of this hill by crawling up until it got to the top, at 3 brandies and 10 cigars.

STEP Select cell O5 and make its background color yellow by clicking the bucket icon in the *Font* group in the *Home* tab.

We are now ready to create a chart. As you know, there are three steps: (1) Select the data, (2) choose the desired chart type, and perhaps most important, (3) clean up the chart.

STEP Select range D1 (notice that this cell is empty, but you need to select it to get all the rows and columns in the table) to Y12. Click the *Insert* tab and click *Recommended Charts*. Click *All Charts* and click *Surface*. Click 3-D *Surface* and click OK.

Excel places a chart that looks like an elongated hill on your spreadsheet. It decided to put cigars (in row 1) on the x-axis because it has more cells, but this is not what we want. We need to clean up this chart.

The first thing to do is to put the brandies axis in the front and the cigars on the side.

STEP Click the *Design* tab (if needed) and click the Switch Row/Column button.

That looks much better, but we have more cleaning up to do.

STEP Remove the legend (select it and press the *delete* key) and add axes titles for each axis. Click the Add Chart Element button and select Axis Titles. Use *Brandies* for the *Primary Horizontal* title, *Cigars* for the *Depth* title, and *Utility* for the *Primary Vertical* title. Change the chart title field text to *Utility Maximization*.

It is now really looking like something we would be proud to put our name on, but we can do one final improvement: Add more color bands to clearly see that it is a hill.

STEP Double-click the *Utility* axis to bring up the *Format Axis: Axis Options* screen on the right. Change the *Major Units* field from 50 to 10.

Your chart now looks like Figure 6.3. The crowded numbers on the Utility axis are not great, but the extra color bands make it easy to see that there is a clear top to this surface.

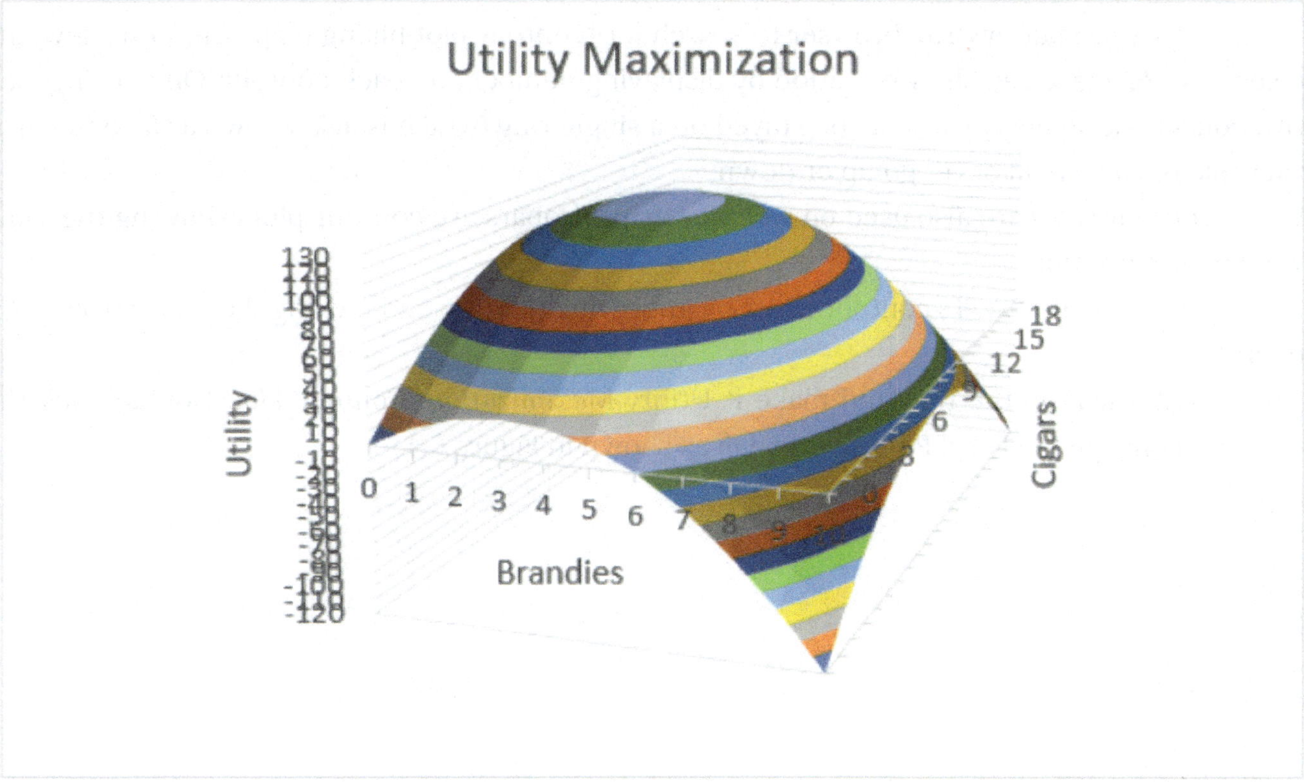

***Figure 6.3*: A 3D visualization of utility maximization.**

Contour Plot

Although a 3D plot like Figure 6.3 is useful, solutions to optimization problems with two endogenous variables often use a 2D contour plot that highlights the choice variables.

A contour plot, also called a level curve, displays a 3-dimensional surface by graphing constant vertical slices of the surface, called contours, on a 2-dimensional chart. It is easier to see what it is than to describe it.

STEP Copy the 3D chart you just made and paste it. In the *Design* tab, click the Change Chart Type button. Click the *Contour Plot* type (with the shaded region that signals the use of color) and click OK.

Comparing the color bands on the two charts makes clear how they are related. The light blue at the top of the hill in the 3D plot is the light blue oval in the contour plot. The orange band is a little lower on the hill, and it is a bigger oval on the contour plot.

It is as if you flew on a plane and looked straight down at the hill. The vertical axis is suppressed on the contour plot, but we could put labels with numbers of the vertical height on each slice. This is exactly what a topographic map does.

STEP Use your favorite browser to search for "contour plot hiking map." Click on a few hits to see how 2D maps can show elevation by displaying numbers on each contour. On a hiking map with concentric squiggly rings, if you stayed on a single ring (which is also known as a contour) as you walked, you would never go up or down.

Contour plots are also used on weather maps. Isobars are contour plots showing the same atmospheric pressure.

Let's clean up Excel's contour chart by improving the title and moving the y-axis from right to left.

STEP Click on the title and make it *Utility Maximization: Contour Plot*. Double-click the y-axis and change the *Label Position* to *High* as shown in Figure 6.4.

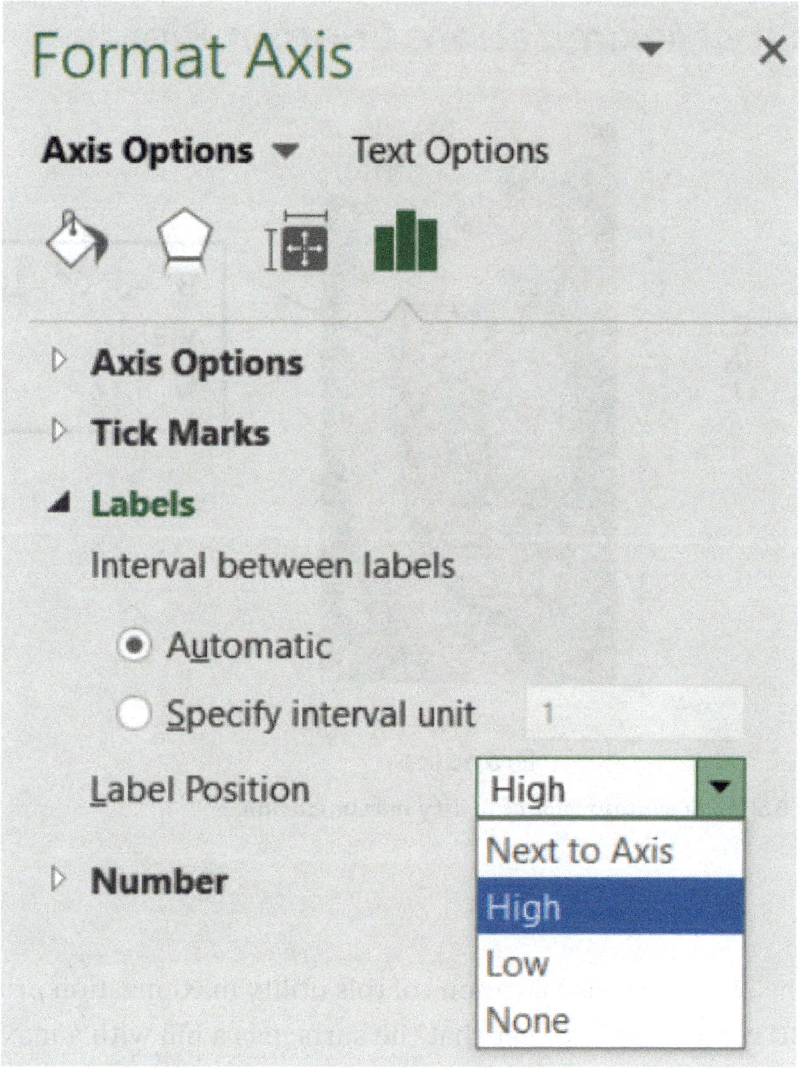

Figure 6.4: Moving the y-axis from right to left.
Source: Screenshot of Excel interface, © Microsoft Corporation.

A final enhancement involves placing a point on the optimal solution and labeling it with a callout box (in the *Shapes* collection in the *Insert* tab), as shown in Figure 6.5.

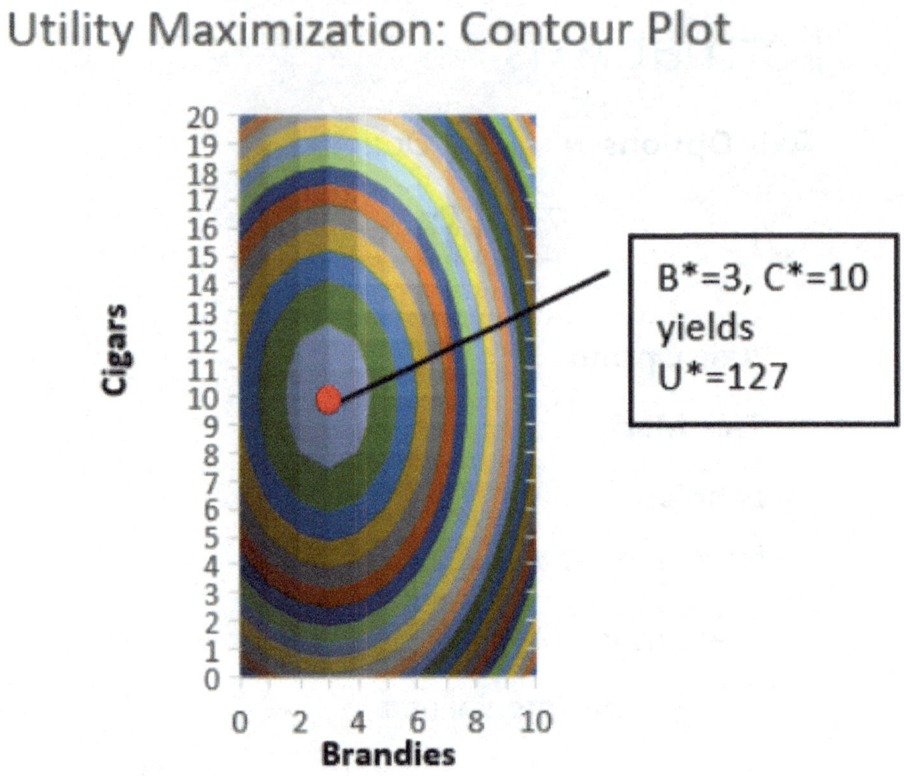

Figure 6.5: **A 2D contour plot of utility maximization.**

Comparing the 3D and 2D visualizations of this utility maximization problem reveals advantages of each. The 3D version makes clear that the surface is a hill with a maximum, but it is difficult to read the optimal number of brandies and cigars.

On the other hand, the 2D contour plot makes it really easy to see the max and the values of brandies and cigars that will maximize utility. The trick is that you have to know how to read a contour plot, and now you do.

Make It Stick

If we used Solver earlier when we did the lifeguard problem, why are we doing it again? Repeating material is a learning strategy that has been proven to work.

Suppose you want to improve your free throw shooting, and you really cared about this, so you decided to practice for one hour per day for two weeks. Most people would think that actually standing at the free throw line and shooting free throws would be the best use of your time, but this is wrong.

A much better use of your one hour per day is to shoot from all over the court—spending 10 minutes in one spot, then moving to another spot, varying distance from, say, 10 to 20 feet (a free throw is 15 feet from the basket). This is called interleaved practice, and it also works for learning!

By doing the lifeguard problem, then doing other things and returning to a slightly different optimization problem, you are burying deeper channels in your brain about Solver and optimization.

Every time you repeat something in Excel, especially in the context of a different situation, you get a little better at it. The novelty of the new problem is important so that you are not doing the exact same thing, but you are making connections and learning.

If you want to know more about the neuroscience behind how you learn and other optimal learning strategies, search for Brown et al.'s 2014 book *Make It Stick*.

STEP Watch dub.sh/howtostudy to see some of these ideas applied to optimal studying.

Takeaways

We revisited work we did earlier using Solver, Excel's numerical optimization add-in.

Excel's Solver easily found the optimal solution to a simple two-variable utility maximization problem.

Solver applies an iteration procedure and stops when it cannot improve by very much. This produces an answer that is not exactly correct, even though the many decimal places it reports seem like it is giving a really precise answer, a phenomenon common to numerical algorithms known as *false precision*.

Two Excel chart types were used to visualize the optimal solution: 3D surface and contour plot.

The 2D contour plot is the best-practice way to display the problem because it highlights the two endogenous variables (one on each axis) and makes it easy to see the numerical values of the optimal solution.

Learning also involves optimization, with better and worse ways to use your time. You definitely want to study and learn optimally.

References

The epigraph is from p. 173 of the 7th edition of Robert Heilbroner's *The Worldly Philosophers*. First published in 1953, this classic tells the story of how economics was born and came to be the mathematical discipline that it is today. It is an easy read, and until *Freakonomics* (by Stephen J. Dubner and Steven Levitt) exploded on the scene in 2009, Heilbroner's *The Worldly Philosophers* had the highest sales of any economics book.

Francis Edgeworth was a key player in the mathematization of economics. *Mathematical Psychics*, published in 1881, was an early application of optimization and comparative statics.

Brown, P., Roediger, H., III, and McDaniel, M. (2014). *Make It Stick: The Science of Successful Learning* (Belknap Press).

Memorize Academy. (2016, Dec. 15). *How to Study Effectively for School or College – Top 6 Science-Based Study Skills* [Video]. YouTube. https://www.youtube.com/watch?v=CPxSzxylRCI.

6.2 Constrained Utility Maximization

Your doctor says that you are killing yourself by smoking too many cigars and drinking too much brandy. She restricts your consumption to a total of 5.

You can have 5 brandies and no cigars or 2, 3, or any other combination that adds up to 5 or fewer. You can choose fractional amounts like one-third of a brandy and four and two-thirds cigars or 1.5 and 3.5.

You cannot, however, maintain your current daily consumption of 3 and 10. That adds up to 13 and violates the constraint.

Your utility function remains the same:

$$U = 18B - 3B^2 + 20C - C^2$$

But we need to add the constraint to properly state this optimization problem. Mathematically, the doctor said that $B + C \leq 5$. Formally, we write the problem like this, where s.t. stands for "subject to":

$$\max_{B,C} U = 18B - 3B^2 + 20C - C^2$$

$$\text{s.t.}\ B + C \leq 5$$

You wonder how you are going to solve this problem. It can be done analytically, but you ask yourself if Solver can do it. Yes, of course it can.

As usual, we will have to implement the problem in Excel. Then we can run Solver to find the optimal solution.

Implementing the Problem in Excel

We have the unconstrained version of the problem already set up, so we start from there.

STEP Make a copy of the sheet in your *UtilityMax.xlsx* workbook by right-clicking the *Sheet1* sheet tab in the bottom left, selecting *Move or Copy . . .*, checking *Create a copy*, and clicking OK. Rename the sheet *ConOpt*.

The new information that we have to implement is the constraint. It is convenient to rewrite the constraint as $B + C - 5 \leq 0$. This way, violations of the constraint occur whenever $B + C - 5$ is positive.

STEP In cell A6, enter the formula =A1+A2-5. In cell B6, enter the label *constraint*.

Now we are ready to call Solver. Excel will include the choices you entered before in the *Solver* dialog box, but we have to add the constraint.

STEP In the *Data* tab, click *Solver*. Confirm that the objective function, max, and changing cells are correct, then click the Add button. From the *Add Constraint* dialog box, click on cell A6 for the *Cell Reference* field, choose *le*, and enter a 0 in the *Constraint* field. Click OK. Notice that Excel adds the constraint to the *Solver* dialog box. Click *Solve*. Excel announces success! Click OK.

We interpret Solver's answer as $B^* = 1$ and $C^* = 4$ and $U^* = 79$, which is the correct answer. To maximize utility subject to the constraint of no more than 5 combined units of cigars and brandies, the best combination is 1 brandy and 4 cigars. This yields a utility of 79 and cannot be beaten by any other combination of brandies and cigars that does not violate the constraint.

Notice that the constraint cell is not exactly zero, but it is very close to zero. Cell A6 shows something like 5.02825E-08. This is a number expressed in scientific notation, and it means 5.02825×10^{-8}. This is a tiny number. You can make it exactly zero if you wish by changing cells A1 and A2 to 1 and 4, respectively.

Visualizing the Optimal Solution

Figure 6.6 displays a 3D surface and contour plot of the constrained utility maximization problem. On the 3D surface plot, the constraint is a barrier that blocks attainment of the unconstrained max at the top of the hill. On the contour plot, the constraint is a line, because if you looked straight down at the barrier from directly above, you would see just a line.

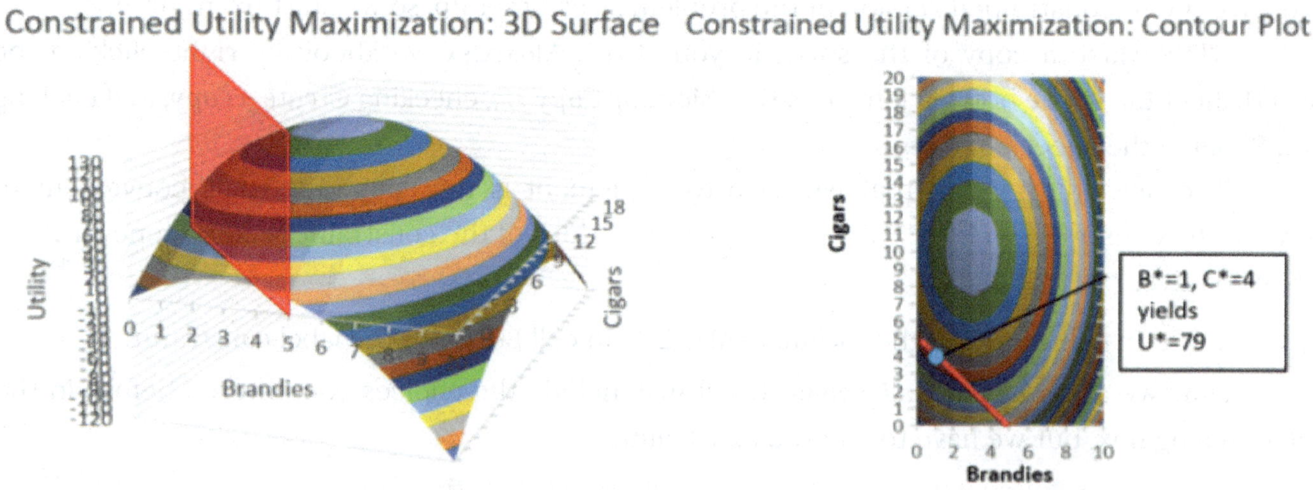

Figure 6.6: Visualizing constrained utility maximization.

STEP Make two separate lists of things you like and do not like for the 3D surface plot and the contour plot. See the appendix if you need help, but do not immediately go there. Try to make the lists yourself before looking at the appendix.

One thing that is extremely important about the contour plot is that it clearly reveals the optimal solution. We can use Excel's wireframe version of the contour plot to see this.

STEP Copy and paste your contour plot, then click *Change Chart Type* in the *Design* tab. Select the *Wireframe Contour* in the *Surface* group of charts.

It is now much easier to see the contour lines. Since there is a contour line for every value of utility, there is actually an infinity of contour lines. Your chart shows only a few of them.

STEP Carefully place a line (use the *Line* object in the *Shapes* collection) from the point 0, 5 to 5, 0 as shown in Figure 6.7.

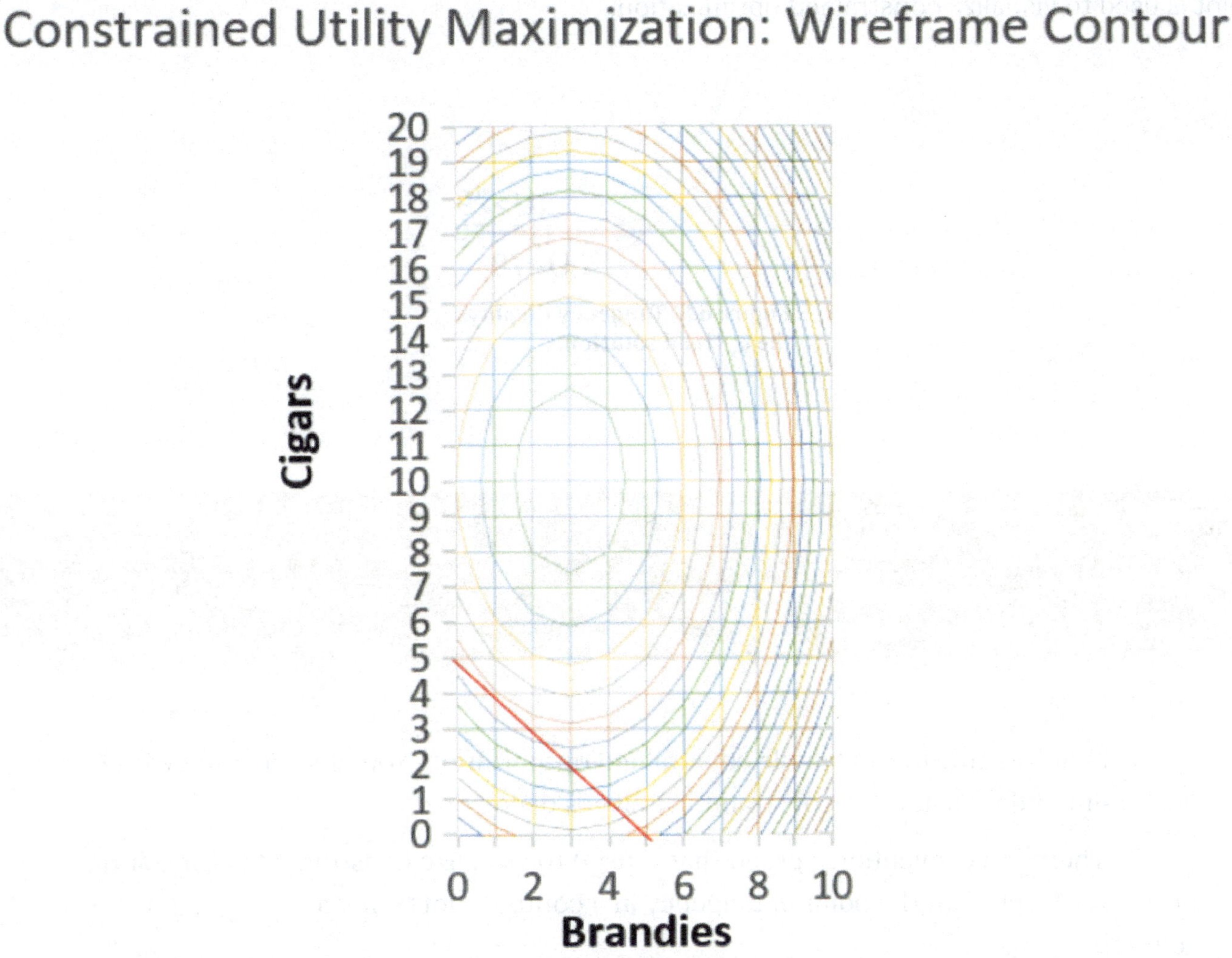

Figure 6.7: Understanding contour lines with the Wireframe chart.

At the optimal solution (at 1, 4), there is a contour slightly above and another below. The curve above has a utility value greater than 79, and the one below is less than 79. There is a curve not shown in Figure 6.7 that is in between the two contours above and below point 1, 4. This contour just touches the constraint line, and it has a utility value of exactly 79. This contour is *tangent* to the diagonal constraint.

A point of tangency means that there is contact at a single point but no crossing. Figure 6.8 shows why tangency is a visualization of the optimal solution.

If the constraint line cuts or intersects a curve, we immediately know this is not the optimal solution. If we are cutting a contour, we can move along the constraint line to reach a higher contour.

In Figure 6.8, the highest curve ($U > 79$) is beyond our reach. The one that just touches the line is the best we can do. Tangency instantly reveals the solution and explains why the 2D contour plot is used to visualize constrained optimization.

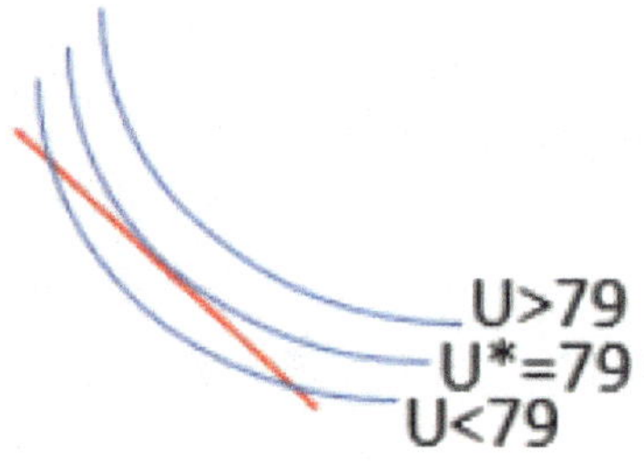

Figure 6.8: Tangency displays the optimal solution.

Takeaways

Excel's Solver add-in can handle constrained optimization. You provide a cell with the constraint and then add the constraint in Solver's dialog box.

There is a conventional graph that is used to visualize constrained optimization problems. It relies on the point of tangency in a contour plot to instantly highlight the solution.

To read a contour plot, remember that it is a top-down view of a 3D surface.

Excel has several 3D surface and contour charts. The chart can be augmented with a variety of drawing objects and text boxes.

Figure 6.9 shows a few pros and cons of the two charts. The only con for the contour plot is the prerequisite knowledge needed to read it.

3D Surface		Contour	
Pro	Con	Pro	Con
Clearly a hill	B*=1, C*=4 unclear	B*=1, C*=4 clear	Contour prereq
Global max clear	U* unclear	U* clear	
Constraint clear	C axis unclear	Constraint clear	

Figure 6.9: Comparing 3D surface and 2D contour plots.

For those in the know, a 2D contour plot is preferred because of the way the tangency draws attention to the optimal solution. It is easy to see the values that solve the constrained optimization problem.

6.3 Comparative Statics with CSWiz

Your doctor is some kind of evil genius (or an economist), and she wants to explore your response to different values of the total allowed units of cigars and brandies.

This is formally known as *comparative statics analysis*. We change one exogenous variable, and we see what effect it has on the optimal solution.

There's an Excel add-in for that—it is called the Comparative Statics Wizard (CSWiz). After explaining comparative statics in more detail, we will use the CSWiz add-in on the constrained optimization version of the cigars-and-brandies problem.

The Logic of Comparative Statics

We did comparative statics analysis earlier with the lifeguard problem (in chapter 2). We turned the lifeguard into a freakish combination of Michael Phelps and Usain Bolt. The optimal solution had us running more, since we were so much faster.

We also did comparative statics analysis when we changed the product price facing the farmer (in section 2.4). As the product price rises, the farmer responds by buying more seed.

There were two more comparative statics examples when we combined Monte Carlo simulation and optimization. The first involved pooled testing (in section 3.3). We lowered the infection rate from 5% to 1%, and this made the optimal group size bigger. The second explored how lowering the cost of searching led to more searches (in section 3.4).

All these examples worked the same way. We solved an optimization problem, then we changed a single exogenous variable and kept everything else the same. We focused on the effect the change had on the optimal solution.

Before we do another example, let's repeat and make crystal clear the logic of comparative statics. It involves a four-step procedure:

1. We set up the problem and find the *initial* solution.
2. We change a single exogenous variable, called the *shock*, holding all other exogenous variables constant. We use a Latin phrase, *ceteris paribus*, as shorthand. This literally means "with other things held equal," and we use the phrase to mean *everything else held constant.*
3. We find the *new* optimal solution.
4. Finally, we *compare* the new to the initial solution to see how the optimal solution responded to the shock.

Comparative statics is the fundamental methodology of economics. It gives a framework for interpreting observed behavior. This framework has been given many names, including the method of economics, the economic approach, the economic way of thinking, and economic reasoning.

As you know, *comparative* clearly points to the comparison between the new and initial solution, but the meaning of *statics* (not to be confused with statistics) is less obvious. It means that we are going to focus on optimal (or equilibrium) positions and not worry about the path of the solution as it moves from the initial to the new point.

We have several ways of comparing the new and initial solutions. A qualitative comparison focuses only on direction (up or down), while quantitative comparisons compute magnitudes of the change in response (as either a difference or a percentage change).

Another Example

$$\max_{B,C} U = 18B - 3B^2 + 20C - C^2$$
$$\text{s.t. } B + C \leq 5$$

We start with the initial constrained optimization problem, which can be formally written like this:

We know that the initial solution is $B^* = 1$ and $C^* = 4$ and $U^* = 79$.

Your doctor surprises you at your next appointment. She is happy with your latest test results and says that you can safely have one more brandy or cigar, so your total allowed amount is now 6. How will you respond to this new development?

STEP From your *ConOpt* sheet in your *UtilityMax.xlsx* workbook, change the 5 in cell A6 to 6. What happens?

The constraint cell is now negative. This means that you are below the constraint. The barrier has moved upward, so you have room to climb higher up the utility hill. But what exactly will you do?

STEP Run Solver. What happens?

With a total of 6 cigars and brandies allowed, your new optimal solution is $B^* = 1.25$ and $C^* = 4.75$, yielding a maximum utility of $U^* = 90.25$.

This makes sense. You take advantage of the loosened constraint to sip a little more brandy and smoke more cigars. That is a qualitative or directional statement. It is like saying that when the price goes down, you buy more.

A quantitative or magnitude statement would be to compute how much more you drink and smoke. You went from 1 to 1.25 brandies as the total amount allowed went from 5 to 6, so that increase is 0.25 brandies. The delta (or difference) for cigars is 0.75, since you went from 4 to 4.75.

There is another way to make a quantitative statement using elasticity. The Comparative Statics Wizard and the results it generates will help us explain how to compute and interpret an elasticity.

The Comparative Statics Wizard

We use a free Excel add-in, *CSWiz.xla*, to do comparative statics analysis. It works with Solver to find the optimal solution given different values of an exogenous variable.

STEP Download the *CSWiz.xla* file from dub.sh/addins and use the Add-ins Manager (File → Options → Add-ins → Go or keyboard shortcut *Alt*, *t*, *i*) to install it. Once installed, click the *Add-ins* tab to see that it is under the *Wizard* group.

To use the CSWiz add-in, we need to modify our Excel implementation of the constrained optimization problem. Instead of hard-coding the total allowed amount of cigars and brandies, we need to make a cell for this exogenous variable.

STEP In cell B8 of your *ConOpt* sheet, enter the label *Total*. In cell A8, enter the number 5. Connect this total value to the constraint cell in A6 by changing the constraint formula to =A1+A2−A8.

We are now ready to run the Comparative Statics Wizard. We will provide information in a series of steps.

STEP Click the *Add-ins* tab, click *Wizard*, and then *Comp Statics*.

As you walk through the steps, be sure to read carefully and think about the information you are providing. The following is the input you need to give as you walk through the steps:

1. Clicking the Input button produces an input box that asks for the objective function cell. Click on cell A4 and click OK. A second box asks for the endogenous variables. Select cells A1 and A2 (both of them) and click OK. The final input box asks for the exogenous variables. Click on cell A8 and click OK. Usually, there is more than one exogenous variable, so you would select all of them. When done, you return to the *Wizard* dialog box, but your inputs are displayed. Confirm that they are correct and click *Next*.
2. Click the Run Solver button to call Solver and run it. Solver needs to successfully find the correct solution to continue. If not, we cannot do comparative statics analysis. When done, you return to the *Wizard* dialog box. Click *Next*.
3. This step is like the first one in that you are asked three questions. Click the Input button. Click cell A8 because this is the cell that we want to vary to see how the optimal solution responds. Click OK. In the second input box, enter the number 1. This will change cell A8 by 1. Click OK. In the final input box, leave the default choice of 5. Click OK. You return to the *Wizard*, and the results of your input are displayed. Confirm that everything is correct and click *Next*.
4. The *Wizard* now has all the information it needs. Clicking the Run Comparative Statics Analysis button will do just that. Excel will solve the problem for total values from 5 to 10 by 1. The *Progress Bar* will advance quickly because this problem is simple, and we only asked for 5 shocks. Click *Next*.

5. Read the message on the final screen and click *Finish*.

You are taken to a new worksheet in your *UtilityMax.xlsx* workbook that displays the results of the comparative statics analysis that you just performed. We use these results to figure out and explain how changing the total allowed amount affects the optimal consumption of brandies and cigars.

STEP We did not name any cells, so the results show cell addresses. We can fix this by entering the names of the variables. Cells A5 and A8 are *Total*. Cells B8, C8, and D8 are Utility*, B*, and C*, respectively. Widen the columns if needed to display the results neatly.

The results confirm our work for *Total* = 5 and 6, but the results extend the comparative statics analysis to total allowed amounts of 7, 8, 9, and 10. Of course, Solver's numbers suffer from false precision, but we know how to interpret them.

STEP Enter the text DB/DTotal in cell E8. In the formula bar, select the first D and change the font to Symbol (in the *Home* tab). Repeat for the second D.

> **EXCEL TIP** Excel allows you to apply formatting to individual characters in a cell. This means you can use different fonts, colors, and sizes for different parts of a cell.

STEP In cell E10, enter the formula =(C10–C9)/(A10–A9) and fill it down.

That is interesting—every time you get an extra total amount allowed, you devote 0.25 of it to brandies (and 3/4 to cigars). In other words, the relationship between optimal brandies and the total amount allowed is linear. We can confirm this with a graph.

STEP Make a chart of B* as a function of *Total*.

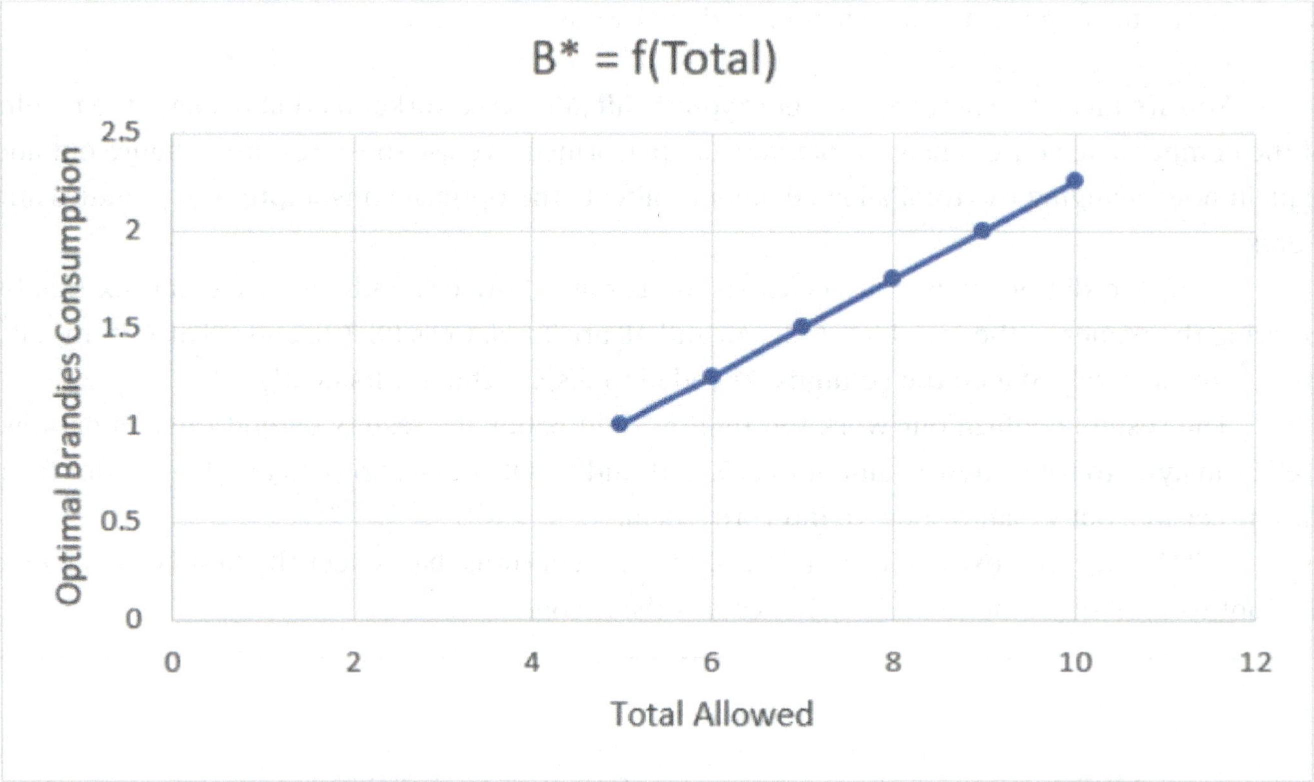

***Figure 6.10**: How brandy consumption responds to the total allowed.*

Your chart should look like Figure 6.10. Notice that we are not displaying an optimal solution. Instead, this chart is tracking how the optimal solution responds to changes in an exogenous variable. This is a common way to present the results of comparative statics analysis.

There is a similar chart of optimal cigars. The relationship is linear, but the slope is bigger, so the line is steeper. It would be good practice to compute the slope and make this chart.

Takeaways

People often think that economics is defined by its content. They think that if you study something like unemployment or money, then you are doing economics.

Actually, modern economics is defined by its methodology. Economists use optimization and comparative statics on anything involving choice. Economics can be applied to war, marriage, and many other "noneconomic" questions.

You can be sure that optimization and comparative statics will be applied if you ever see a title that begins with "An Economic Analysis of"—this means that whatever is being studied will be analyzed and seen as an optimization problem.

We use comparative statics to interpret changes in behavior (you sipped more brandy when the constraint loosened) and to predict responses (lowering the price will trigger an increase in quantity demanded).

The Comparative Statics Wizard is a numerical approach, as opposed to analytical approaches that use mathematics.

CSWiz.xla is an Excel add-in that takes advantage of Excel's Solver add-in. The user provides information about the problem and which variable is to be shocked. CSWiz does the tedious work of solving the problem at different values of the exogenous variable and keeps track of the optimal solutions.

Once you have the results, further analysis can be performed. Often, we are interested in the relationship between variables, and we draw graphs to visualize how an endogenous variable responds to an exogenous shock.

6.4 Elasticity

You probably have heard of the price elasticity of demand, but you may not know what it means or how to use the concept.

Our goal is to truly understand elasticity and be comfortable using it. At its most fundamental level, it is simply a numerical measure of responsiveness.

In the initial version of the lifeguard problem, the lifeguard entered the water after running roughly 56 meters. When maximum running speed doubled to 10 m/sec, *ceteris paribus*, the optimal solution changed to running almost 80 meters. We can (and did) show this on a graph, but is there a faster way to summarize comparative statics analysis? Yes—in a word, *elasticity*.

We have been working on a constrained optimization problem where you sipped 1 brandy and smoked 4 cigars when the doctor set a limit of 5 total brandies and cigars. When that limit was relaxed and you were allowed a total of 6 units, you chose 1.25 brandies and 4.75 cigars. Again, we can (and did) show this on a graph, but elasticity captures the relationship between the amount consumed and the total allowed in a single number.

We proceed by reviewing a few general ideas about elasticity and what it is trying to convey. Then we move to actual computations and practice interpreting elasticity values.

The more examples you see, the more the concept will stick. Be sure to keep an eye out for the repeated pattern in the elasticity. We always have an optimal solution that is responding to a shock, and the elasticity measures if the response is weak or strong.

Elasticity Basics

Elasticity is a pure number (it has no units) that measures the sensitivity or responsiveness of one variable when another changes. *Elasticity*, *responsiveness*, and *sensitivity* are synonyms. An elasticity number expresses the impact one variable has on another. The closer the elasticity is to zero, the more insensitive or inelastic the relationship is between two variables.

Elasticity is often expressed as "the something elasticity of something," like the price elasticity of demand. The first something, the price, is always the exogenous variable; the second something—in this case, demand (the amount purchased)—is the response or optimal value being tracked.

A less common, but perhaps clearer, way to express the cause and effect is to say, "The elasticity of something with respect to something." The elasticity of demand with respect to price makes it clear that demand depends on and responds to the price.

Unlike the difference between the new and initial values, elasticity is computed as the ratio of percentage changes in the values. The endogenous or response variable always goes in the numerator, and the exogenous or shock variable is always in the denominator. Thus, the x elasticity of y is .

The percentage change, $\frac{new - initial}{initial}$, is the change (or difference), new minus initial, divided by the initial value. This affects the units in the computation. The units in the numerator and denominator of the percentage change cancel, and we are left with a percent as the units. If we compute the percentage change in apples from 2 to 3 apples, we get a 50% increase. The change (or delta), however, is +1 apple.

If we divide one percentage change by another, as we do with an elasticity computation,

, the percentages cancel, and we get a unitless number. Thus, elasticity is a pure number with no units. So if the price elasticity of demand for apples is –1.2, there are no apples, dollars, percents, or any other units. It's just –1.2.

The –1.2 can be used to compute the percentage change in apples if the price of apples increases by 10%. We simply multiply –1.2 by 10% to get –12%. Or if the price of apples falls by 20%, we know that the quantity demanded of apples will rise by 24% (–1.2 × –20%).

We can also use an elasticity to compute the exogenous shock needed to produce a given percentage change in the endogenous variable. If ApplesRUs Inc. knew that the price elasticity of demand for apples was –1.2 and they wanted to increase apples sold by 6%, then they would lower prices by 5% (6% divided by –1.2).

Elasticity is a ratio of percentage changes, so there are three numbers involved: the elasticity, the percentage change in the numerator, and the percentage change in the denominator. We are given and use two of the three to find the third one:

1. Given $\%\Delta x$ and $\%\Delta y$, find the elasticity: $\frac{\%\Delta y}{\%\Delta x}$

2. Given $\%\Delta x$ and elasticity, find the $\%\Delta y$: $elasticity \times \%\Delta x$

3. Given $\%\Delta y$ and elasticity, find the $\%\Delta x$: $\frac{\%\Delta y}{elasticity}$

The lack of units in an elasticity measure means we can compare wildly different things. No matter the underlying units of the variables, we can put the dimensionless elasticity number on a common yardstick and interpret it.

Figure 6.11 shows the possible values that an elasticity can take, along with the names we give particular values.

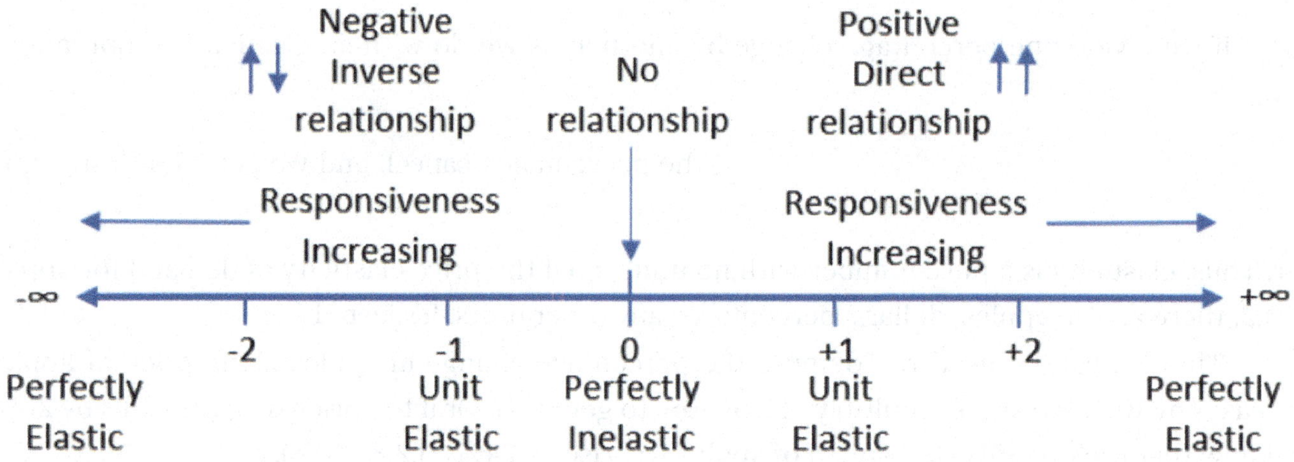

Figure 6.11: Elasticity on the number line.

Empirically, elasticities are usually low numbers around 1 (in absolute value). An elasticity of +2 is extremely responsive or elastic because the response is twice the shock. It means that a 1% increase in the exogenous variable generates a 2% increase in the endogenous variable.

The sign of the elasticity indicates direction (a qualitative statement about the relationship between the two variables). Zero means that there is no relationship—that is, the exogenous variable does not influence the response variable at all. Thus, −2 is extremely responsive like +2, but the variables are inversely related, so a 1% *increase* in the exogenous variable leads to a 2% *decrease* in the endogenous variable.

One (both positive and negative) is an important marker on the elasticity number line because it tells you if the given percentage change in an exogenous variable results in a smaller percentage change (when the elasticity is less than 1), an equal percentage change (elasticity equal to 1), or greater percentage change (elasticity greater than 1) in the endogenous variable.

The adjective *perfectly* is used to identify two extreme cases. If the elasticity is 0, it is perfectly inelastic, and this means there is no response at all to a shock. This is rare; usually optimal values of endogenous variables adjust to changes in the environment.

"Perfectly elastic" means the elasticity measure is infinity (positive or negative). This means that the tiniest little change in an exogenous variable triggers a massive response in the endogenous variable. Again, this is a rare, limiting case for elasticity.

Elasticities can be confusing. There is a lot to remember. The following are six common misconceptions and issues surrounding elasticity. Reading these typical mistakes will help you better understand this fundamental but easily misinterpreted concept.

1. Elasticity is about the *relationship* between two variables, not just the change in one variable. Thus, do not interpret a negative elasticity as meaning that the response variable must decrease. The negative means that the two variables move in opposite directions. So if the age elasticity of time playing sports is negative, that means that both time playing sports falls as age increases and time playing sports rises as age decreases.
2. Elasticity is a *local phenomenon*. The elasticity will usually change if we analyze a different initial value of the exogenous variable. Thus, any one measure of elasticity is a local or point value that applies only to the change in the exogenous variable under consideration from that starting point. You should not think of a price elasticity of demand of −0.6 as applying to an entire demand curve. Instead, it is a statement about the movement in price from one value to another value close by—say, \$3.00/unit to \$3.01/unit. The price elasticity of demand from \$4.00/unit to \$4.01/unit may be different. There are constant elasticity functions, where the elasticity is the same all along the function, but they are a special case.
3. Elasticity can be calculated for *different size changes*. To compute the x elasticity of y, we can go from one point to another, $\frac{\%\Delta y}{\%\Delta x}$, but the size of the change in x can vary. The computed elasticity will be different depending on the size of the shock if the relationship is nonlinear.
4. Elasticity always puts the *response variable in the numerator*. Do not confuse the numerator and denominator in the computation. In the x elasticity of y, x is the exogenous or shock variable and y is the endogenous or response variable. Students will often compute the reciprocal of the correct elasticity. Avoid this common mistake by always checking to make sure that the variable in the numerator responds to or is driven by the variable in the denominator.
5. Remember that elasticity is *unitless*. The x elasticity of y of 0.2 is not 20%. It is 0.2. It means that a 1% increase in x leads to a 0.2% increase in y.
6. Perhaps the single most confusing thing about elasticity is its relationship to the slope: *Do not confuse elasticity with slope*. This is easy to forget and deserves careful consideration. Remember that elasticity is a *percentage* change calculation, $\frac{\%\Delta y}{\%\Delta x}$, while a slope is merely the rise over the run, $\frac{\Delta y}{\Delta x}$.

Economists, unlike chemists or physicists, often gloss over the units of variables and results. If we carefully consider the units involved, we can ensure that the difference between the slope and elasticity is crystal clear.

The slope is a quantitative measure in the units of the two variables being compared. If $Q^* = \frac{P}{2}$, then the slope $\frac{\Delta Q^*}{\Delta P} = \frac{1}{2}$. This says that an increase in P of \$1/unit will lead to an increase in Q* of 1/2 a unit. Thus, the slope would be measured in units squared per dollar (so that when multiplied by the price, we end up with just units of Q).

Elasticity, on the other hand, is a quantitative measure based on percentage changes and is therefore unitless. The P elasticity of Q* = 1 says that a 1% increase in P leads to a 1% increase in Q*. It does not say anything about the actual numerical \$/unit increase in P, but it does speak of the percentage increase in P. Elasticity focuses on the percentage change in Q*, not the change in terms of number of units.

Thus, elasticity and slope are two different ways to measure the responsiveness of a variable as another variable changes. Elasticity uses percentage changes, $\frac{\%\Delta y}{\%\Delta x}$, while the slope does not, $\frac{\Delta y}{\Delta x}$. They are two different ways to measure the effect of a shock, and confusing them is a common mistake.

Computing Elasticity

When the total allowed for B and C went from 5 to 6, you changed B^* from 1 to 1.25 and C^* from 4 to 4.75. We can compute two elasticities with these numbers.

The total allowed elasticity of brandies is

$$\frac{\%\Delta B^*}{\%\Delta T} = \frac{\frac{\Delta B^*}{B^*}}{\frac{\Delta T}{T}} = \frac{\frac{newB - initialB}{initialB}}{\frac{newT - initialT}{initialT}} = \frac{\frac{1.25-1}{1}}{\frac{6-5}{5}} = \frac{0.25}{0.2} = 1.25$$

The total allowed elasticity of brandies is 1.25 because we had a 20% increase in T (from 5 to 6), and this led to a slightly bigger 25% increase in brandies (from 1 to 1.25). Thus, we say that the brandies response is elastic, or pretty responsive. Figure 6.11 shows that any elasticity greater than 1 in absolute value is said to be elastic.

The total allowed elasticity of cigars is

$$\frac{\%\Delta C^*}{\%\Delta T} = \frac{\frac{\Delta C^*}{C^*}}{\frac{\Delta T}{T}} = \frac{\frac{newC - initialC}{initialC}}{\frac{newT - initialT}{initialT}} = \frac{\frac{4.75-4}{4}}{\frac{6-5}{5}} = \frac{0.1875}{0.2} = 0.9375$$

The total allowed elasticity of cigars is 0.9375 because we had a 20% increase in T (from 5 to 6), and this led to a slightly smaller 18.75% increase in cigars (from 4 to 4.75). Thus, we say that the cigars response is inelastic, or unresponsive. Figure 6.11 shows that any elasticity less than 1 in absolute value is said to be inelastic.

Since we know the slope of the optimal brandies as a function of total allowed is 0.25 and the total allowed elasticity of brandies is 1.25, that is conclusive proof that elasticity and slope are different. Another way we can show the difference is with a little algebra:

$$\frac{\%\Delta B^*}{\%\Delta T} = \frac{\frac{\Delta B^*}{B^*}}{\frac{\Delta T}{T}} = \frac{\Delta B^*}{B^*}\frac{T}{\Delta T} = \frac{\Delta B^*}{\Delta T}\frac{T}{B^*}$$

The last term shows we can compute the elasticity by multiplying the slope by $\frac{T}{B^*}$. This shows that elasticity is slope times the ratio of the exogenous to the endogenous to the endogenous variable values. In this example, 0.25 times 5/1 is 1.25.

We can also show that elasticity changes as you change the point from which it is measured.

STEP In your CS1 sheet, put the label %DB/%DT in cell F8 and then change the two Ds to Symbol font. In cell F10, enter the formula =((C10−C9)/C9)/((A10−A9)/A9) and fill it down.

Cell F10 reproduces the 1.25 elasticity we computed earlier, but notice how the elasticities get smaller as T rises. Again, this shows that elasticity is not slope, since the slope stays constant while the elasticity changes.

Elasticity Practice

Work on these elasticity computations and questions to improve your understanding. Answers are provided in the appendix (according to step number).

STEP 1. Compute the max run speed elasticity of distance on sand in the lifeguard problem as max run speed is increased from 5 m/sec to 10 m/sec. Interpret your result.

STEP 2. Compute the IR (infection rate) elasticity of group size as IR falls from 5% to 2%. Recall that optimal group size rose from 5 to 8. Interpret your result.

STEP 3. Compute the slope of $C^* = f(T)$ and use it to compute the total allowed elasticity of cigars at $T = 5$. Does your number agree with the 0.9375 value we found earlier?

STEP 4. Compute the slope of $C^* = f(T)$ and the total allowed elasticity of cigars from $T = 9$ to 10. Does the slope or elasticity change compared to the elasticity from $T = 5$ to 6? What does this show?

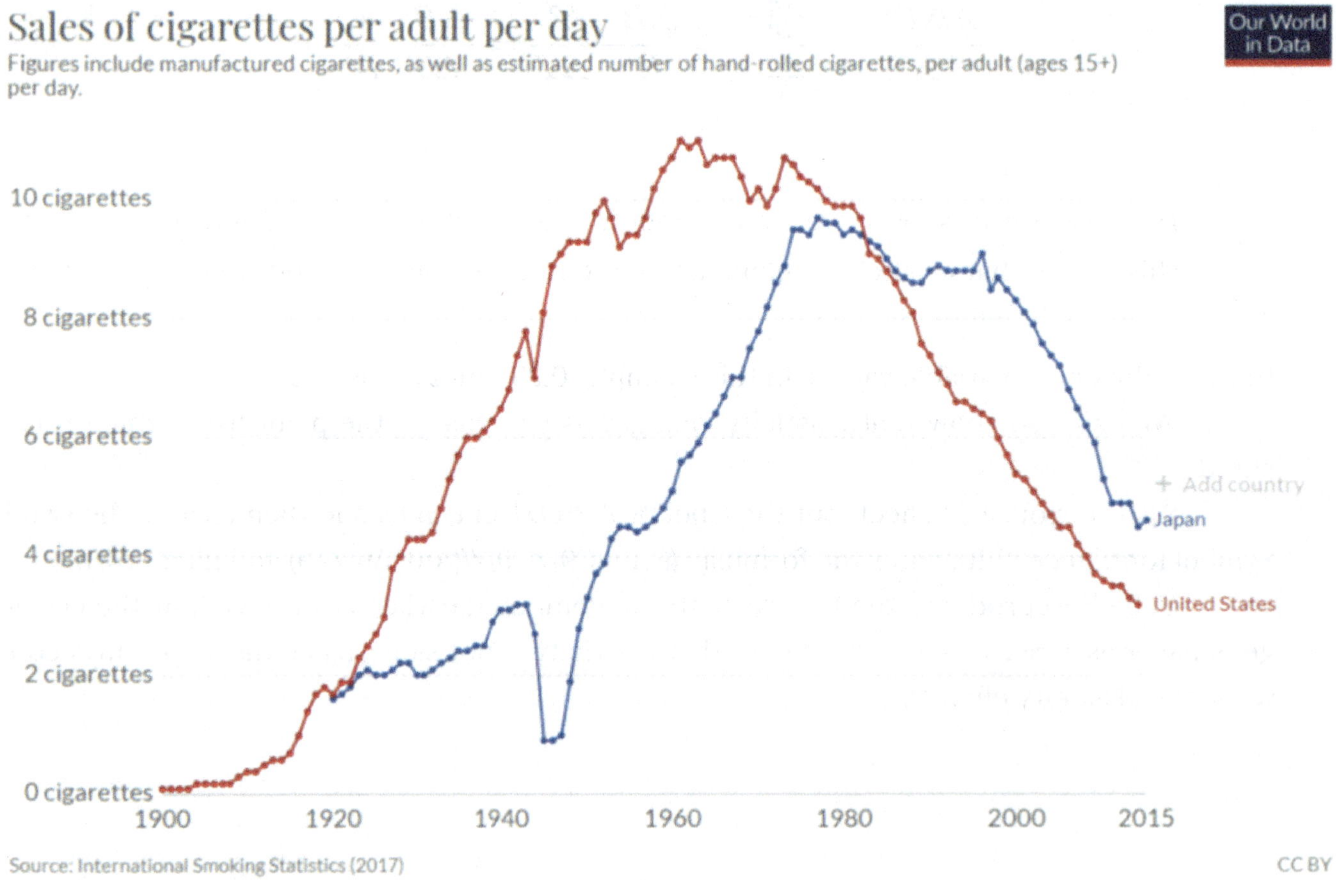

Figure 6.12: Smoking rates in Japan and the United States. Source: Our World in Data / CC BY 4.0.

Cigarettes have been extensively studied. The average number of cigarettes sold per day in the United States and Japan since 1900 is shown in Figure 6.12.

Visit ourworldindata.org/smoking to see an interactive version of this chart and to add other countries. The pattern is the same around the world—rising smoking rates reach a peak, then they decline. Today, a little over 10% of American adults smoke, down from 40% at the peak.

Governments want to reduce cigarette consumption to improve public health. Banning advertising is common, as is taxing cigarettes. The idea is that increasing the total price consumers must pay (the price plus the tax) will reduce consumption. Whether this works depends on the price elasticity of demand (the quantity purchased).

STEP 5. To reduce cigarette consumption in response to a tax, what are governments hoping is true about the price elasticity of demand for cigarettes?

STEP 6. What do you think is a good guess for the price elasticity of demand for cigarettes? Explain your answer.

STEP 7. How do you think the price elasticity of demand for cigarettes compares between adult and teenage smokers? Explain your answer.

Takeaways

Comparative statics is how economists view the world, and elasticity is how they communicate comparative statics results.

You want to be able to interpret and compute it:

Interpret: The closer an elasticity is to zero, the less responsive the endogenous variable is to a particular shock.

Compute: The exogenous variable elasticity of the endogenous variable is always the percentage change in the endogenous variable divided by the percentage change in the exogenous variable.

There are other ways to compute elasticities. The ratio of percentage changes is the simplest, most basic approach.

References

The economics literature on cigarette smoking is vast: Sloan, F. A., Smith, V. K., and Taylor, D. H. (2002). "Information, Addiction, and Bad 'Choices': Lessons from a Century of Cigarettes." *Economics Letters* 77, pp. 147–155, is an accessible, informative starting point.

For a broader, historical review, see Brandt, A. M. (2007). *The Cigarette Century: The Rise, Fall, and Deadly Persistence of the Product That Defined America* (Basic Books).

Appendix

1. The max run speed elasticity of distance on sand is 0.43 and this is quite inelastic, or unresponsive. Max run speed was doubled (so a 100% increase), and distance on sand did increase, but only by 43%.
2. The IR elasticity of group size is –1, and this is unit elastic. IR fell by 60% (from 5 to 2), and group size rose by 60% (from 5 to 8). The minus sign means the two variables are inversely related.
3. The slope of $C^* = f(T)$ is 3/4, so multiplying this by 5/4 is 15/16, which does agree with the 0.9375 value in the text.
4. The slope of $C^* = f(T)$ stays constant at 0.75, but the elasticity increases from 0.9375 to roughly 0.9643. This shows that elasticity is a local phenomenon that changes depending on the value of the exogenous variable at which it is computed.
5. Governments hope that the cigarette demand is elastic, meaning that the price elasticity of demand is high. This way, small increases in taxes will produce big decreases in cigarette consumption.
6. Many studies have produced a variety of results, but the price elasticity of demand for cigarettes is expected to be inelastic, so less than 1 in absolute value. A good guess would be –0.6.
7. Teenage smokers are more price sensitive, since they are not as addicted yet and typically have lower incomes than adults. If adults are at –0.6, teenagers might be at –1.4.

6.5 Cost Minimization

You are on the factory floor of a manufacturing business. The CEO calls and says, "We need to make 300 units today."

Your production function is simple: $Q = \sqrt{L} + \sqrt{K}$, where L is the amount of labor hours and K is the number of machines. You get to choose how much L and K to use, but you must produce 300 units.

You could, for example, use 90,000 hours of labor and no machines or 40,000 machines and 10,000 hours of labor. There are many other combinations of L and K that would meet the required quantity of output (Q).

You have to pay for the inputs. The wage rate (*w*) is $20 per hour, and the rental rate of machines (*r*) is $40 per machine.

Your goal is to find the L and K that minimize TC (total costs of production). Formally, your constrained optimization problem looks like this:

$$\min_{L,K} TC = 20L + 40K$$

$$\text{s.t.} \sqrt{L} + \sqrt{K} = 300$$

Implementing the Problem in Excel

You know that optimization problems always have three parts:

1. Goal (objective function) → min TC.
2. Endogenous variables → L, K.
3. Exogenous variables → w, r, q, and the function $\sqrt{L} = \sqrt{K} = q$.

We will organize our spreadsheet with these parts, but first we want to visualize the problem.

STEP In cell A1, enter the label L, and in cell B1, enter the label K. In cells A2 to A20, enter numbers 0 to 90000 by 5000. In cell B2, enter the formula =(300-SQRT(A2))^2 and fill it down. Finally, make a *Scatter* chart of the data in cells A1:B20.

Your chart is displaying an *isoquant*. Since the prefix *iso* means equal (like an isosceles triangle), an isoquant shows all the combinations of L and K that make the same amount of output.

There are many isoquants, one for each level of output. Your chart shows the isoquant for 300 units of output. It is the constraint for this optimization problem. The solution is on the isoquant, but we do not know which combination of L and K is the least expensive.

STEP Add a point on the chart and a scroll bar on the sheet to visualize that you can choose any combination on the isoquant. See the appendix if you need help.

So how do we find the cheapest combination of L and K that produces 300 units of output? With Solver, of course, but first we have to implement the problem in the spreadsheet.

STEP Label cells N1 and N2 as L and K, respectively. Cells N4, N5, and N6 have labels w, r, and q, respectively. Cell N8 is TC and N10 is the constraint. In cells M4, M5, and M6, enter the exogenous variable values. In cells M8 and M10, enter formulas. See the appendix if you need help.

Now you are ready to run Solver.

STEP Properly configure Solver and run it to find the optimal solution. See the appendix if you need help.

Solver should find a solution close to the exact answer of L* = 40,000 and K* = 10, 000 with a TC* = $1,200,000. This solution makes sense, since L and K are equally productive, but capital is twice as expensive as labor.

We can see that this solution is correct by computing the total cost of the points on the isoquant in columns A and B.

STEP In cell C1, enter the label *TC*. In cell C2, enter the formula =20*A2+40*B2 and fill it down.

It is easy to see that the cheapest way to make 300 units of output is the 40,000 and 10,000 combination.

Visualizing the Optimal Solution

Recall that the cigars-and-brandies utility maximization problem was visualized with a tangency condition between the utility contours and the constraint. Does the same apply here? Yes, it does.

We first create 3D surface and 2D contour plots of the total cost function, then we can draw a graph of the optimal solution.

STEP Copy cells A2:A20, insert a new sheet in your workbook, select cell A2, and paste. Select cell B1 and paste transpose (click the *Paste* down arrow and select the *Transpose* icon as shown in Figure 6.13). Enter a formula that computes the total cost for the given labor in column A and capital in column B. See the appendix if you need help. Make *3D Surface* and 2D contour plots.

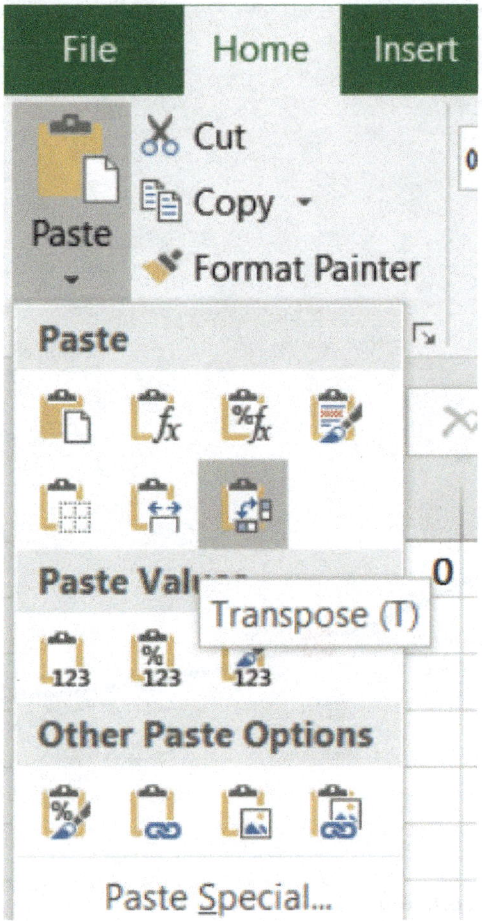

Figure 6.13: Paste transpose.
Source: Screenshot of Excel interface, © Microsoft Corporation.

The surface is like a sheet of paper, and the contours are straight lines. Each contour is called an *isocost* because it represents combinations of L and K with the same cost.

STEP Use Excel's *Shapes* group of drawing objects to add straight lines to your isoquant chart. Your lines must have a slope of 0.5 because w/r is 20/40. The lowest feasible isocost is a line with K-intercept of 30,000 and L-intercept of 60,000. All your isocost lines must be parallel.

Figure 6.14 shows a visualization of the optimal solution. The curve is the constraint and the lines are isocosts. You want to be on the lowest isocost on the constraint.

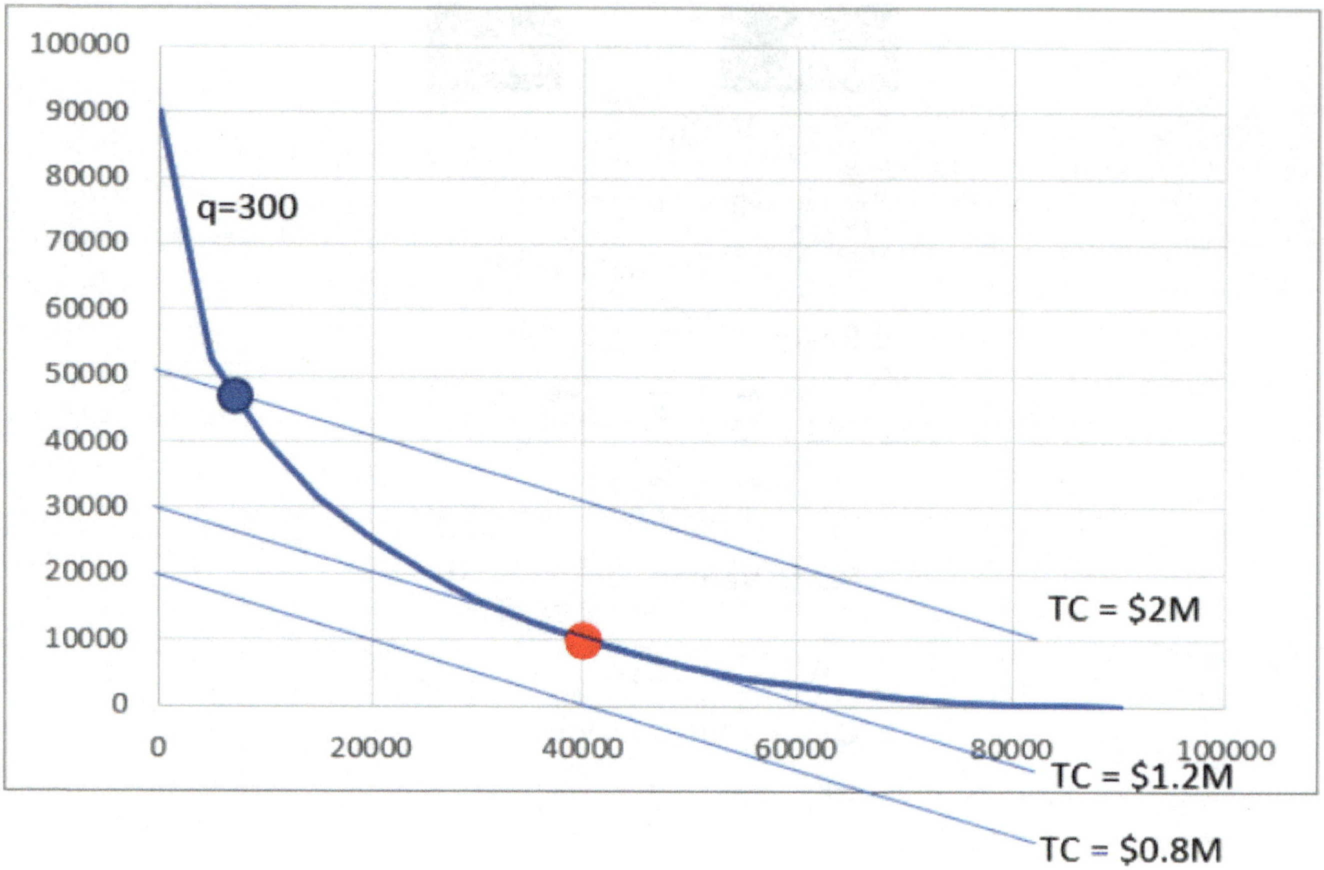

Figure 6.14: Visualizing the optimal solution.

There are many more isocost lines than the three shown. The point on the isoquant and the highest isocost is feasible in that you could make 300 units with this combination of L and K, but you would not be minimizing costs. The lowest isocost has lower costs than the optimal solution (40,000 hours of labor and 10,000 machines), but since it is below the isoquant, it violates the constraint, and no combination of inputs on that isocost is an eligible solution.

STEP Return to your chart and make sure you have an isocost line that is tangent to the isoquant at the optimal solution. Add a red dot (use Excel's *Shapes* objects again) at point L = 40,000 and K = 10,000 (as shown in Figure 6.14). Finally, improve Figure 6.14. What is it missing? See the appendix if needed.

Comparative Statics

We finish this problem by considering what would happen if the CEO called and changed the needed output level. We will compute the output elasticity of total cost.

STEP Use the Comparative Statics Wizard to explore how the optimal solution changes as you vary q from 300 to 400 by 10. Make a chart of the minimum total cost as a function of quantity.

You have made a graph of the cost function. This tells us how costs of production vary as output changes.

STEP Use your CSWiz results to compute the slope of the cost function and the output elasticity of total cost as q rises by 10.

The slope of the cost function is rising slowly as quantity increases, which agrees with the shape of your cost function (it is increasing at an increasing rate). The output elasticity of total cost is decreasing as quantity goes up, but very slightly. Of more importance is its value of a little over 2—this means that total cost is quite responsive to output in this example.

Takeaways

Input cost minimization is a constrained optimization problem where we are asked to find the cheapest way to produce a given output.

Solver can do this problem, and the Comparative Statics Wizard can be used to explore how the optimal solution changes as quantity changes.

The optimal solution is visualized as a tangency between the isoquant and isocost lines.

Notice how many other concepts and skills were repeated as you worked through this problem. Once you get the pattern, it is easier to understand other applications.

Appendix

To add controls to a spreadsheet, the *Developer* tab needs to be visible on the *Ribbon*. If it is not, click *File*, click *Options*, then click *Customize Ribbon*, and check the *Developer* item.

STEP Copy cell range A2:B2 and paste it below your chart. To add this one point to your chart, copying, pasting, and editing the SERIES formula is an easy way to do this. You need to replace the x– and y-axis arguments in the pasted SERIES formula with the cell that has the x-axis value and the cell that has the y-axis value.

Next, we add the *Scroll Bar* control, but it has a maximum value of 30,000. As a simple work-around, we can connect the scroll bar to a different cell—say, the cell below the 0 value (that you should have as the x-coordinate value)—and then the control can be connected to that cell.

Suppose your x-y coordinate pair is in cells F22 and G22. Change the 0 value in cell F22 to 10 times the cell below it by entering the formula =10*F22 in cell F23. Right-click the *Scroll Bar* control and make the cell link be F23 by entering F23 in the *Cell link* input box. Finally, the scroll bar maximum should be set to 9000.

Now when you set cell F23, for example, to 5,000, cell F22 is 50,000. Thus, the *Scroll Bar* control can range from 0 to 9,000 in cell F23, and this produces values from 0 to 90,000 in cell F22.

STEP Click the *Developer* tab on the *Ribbon*, click the down arrow in the Insert button, and select the scroll bar icon (in the top, form control group). Click and drag on the spreadsheet (roughly under the chart) to create the *Scroll Bar* control and link it to the appropriate cell on your spreadsheet.

Be careful to avoid selecting the *Spinner* control instead of the *Scrollbar*. When you click the down arrow on the Insert button, if you float the cursor over each control, Excel displays its name. This helps you choose the right control.

To use Solver to find the cost-minimizing combination of L and K, cells M4, M5, and M6 are 20, 40, and 300, respectively. Cell M8 has formula =M4*M1+M5*M2 and should be formatted as $. The constraint is in cell M10 with the formula =SQRT(M1)+SQRT(M2)-M6.

For Solver, the objective function is M8, the *Min* radio button should be checked, and the changing cells are M1 and M2. The constraint should be that M10 = 0.

The formula in cell B2 needed to make a 3D chart is =20*$A2+40*B$1. Format as $ with no decimals and fill down and right.

Figure 6.14 can be improved by adding an appropriate title and labeling the axes.

7. Yield Curve

> "Yo word is yo bond," which in today's Hip Hop Culture has become word is born.
>
> Geneva Smitherman

7.1 Bond Basics

It is January 1, 2030. You give XYZ Inc. $1,000 today, and they promise to pay you back in two years. Congratulations, you just bought a *bond*!

The $1,000 is called the *face* or *par value*, and the *maturity date* is two years from now, January 1, 2032 (when you get the face value back). Not surprisingly, you own a two-year bond.

Of course, you must be compensated for the time value of money—$1,000 two years from now is worth less than $1,000 right now. So XYZ also promises to pay you interest at regular intervals—say, every six months. The *coupon rate*, say 5%, tells you the interest you will be paid in a year. Five percent of $1,000 is $50, so you will get two payments of $25.

Because the coupon (interest) and final payments are on a strict schedule, bonds are called *fixed-income securities*. Bonds are *debt*, and they give investors a safer but lower return, on average, than stocks which are *equity* (since they involve ownership of a corporation).

The jargon—special words or technical language used by professionals—can make financial products and choices difficult to understand. We can make your bond come to life with Excel. As you enter the information, think about the trade-off involved here—the lender (you) gives up money now in return for future payments from the borrower (XYZ). This is the core idea.

STEP Open a blank Excel workbook and save it as *YieldCurve.xlsx*. In cells A1 to A5, enter the dates 1/1/2030, 7/1/2030, 1/1/2031, 7/1/2031, and 1/1/2032, respectively. In cell B1, enter -$1000; this is the amount you invested in the bond (hence the minus sign). Cells B2, B3, and B4 represent the coupon payments, so enter 25 for each of those cells. At the end, you get the last interest payment plus the face value back, so cell B5 is 1,025.

Your spreadsheet now looks quite familiar, given the work we did on present value and the internal rate of return (IRR). That's right; a bond is just another application of those ideas. You start with a negative number that represents your investment, then get a stream of income over time that is your return on investment.

The IRR is a measure of the quality of an investment; the bigger it is, the better the investment. We can compute the IRR for these cash flows at these dates using Excel's XIRR function. It incorporates the dates at which the flows are paid and received and returns the annualized internal rate of return.

STEP Enter the formula =XIRR(B1:B5,A1:A5) in cell C1 and format it as a % with two decimal places. In cell D1, enter the label IRR = YTM so that your spreadsheet replicates Figure 7.1.

	A	B	C	D
1	1/1/2030	($1,000)	5.06%	IRR = YTM
2	7/1/2030	$25		
3	1/1/2031	$25		
4	7/1/2031	$25		
5	1/1/2032	$1,025		

Figure 7.1: Understanding a bond.

The IRR is a little over 5% because you received the annual interest payment of $50 a little ahead of time: $25 halfway through the year and another $25 at the end of the year instead of all $50 at the end of the year.

STEP Confirm this by changing cells B2 and B4 to 0, cell B3 to $50, and cell B5 to $1,050.

Cell C1 now shows the IRR as 5.00%. This shows that the XIRR function is working as advertised. It also shows that the timing of the coupon payments is critical. Your spreadsheet is now displaying a different bond than the one in Figure 7.1. The IRR of the bond in Figure 7.1 is higher than the one on your spreadsheet because of the timing of the interest payments.

The IRR for a bond is called the *yield to maturity* (YTM). It is calculated as if the investor will hold the bond until the maturity date. But they might not. Bonds can be traded before they mature in the *secondary market*.

A *zero-coupon bond*, also called a *strip*, is just what it says—it has no interest payments.

STEP Change the value in cell B3 to 0 (so the values in cells B2, B3, and B4 are all 0), and make cell B5 $1,000.

The YTM is now zero. That's terrible. No investor would buy this bond. To entice buyers, the issuer must sell the bond at a discount (or below par).

STEP Change cell B1 to -$900.

That's better. Now the YTM is about 5.4%. Investors are compensated for lending $900 today by getting the face value of the bond, $1000, in two years. Someone might be willing to buy this bond and lend the issuer $900.

Bonds are complex financial assets. They have many variations, and the jargon is intimidating, but no matter how complicated it gets, the idea is that a bond is a promise—money in the future is promised in return for money now.

Yield Data

With a basic understanding of a bond and how it works, we can get yield data and create visualizations, including that of our ultimate goal: the yield curve over time.

We will work with US Treasury securities with different maturity dates. They all work like bonds, but they have different names depending on their maturity dates: Treasury *bills* mature in 1 year or less, Treasury *notes* in two to 10 years, and Treasury *bonds* in 20 or 30 years.

First, we will examine a single security over time, but our eventual goal is to visualize a richer dataset with yields for different maturities over time. This will give us the yield curve.

STEP Insert a sheet in your workbook, rename it GS1, and enter the Series ID GS1 (for government security maturing in 1 year) in cell A1. Use the FRED Excel add-in to get the data. Use FRED's charting tools to make a chart with recession shading, like Figure 7.2 (made in October 2023). Refer back to the work we did using FRED to get unemployment data (in chapter 5) if needed.

Figure 7.2 shows the yield on a one-year US Treasury bill on a monthly frequency from April 1953 to September 2023. Your spreadsheet will have this series up to the previous month in which you created it.

Figure 7.2: One-year US Treasury bill yield over time.
Source: Board of Governors of the Federal Reserve System (US) via FRED, Public Domain Data / FRED Terms.

Unlike the unemployment rate, which rose in every recession, one-year US Treasury bill yields are mostly falling when they enter the shaded bars. This is because the government is actively trying to use monetary policy to lower interest rates to stimulate the economy.

The US Federal Reserve (Fed) acts as a central bank and influences many different interest rates, including bond yields, by controlling the *federal funds rate* (the interest rate at which banks lend reserves to each other).

The key point for our yield data is that one-year US Treasury bill yields are not directly controlled by the Fed. They are the outcome of supply and demand. Bonds, including US Treasury securities, can be traded before their maturity dates. It is the bond market that determines yields.

It is easy to see in Figure 7.2 that in the early 1980s, yields were very high, in double-digit territory. Why? Certainly, a contributing factor was high inflation at that time. The yield had to be high to entice the lender to part with money now to be paid back later.

STEP Return to your bond demonstration sheet. You should see the zero-coupon bond. You part with $900 now and get $1,000 in two years, which has a YTM of about 5.4%.

In the early 1980s, there would be no way you would give anyone (XYZ or the US government) $900 in return for $1,000 in two years. The $1,000 you got back two years later would be so watered down by the high inflation at that time that you would refuse that deal. So the issuer would need to raise the yield by lowering (discounting) the bond by more than $100.

STEP Change cell B1 to –$800. What happens?

Not surprisingly, the YTM increases to almost 12%. Is that enough to get you to make the trade? Not in August 1981.

STEP Return to the GS1 sheet. Enter the formula =MAX(B:B) in cell C8 to see the highest yield in the dataset. Scroll down to find when it occurred.

In August 1981, the market, or equilibrium, yield was 16.7%. You would not lend unless you got that yield, just like you would not buy apples from a particular seller if their price was higher than the market price that many other sellers were selling apples for.

STEP Return to the sheet with the simple two-year bond we were playing with and use Solver to find the discount in the bond price needed to produce a yield of 16.7%. Be sure to uncheck (if needed) Solver's *Make unconstrained variables nonnegative* option, since we want a negative number in cell B1.

You should find that the bond price is roughly $734, so it is a discount of $266 from the par value.

The inverse relationship between the yield and the bond price is a fundamental concept in the bond world. The Excel implementation of a bond makes it easy to see: The lower the price (the bigger the discount) in cell B1, the higher the yield.

Yields for Different Maturities

Just like GS1, the yield on a 1-year US Treasury bill, FRED has data for yields on US Treasury securities with different maturities, also known as the *term structure*. We will get data on US Treasuries from 3-month to 30-year terms.

STEP Insert a sheet in your workbook and name it *TermStructure*. In individual cells in the top row, enter the following *Series IDs*: GS3M, GS6M, GS1, GS2, GS3. GS5, GS7, GS10, GS20, and GS30. The M stands for months, and the numbers indicate the length of time. So GS6M is a 6-month US Treasury bill, and GS20 is a 20-year Treasury bond. Click the Get FRED Data button.

The series start at different dates. We need to find the latest date and start them all from that point so that we can see how the yields varied by maturity on the same date.

STEP The latest starting date in row 8 is 9/1/1981. Copy this cell and paste it in cells E4, G4, and so on until S4. Update the data.

Each row has yields for differing maturities of US Treasury securities for a particular point in time. Thus, each row has the data for the yield curve for that month.

Here is how the Fed describes the yield curve:

> Investors can trade Treasury securities freely between issuance and maturity. As the market price of Treasury securities varies over time, so does their implied yield—their return relative to their price. At any given time, there is a wide range of Treasury securities with different maturities outstanding. Market forces tend to ensure that the yields on securities with similar maturities are not dramatically different from each other. This feature makes it possible to summarize the information contained in the cross section of market-implied yields by a smooth curve of yield as a function of maturity—the yield curve.[1]

Thus, the yield curve shows yield by maturity. Let's make one.

STEP Copy the *TermStructure* sheet and rename it *YieldCurve*. Change each of the *value* labels in row 7 to the corresponding length of time in years. Cell B7 is 0.25 (you may have to increase the decimal places displayed), cell D7 is 0.5, cell F7 is 1, and so on. Delete rows 1 to 6. Delete the date columns, starting with column C (so C, E, G, and so forth, all the way to S). Finally, select the yield data (from B2 to the last row in column K) and display two decimal places.

You now have a dataset that looks like Figure 7.3. It has dates in column A, lengths of maturity in years in row 1, and yields for each month by maturity. These are the inputs needed to make a yield curve.

	A	B	C	D	E	F	G	H	I	J	K
1	date	0.25	0.5	1	2	3	5	7	10	20	30
2	09/01/1981	15.61	16.36	16.52	16.46	16.22	15.93	15.65	15.32	15.07	14.67
3	10/01/1981	14.23	15.06	15.38	15.54	15.50	15.41	15.33	15.15	15.13	14.68
4	11/01/1981	11.35	12.12	12.41	12.88	13.11	13.38	13.42	13.39	13.56	13.35
5	12/01/1981	11.32	12.44	12.85	13.29	13.66	13.60	13.62	13.72	13.73	13.45

Figure 7.3: Data to make a yield curve.

STEP Select cells A1:K2 and insert a *Scatter with Straight Lines and Markers* chart. Add a title, *Yield Curve*, and label the axes *Yield (%)* and *Maturity (years)*.

You just made your first yield curve. It is not common. Usually, it is upward sloping. The longer the maturity, the higher the yield, because lenders have to be rewarded for locking up their money for longer periods of time.

The 1980s were certainly exceptional economic times. The yield curve was *inverted* because yields for shorter maturities were higher than those for longer maturities. This usually means bad tidings for the economy.

There is another step we could take to make our yield curve a true curve: We could fit a smooth curve to the data. The smoothed curve version of yield as a function of maturity is what

1. Source: https://www.federalreserve.gov/data/nominal-yield-curve.htm

most people call a yield curve. There are many ways to fit such a curve, and it gets complicated, so we will stay with our rudimentary version that connects the data with straight lines.

We can easily make another yield curve so we can understand what the yield curve is telling us. We work smart by using the edit SERIES formula approach.

STEP Copy and paste the chart. Click on the data and edit the SERIES formula by changing the 2 to 222 in the y-axis part of the formula, *YieldCurve!$B$222:$K$222.*

You just produced a yield curve for January 2000. Unlike September 1981, it rises fast, then stretches out. Figure 7.4 compares the two yield curves.

While the slightly lower yield for 30 versus 20 years is unexpected, the January 2000 yield curve (on the right) is a typical yield curve. As the yield to maturity rises from very short term (starting at 30 days) to 2 years, yields rise quickly, but then they rise much more slowly as maturity increases.

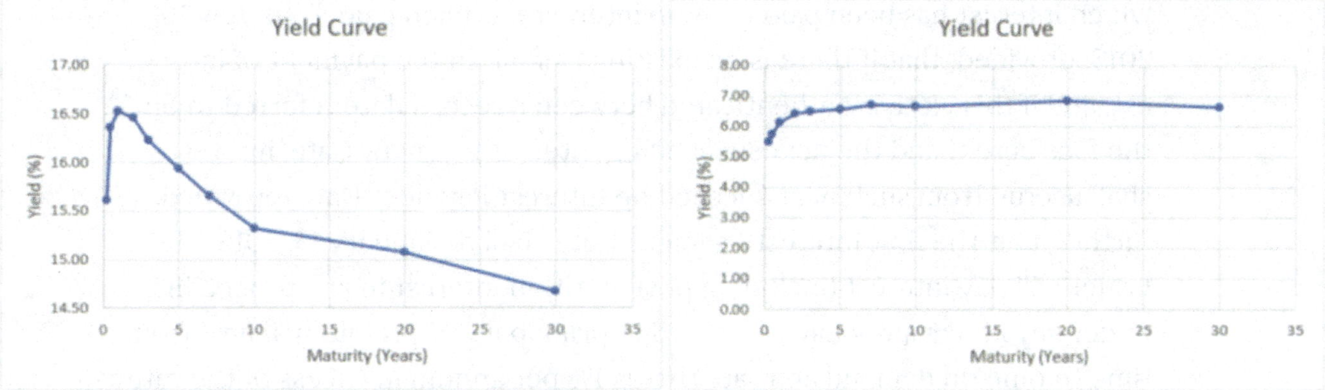

Figure 7.4: September 1981 (left) and January 2000 (right) yield curves.

We learned about bonds and yields, got yield data, and created yield curve charts. Next up, we work on fancier visualizations of yield curve data.

Takeaways

In everyday English, a bond is a connection between people (a bond of friendship) or objects (to bond is to glue things together). In finance, the connection is between lender and borrower.

A bond is a security in which a borrower (e.g., a firm or government) promises to pay back the face value at the maturity date and make interest payments at specific dates (to compensate the lender for the time value of money).

Unlike the two-year bond we implemented in Excel, most bonds are on a 30/360 calendar and have a high threshold of legalese, like this example:

> (1) Interest. Ventas Realty, Limited Partnership (the "Issuer") promises to pay interest on the principal amount of this Note at 4.125% per annum from July 16, 2015 until maturity. The Issuer will pay interest semi-annually in arrears on January 15 and July 15 of each year, or if any such day is not a Business Day, on the next succeeding Business Day (each, an "Interest Payment Date"). Interest on the Notes will accrue from the most recent date to which interest has been paid or, if no interest has been paid, from July 16, 2015; provided, that if there is no existing Default in the payment of interest, and if this Note is authenticated between a record date referred to on the face hereof and the next succeeding Interest Payment Date, interest shall accrue from such next succeeding Interest Payment Date; provided, further, that the first Interest Payment Date shall be January 15, 2016. The Issuer will pay interest (including post-petition interest in any proceeding under any Bankruptcy Law) on overdue principal and premium, if any, from time to time on demand at a rate that is 1% per annum in excess of the rate then in effect; the Issuer will pay interest (including post-petition interest in any proceeding under any Bankruptcy Law) on overdue installments of interest (without regard to any applicable grace periods) from time to time on demand at the same rate to the extent lawful. Interest will be computed on the basis of a 360-day year of twelve 30-day months.[2]

A bond is a way for borrowers to raise money. Firms often use bonds to fund operations, while government bonds pay for deficit spending (when outlays are greater than tax revenues).

The funds raised by issuing bonds are debt because the issuer has to pay the lenders back, just like they would pay back a bank loan.

The jargon in the bond world is intense. Knowing things like the difference

2. Source: EDGAR filing at the Securities and Exchange Commission website, www.sec.gov/Archives/edgar/data/740260/000110465915051467/a15-1495311ex4d2.htm

between the coupon rate and the yield to maturity is critical for those who live in the bond world.

It is important to understand that the contract is ironclad, so the coupon rate and promised cash flows do not change as interest rates change. You might buy a bond in the secondary market above or below par value, so the *spot rate* (the IRR at the time you buy the bond) does change.

Higher interest rates produce lower bond prices. This fundamental law of bonds is easiest to see in a strip because there are no interest payments. The bond price will always be lower than the face value, but as the bond price (the amount you pay to buy the bond) gets farther from the face value (the amount you get at maturity), the higher the yield: "The U.S. Treasury yield curve is of tremendous importance both in concept and in practice. From a conceptual perspective, the yield curve determines the value that investors place today on nominal payments at all future dates—a fundamental determinant of almost all asset prices and economic decisions" (Gürkaynak et al., 2006, p. 1).

References

The epigraph is from p. 8 of Geneva Smitherman's *Black Talk: Words and Phrases from the Hood to the Amen Corner*, Houghton Mifflin (1994). Here is the full entry for word is born!:

"An affirmative response to statement or action. Also, *Word!*, *Word up!*, *Word to the mother!* A resurfacing of an old, familiar saying in the Black Oral Tradition, "Yo word is yo bond," which was popularized by the five percent nation in its early years. *Word is born!* reaffirms strong belief in the power of the word, and thus the value of verbal commitment. One's word is the guarantee, the warranty, the *bond*, that whatever was promised will actually occur. *Born* is the result of the AAE [African American English] pronunciation of "bond"; see Introduction."

Board of Governors of the Federal Reserve System (US), *Market Yield on U.S. Treasury Securities at 1-Year Constant Maturity, Quoted on an Investment Basis* [GS1], retrieved from FRED, Federal Reserve Bank of St. Louis; https://fred.stlouisfed.org/series/GS1.

The yield data in FRED are produced by the Fed, and it is a complicated process. A good source for digging into the details is Refet S. Gürkaynak, Brian Sack, and Jonathan H. Wright (2006) "The U.S. Treasury Yield Curve: 1961 to the Present," Finance and Economics Discussion Series, Divisions of Research & Statistics and Monetary Affairs, Federal Reserve Board, Washington, DC.

7.2 Yield Curve Visualizations

We begin our visualizations of the yield curve with a clever way to easily control which month-year yield curve to display. Our strategy will be to use a *Combo Box* form control to enable the user to select a date. The selected month-year will be connected to a cell in the sheet, which we will use to get the yields via the OFFSET function. Finally, we will tie the chart to the selected yields by directly editing the SERIES formula. This will all make more sense as we actually do it.

STEP With yield curve data in columns B through K, dates in column A, and labels in row 1, click the *Developer* tab, then the *Insert* group, and select the *Combo Box* form control as shown in Figure 7.5. Click on the spreadsheet under your yield curve chart, and drag to place the control on the sheet. Right-click the control and choose *Format Control*. For the *Input range*, select from cell A2 to the last row with data in column A. For the cell link, select cell M1.

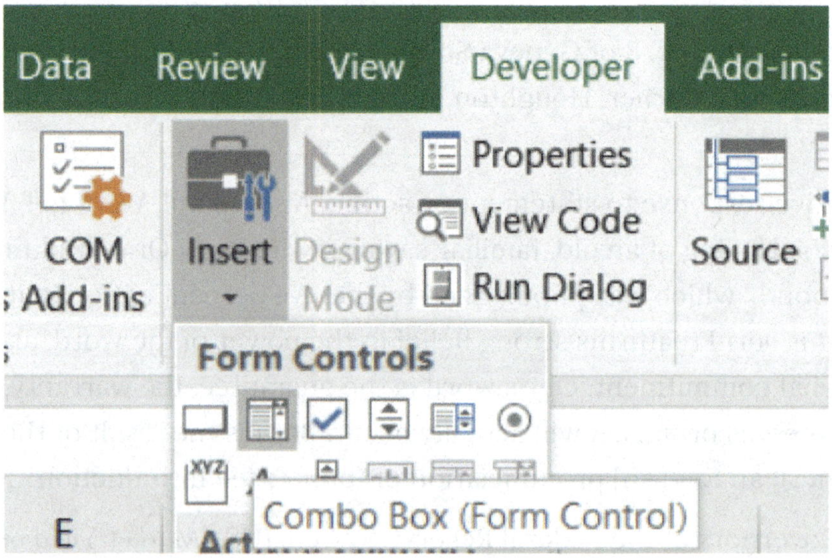

***Figure 7.5:* Selecting the Combo Box control.**
Source: Screenshot of Excel interface, © Microsoft Corporation.

It does not look like we have done anything, but we have. Our Combo Box is loaded with the dates in column A.

STEP Click on any cell in the sheet so that the Combo Box is not selected and then click the *Combo Box* control. Select any date.

Cell M1 now shows the row number of the date you selected. Next, we get the yield data for the chosen date.

STEP Enter the formula =OFFSET(A1,$M$1,0) in cell N1.

Excel displays the date for that row. The OFFSET function works by taking you to cell A1 and then going down however many rows are in cell M1 while staying in column A (that is what the zero says to do).

STEP Change cell M1 to 10. What happens?

Not only does the date in cell N1 change to the date in cell A10, but notice that the *Combo Box* control has also changed. Cell M1 is connected to the Combo Box, so you can use the Combo Box to set cell M1's value or do the reverse and set the Combo Box's value by entering a number in cell M1.

STEP Select cell N1 and fill it right to cell X1.

Now you are displaying the yields for each maturity for that month-year. This means all we have to do is edit the chart's SERIES formula to display the yields in cells O1:X1.

STEP Click a point on the yield curve to see the SERIES formula in the formula bar. Remove the legend text and edit the y-axis so that the SERIES formula is =SERIES(,*YieldCurve*!$B$1:$K$1, *YieldCurve*!$O$1:$X$1,1).

We are ready to test our dynamic visualization of the yield curve.

STEP Click the *Combo Box* control and pick a date.

The chart immediately updates and shows you the yield curve for that date! The *Combo Box* control is an effective way to get user input.

STEP Use the *Combo Box* control to display yield curves from several dates. Try one from each decade. Definitely visualize the last row so you can see the current state of the yield curve.

If you play around a bit, you will see that the yield curve is usually upward sloping, but there are a variety of shapes. Inversion is when yields for longer maturities are lower than those for shorter maturities. This does happen, but it is not the usual shape of the yield curve. Before we discuss the interpretation of inversion, we will do some 3D visualizations.

3D Viz in Excel

What if we visualized all the month-year yield curves at once, in one chart? The yield would be the vertical axis in a 3D plot, with time and the maturities as the two horizontal axes.

STEP Delete the *date* text from cell A1 (the top-left corner of the data must be an empty cell). Select from cell A1 to the last row in column K. Click *Insert* and *Recommended Charts* and then select *3D Surface*.

Excel puts a chart on your spreadsheet, but it certainly needs some cleaning up. What follows are the steps to produce Figure 7.6.

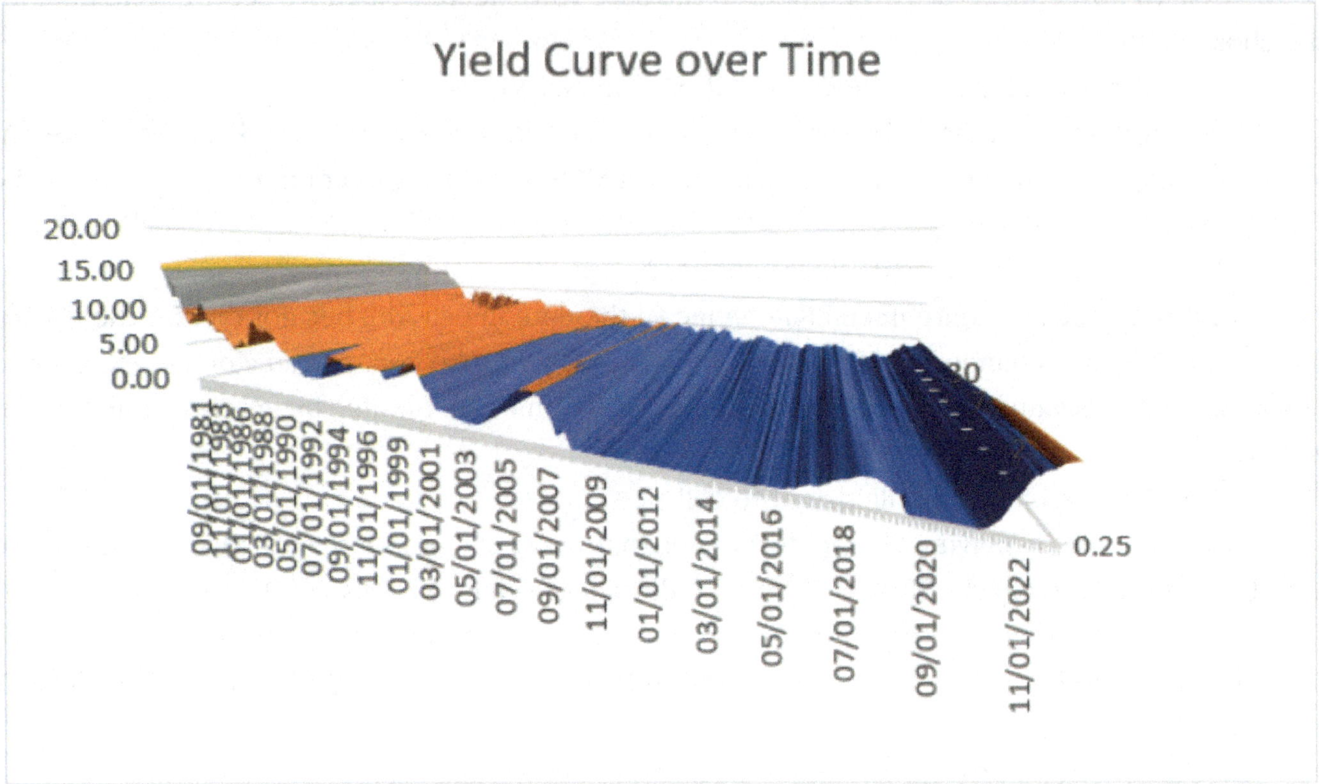

Figure 7.6: 3D surface Excel chart of the yield curve.

STEP Make the title *Yield Curve over Time* and delete the legend.

The problem with the chart on your screen is that the time axis (near the front) is long and the maturity axis is too narrow. This is because there are many more rows than columns. We need to widen the maturity axis.

STEP Right-click the surface and select *3-D Rotation. . . .* Repeatedly click the up arrow in the *Depth (% of base)* setting until you start to see the maturity axis start to widen. You can go up to 2,000, so directly enter this value.

Your chart should now look like Figure 7.6. It still needs more work. The maturity axis labels are unclear, and too many dates are displayed. The vertical axis needs a label, and the way it is angled is not helpful. We will not bother trying to fix these issues because there is a big problem with Excel's charting interface: Rotation is clumsy.

Excel provides X, Y, and Z rotation controls, and you can try them, but they are difficult to work with. We want to be able to easily spin the chart with the cursor. To do this, we will use Python.

3D Viz in Python

Python is "an interpreted, object-oriented, high-level programming language with dynamic semantics" (www.python.org/doc/essays/blurb/). That sounds complicated, but do not worry; Python is really easy to access and use. It is open-source (free), and its many users provide a strong support system.

As of this writing, generative AI (especially ChatGPT) can be used to write effective Python code.

Although you can download and install it on your personal device, we will use an even simpler approach, Google's Colab environment.

STEP Click the link colab.research.google.com/ or enter it into your favorite browser. If needed, login to Google when prompted. Click on the *Welcome to Colab* link and read it.

The Colab notebook that you read is composed of executable and text cells. Across the top of the Colab screen are the usual menu items, and on the left is a table of contents with the sections in the notebook.

The yield data in the *YieldCurve.xlsx* workbook were uploaded to Google Drive. A few lines of Python code create a 3D plot that is easy to rotate and spin.

STEP Click the link dub.sh/3DVizYieldCurve or enter it into your favorite browser to see a Colab notebook that creates a 3D visualization of the data. Follow the instructions to spin the plot.

Figure 7.7 shows the Python visualization of the yield curve over time. Of course, the online version is live in the sense that you can spin it and use the cursor to get values at specific points on the surface.

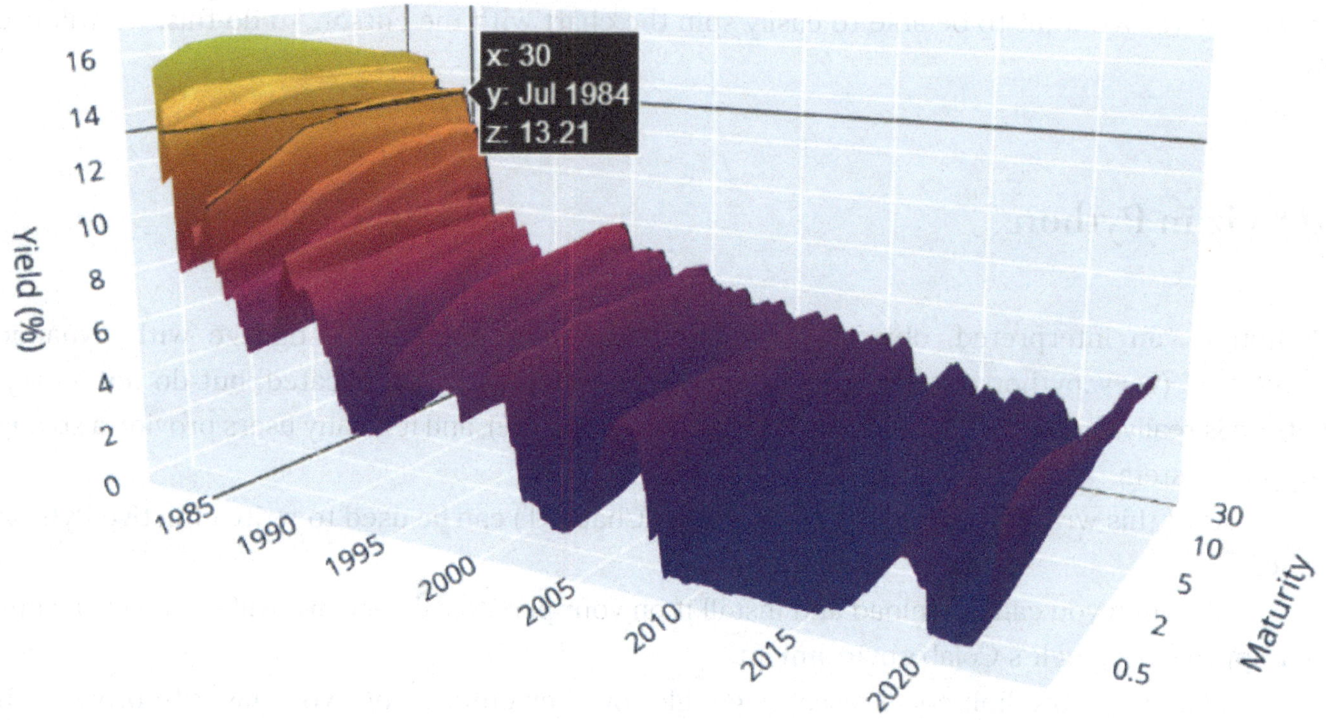

Figure 7.7: 3D chart in Python.

Yield Curve Meaning

Our yield curve visualizations are certainly eye-catching, but what does the yield curve actually tell us? There are several ways to answer this question, but the most important use of the yield curve is as the market's expectation of future economic performance.

Before we dig into how the yield curve can be used as a predictor, consider this: You follow a sports team that is expected to be really good this year, but they have aging stars at key positions. Then the betting odds of your team winning a championship would be higher for this season than a few years from now.

Conversely, if your team was bad now but had young players who could develop into superstars, their odds of winning in future years are higher than now.

You can stretch the time horizon even farther and think about odds a decade or longer from now. For so far into the future, all the teams would have similar odds (almost none of the current players would be active) unless there is some reason to believe that the ownership or management of a team is especially good or bad.

This thought exercise is quite similar to what the yield curve is doing. The yields are produced by supply and demand for each maturity. In a real sense, the yields for different maturities reflect the market participants' overall outlook on the economy at different times in the future.

When the yield curve inverts and longer maturities have lower yields than shorter ones, it means that investors think yields and interest rates will be lower in the future. This is interpreted as pessimism because low interest rates are associated with the Fed trying to stimulate an economy in recession.

So is the yield curve any good at predicting the future?

STEP Return to your *YieldCurve.xlsx* workbook and insert a blank sheet. Use FRED's *Data Search* tool to search for *yield curve*. Select the top 2 hits, T10Y2Y and T10Y2YM. Get the data and make separate charts with recession shading.

The daily chart is more jagged, but it tells the same story as the monthly frequency chart, shown in Figure 7.8. When the series dips below zero (so 2-year yields are higher than 10-year yields), the yield curve is inverted.

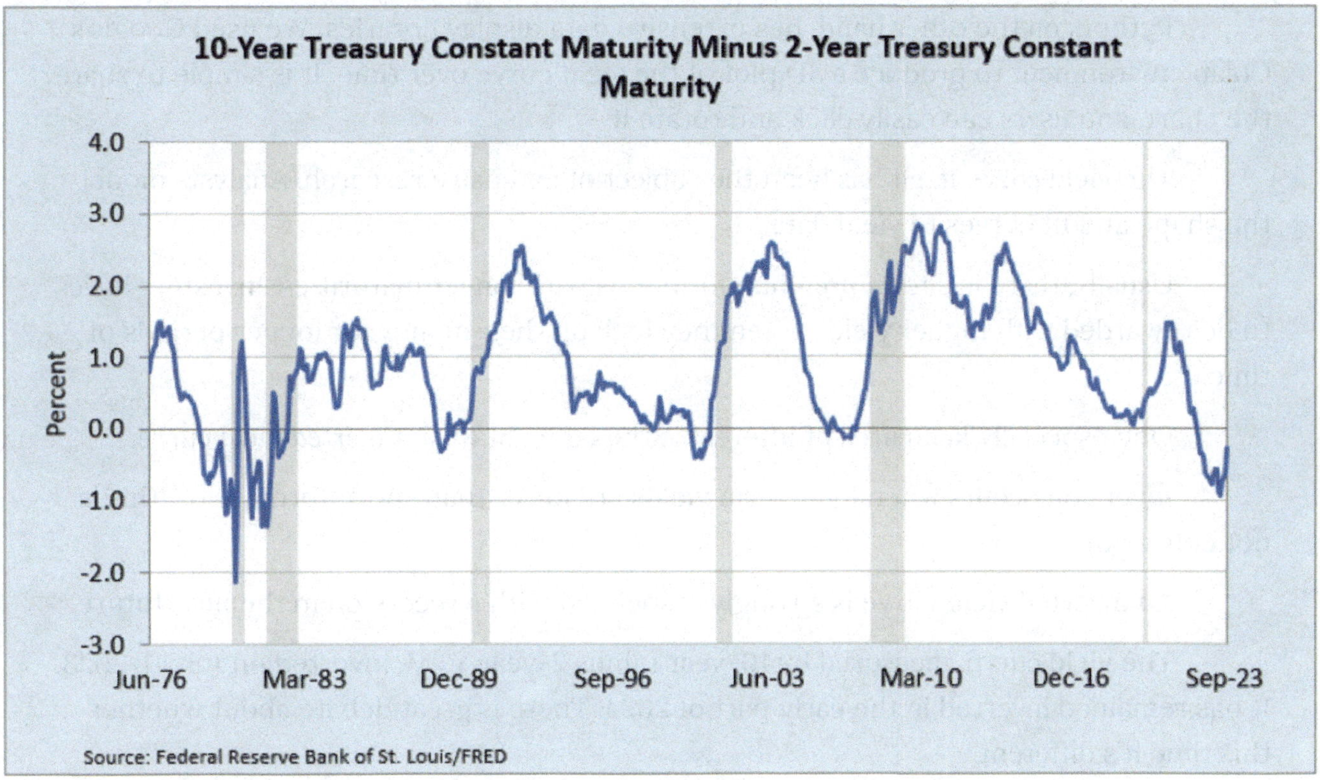

***Figure 7.8*: FRED Series ID T10Y2YM: Inversion when below zero.**
Source: Federal Reserve Bank of St. Louis via FRED, Copyrighted Data / FRED Terms.

Since 1969, an inverted yield curve has correctly predicted recessions shortly after the inversion (roughly within 15 months). Figure 7.8 shows that when the series goes below zero, a shaded bar soon follows—except the last one.

Is this time different? As of this writing, in 2024, the yield curve has been inverted for a record long time (www.google.com/search?q=yield+curve+record), yet the US economy seems strong. Will the yield curve be right again?

Takeaways

Excel can be used to make charts, and adding controls can make an Excel chart responsive to user input. We used a *Combo Box* control to allow the user to display the yield curve for a particular month-year.

Excel is not, however, strong data visualization software. In particular, its ability to manipulate charts, such as spinning a 3D plot, is quite limited.

Python, on the other hand, has extensive data display libraries. We used Google's Colab environment to produce a 3D plot of the yield curve over time. It is simple to share the chart, and users can easily click and rotate it.

The yield curve itself has been the subject of extensive research. Analysts model the shape and fit curves to yield data.

Usually, there is a *term premium* for bonds with longer maturities. Investors have to be rewarded with higher yields when they lock up their money for longer periods of time.

One especially keen area of interest is the concept of an *inverted yield curve.*

Inversion occurs when long-term yields are lower than short-term yields (this is not common).

An inverted yield curve is strongly associated with a recession in the near future.

The yield curve, measured by 10-year minus 2-year YTM, inverted on July 11, 2023. It has remained inverted in the early part of 2024. There is great debate about whether this time it's different.

References

For an overview of the yield curve with excellent graphics and an explanation of the meaning of the yield curve, see Bruce-Lockhart, C., Lewis, E., and Stubbington, T. "An Inverted Yield Curve: Why Investors Are Watching Closely." *Financial Times*, April 6, 2022, ig.ft.com/the-yield-curve-explained/.

Federal Reserve Bank of St. Louis, *10-Year Treasury Constant Maturity Minus 2-Year Treasury Constant Maturity* [T10Y2YM], retrieved from FRED, Federal Reserve Bank of St. Louis; https://fred.stlouisfed.org/series/T10Y2YM.

8. National Income Accounting

> The NIPAs trace their origin back to the 1930s, when the lack of comprehensive economic data hampered efforts to develop policies to combat the Great Depression. In response to this need, the U.S. Department of Commerce commissioned future Nobel Laureate Simon Kuznets to develop estimates of national income.
>
> Bureau of Economic Analysis (BEA) documentation

8.1 GDP and Macroeconomic Volatility

Just like a business needs an accounting system to keep track of what is going on, the National Income and Product Accounts (NIPAs) measure how the economy is doing. Before the 1930s, policy makers were flying blind—no one really knew how the economy was performing.

Gross domestic product (GDP) is the market value of all final goods and services produced within a country in a given period of time. This is the most fundamental measure of economic activity.

The bedrock accounting equation is GDP = C + I + G + NX. There are several ways to compute GDP, but this equation focuses on spending. It says that GDP can be computed as the sum of consumption (C), investment (I), government (G) spending, and net exports (NX).

STEP Open Excel and save a workbook as *GDPInvestment.xlsx*. Enter these *Series IDs* in the top row: GDP, PCEC, GPDI, GCE, and NETEXP. Use the FRED Excel add-in to get the data (refer to previous work with FRED if needed). In cell K8, enter the formula =B8-D8-F8-H8-J8. That is GDP − C − I − G − NX. Display three decimal places.

Excel shows 0.000—GDP really and truly is the sum of spending by consumers, firms, and governments (local, state, and federal) plus net exports.

STEP Fill cell K8 down. Scroll down and look at the values.

Yes, GDP = C + I + G + NX is always true, with a little *rounding error*—a small numerical discrepancy. For example, adding 1.3 and 1.6 gives 2.9. If we round to the integer before adding, we get 1 plus 2 equals 3. Rounding errors are often found when the sums of percentages are slightly more or less than 100% in a table.

With three decimal places displayed, you can see that sometimes column K shows a plus or minus 0.001. That is a rounding error in the GDP aggregates (C, I, G, and NX).

GDP is a flow, not a stock. GDP measures *output per time period* (usually a quarter or a year), not a total accumulated at a point in time. Imagine water flowing into a bathtub—GDP is how much water is pouring in (so liters or gallons per minute), not how much water is in the tub.

C, I, and G are the total spending (purchased final goods and services) made by consumers, firms, and governments, respectively. A computer can be C, I, or G depending on who bought it. It is C if you or I bought it for personal use, I if a firm bought it, and G if a government agency bought it.

Every buyer is either a consumer, firm, or government. By tracking the spending of these three categories of buyers, we get a total of the value of all final goods and services produced in a given time period.

But GDP is certainly not perfect. It misses things that are produced but not sold, like household work. Imagine if millions of moms stayed at home and cooked, cleaned, and took care of kids, then society changed, and many of those moms went to work and paid others to cook, clean, and take care of the kids. Before, none of that work was counted, and after, it was.

GDP is also criticized because it says nothing about how the economy's output is distributed. It is a measure of total output and is silent on important issues of inequality and poverty.

It is easy to forget that G does not include transfer payments (such as Social Security benefits). "Government spending" in the macroeconomic sense means the purchase of final goods and services by governments (e.g., roads, schools, and military gear).

It is even harder to remember that in macroeconomics, I does not represent investing in stocks or other speculative activity. Instead, investment is a subcategory of total spending focusing on goods and services purchased by firms.

While the core meaning of investment is the purchase of new tools, plant, and equipment by firms, it also includes residential investment (new housing construction) and changes in business inventories (produced but unsold output).

STEP Insert a new sheet and, in the top row, enter these *SERIES IDs*: *GPDI*, *PNFI*, *PRFI*, and *CBI*. Get the data. In cell I8, enter the formula =B8-D8-F8-H8 (*Gross Private Domestic Investment* minus *Private Nonresidential Fixed Investment* minus *Private Residential Fixed Investment* minus *Changes in Business Inventories*). Display three decimal places and fill down. Scroll to the last row and keep an eye on column I as you scroll.

Once again, with a bit of a rounding error (+/− 0.001), the data show that total investment really is the sum of those three subcategories.

The first of the three investment categories is what we might call true investment in the sense of tools, plant, and equipment purchased by firms. It is by far the largest type of investment.

The second category, new housing construction, could have been included in C (consumers buy homes), but by convention it is considered investment. There are many types of dwellings (think houses, condos, apartment buildings, and more), and the supply of housing is fundamental for every economy.

By the way, sales of *existing* homes (or cars or anything used) are not expenditures on goods produced during the given time period, so they are not counted as part of GDP. This makes sense, since we only want to measure the production of goods and services, and we do not care if previously produced items are exchanged.

The final category, changes in business inventories, covers the fact that some things are produced in a given year but sold later. By keeping track of inventories, we properly account for goods and services produced in a given time period. You can see in the data that this category is a small percentage of total investment.

So C, I, and G are what consumers, firms, and governments buy, but what about NX? What do exports minus imports have to do with GDP? We have to make sure we count things produced at home but exported (so there is no domestic spending for these items), and we want to subtract things we buy that were not made by us. NX is like CBI, a category that makes sure we are correctly counting everything.

A quick look at the data will show that, perhaps surprisingly, net exports do not matter much in the grand scheme of things.

STEP Return to the first sheet and scroll down to the last row. In a row below the last row, compute the share of GDP that is C. For 07/01/2023 it would be =D314/$B$314. Repeat for I, G, and NX.

The data show that C is by far the largest share of GDP, roughly 2/3, while I and G are usually about 1/6. Even though the United States is a relatively open economy, and we live in an era of globalization, NX is a small share of GDP—just a few percentage points.

During the Great Depression, it became clear that we needed a way to measure how the economy was doing. Obviously, the economy was doing badly, but there was no objective, quantitative information on how bad it was and how different areas of the country were doing. National income accounting is much more complicated than the overview presented here, but at its core it measures economic performance by

$$GDP = C + I + G + NX.$$

Short- and Long-Run Macroeconomics

The 1930s were so traumatic that the Great Depression not only led to the creation of government agencies to measure output and unemployment, but a whole new area of economics was born. Macroeconomics, the study of the overall economy, is split into two parts: short and long run.

In previous work (in section 4.2), we used Maddison's data to explore the long-run economic performance of different countries and compare CAGRs. The variability over many years was staggering, with some countries enjoying decades of sustained growth while others continue to languish.

We will use FRED data to examine short-run economic performance. GDP and its subcategories will be the stars of the show. Although we have learned some things about managing the economy in the short run, a great deal remains mysterious, and we do not know exactly why a market economy is so unstable and volatile.

The stylized graph in Figure 8.1 shows a market economy's actual performance (the thin squiggly line) moving around its long-run path, also known as *potential* GDP.

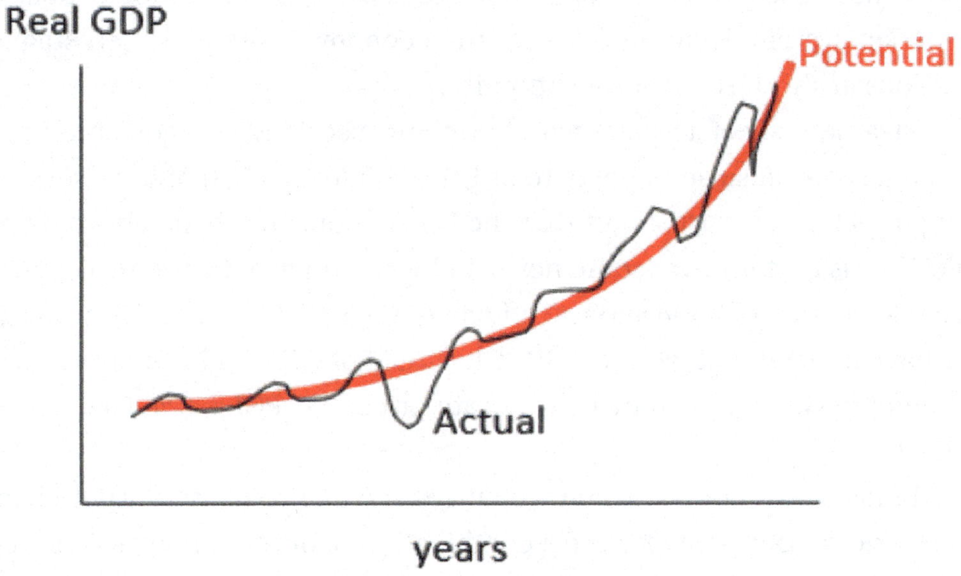

***Figure 8.1**: Short- and long-run macroeconomics.*

Figure 8.1 has good news and bad news. The good news is growth—over time, real GDP has increased, and the curved nature of the path portends big increases in the future. Figuring out how the market system delivers such growth in output over time remains a central unsolved problem in economics.

The bad news is the fluctuations in output—every drop in actual real GDP causes pain via job loss and firm collapse. Understanding why the market system is so erratic is another central unsolved problem in economics.

These two fundamental properties of market economies, long-run growth and short-run fluctuations, drive the organizational structure of macroeconomics. For long-run analysis, we use growth theory models and focus on the trend of real GDP per person with a time scale of decades or more. An important goal is to make output per person grow fast, with 2% per year considered very good for rich countries. Seemingly small percentage point increases in CAGR produce huge gains over long periods of time.

Short-run macroeconomics pays little attention to population growth, since it remains roughly the same from one quarter to the next, and focuses on explanations for rising and falling GDP from one quarter to the next. Instead of CAGR over many years, the most common measure is the annualized percentage change in GDP from one time period to the next. When positive, the economy is booming, while negative percentage changes indicate recession.

In the short run, more variables come into play, such as prices, interest rates, and future expectations, because they seem to impact the boom-bust cycle. A key goal is to stabilize the economy. Government policy makers actively attempt to manipulate the economy so as to even out the variability and reverse downturns. We want not only acceleration but a smooth ride.

Figure 8.1 is not based on actual data, but the roller coaster or boom-bust depiction is a feature of the market system. Figuring out why the economy roars and then stagnates is one of the central questions in short-run macroeconomics.

STEP Insert a new sheet in your workbook and use FRED to get data on *GDPPOT* and *GDPC1*. Make a single chart (use an initial date of 1/1/1950 for *GDPC1*) of both series.

Unlike Figure 8.1, your chart shows that the US economy has been above its path (potential GDP) for a while. This is certainly welcome news and will influence future projections of potential output. The Great Recession of 2008 and the effects of the COVID-19 pandemic are clearly visible.

You may have noticed that we used *GDPC1* instead of *GDP* (as in the previous section). The difference between the two is how they incorporate prices. *GDPC1* is *real GDP* and *GDP* (without the C1) is *nominal GDP*.

Real GDP holds prices constant, so its changes are due solely to output changes. Nominal GDP uses current prices, so its changes are a combination of output and price changes.

GDPC1 uses *chained dollars* (hence the C) to hold prices constant. Because buyers respond to changing prices and innovation creates new products, it is impossible to maintain a truly fixed basket of items with which to construct a price index. Chained dollars are a way around this problem, and they are used for many other macro variables—whenever you see "chained dollars," that means the variable has prices held constant and is in real terms.

Real GDP is the correct GDP to use when you are interested in how the economy is doing over time. If you use nominal GDP and there is inflation, you might conclude that the economy is growing rapidly when it is just rising prices making nominal GDP increase.

Who's Responsible?

Let's dive down into real GDP and explore its components. Our goal is to see if we can figure out why real GDP is so volatile. Is it C, I, or G? In other words, are consumers, firms, or governments responsible for the business cycle?

This is not a mystery novel, but we like surprises, so we will wait for the big reveal. You might want to pick one and see if you get it right.

STEP Insert a new sheet in your workbook and enter GDPC1, PCECC96, GPDIC1, and GCEC1 in the first row. Enter *pca* in the second row (under each SERIES ID). Get the data.

You are looking at the annualized percentage change (that is what *pca* does) for each macro aggregate. We need to visualize the data to understand what is going on. We start with real GDP.

STEP Use FRED's charting tool to make a graph of annualized percentage changes in GDPC1 over time.

Figure 8.2 shows what your chart should look like. There are two things to notice. First, the percentage change is negative in every recession. This makes sense, since the definition of a recession is a downturn in the economy. Second, before 1980, it seems the economy was more volatile than after 1980. Look carefully at how the spikes hit and exceed 10.0 percentage points before 1980, but they are more tamped down after the recession in the early 1980s.

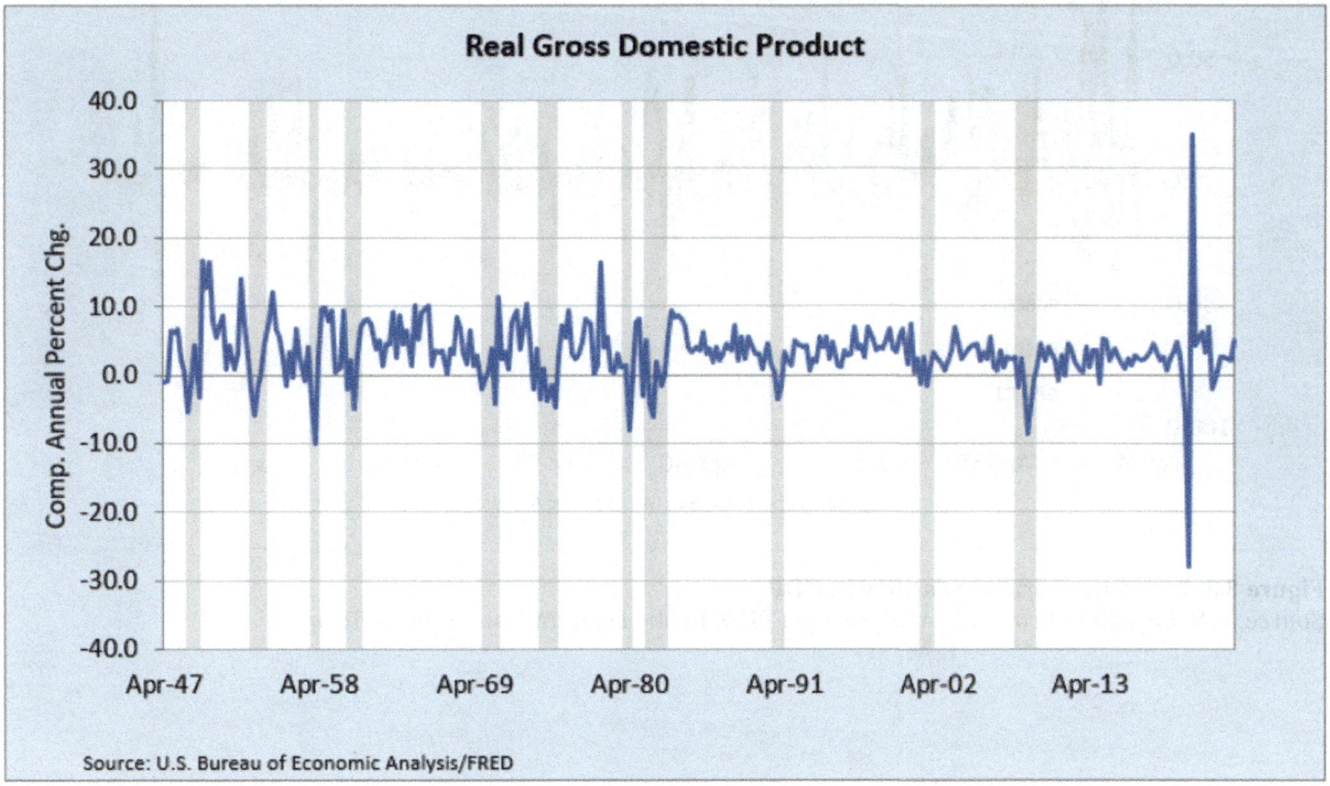

Figure 8.2: Annualized percentage change in real GDP over time.
Source: U.S. Bureau of Economic Analysis via FRED, Public Domain Data / FRED Terms.

So which of the three macro aggregates—C, I or G—is responsible for this? You get one last chance to guess before the big reveal.

STEP Create three individual charts of C, I and G. Stack them on top of each other.

At first, they seem similar, but look carefully at the *y*-axis of each chart. We need to standardize them to compare them correctly.

STEP Change the y-axis min and max to −100 and 150 in the C and G charts so that the three charts have the same y-axis.

The result is dramatic. It is easy to see that investment is much more volatile than consumption or government spending.

STEP Another way is to create a single chart with C, I, and G. Use FRED's *Create Multiple Series Graph* to do this.

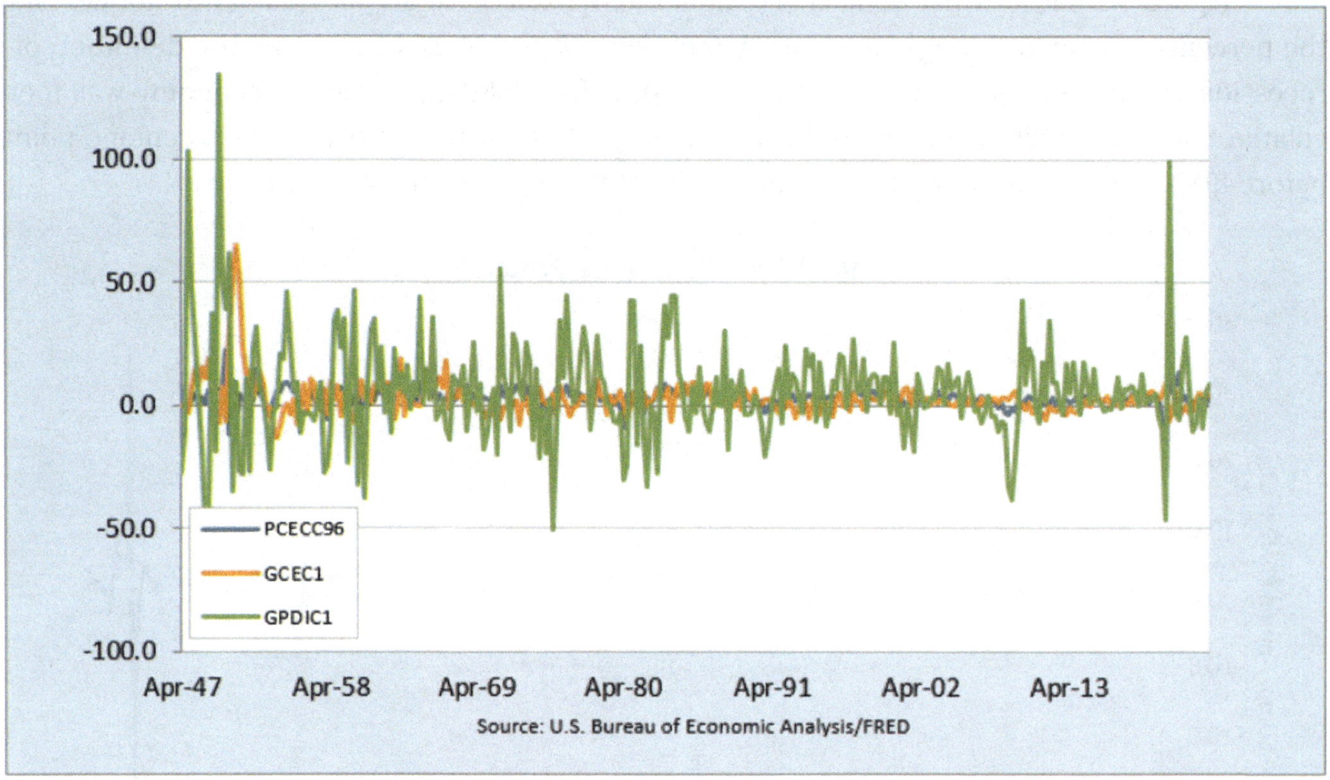

Figure 8.3: Investment drives volatility in GDP.
Source: U.S. Bureau of Economic Analysis via FRED, Public Domain Data / FRED Terms.

Your chart (the same as Figure 8.3) clearly shows investment volatility swamping consumption and government spending. It is not that C and G do not matter—in fact, a great deal of effort is devoted to explaining how C changes. Forecasting consumer sentiment and spending is important.

But there is no question that a critical source of the volatility in GDP is coming from I. The question then becomes, Why is investment so volatile?

We know investment depends on interest rates from our previous work on IRR. For a project to be undertaken, the IRR must be greater than the appropriate discount rate. Often, this is a cost of funds measure or market interest rate. Thus, as interest rates fall, investment rises and vice versa.

Thus, conventional wisdom says that investment is volatile because interest rates bounce around a lot. But there is another important factor affecting investment: emotion.

John Maynard Keynes, the leading economist of the first half of the 20th century, argued that interest rates alone could not explain the volatility of investment. He coined the term *animal spirits* to capture the instinctual and primitive forces that help drive decision-making:

> Even apart from the instability due to speculation, there is the instability due to the characteristic of human nature that a large proportion of our positive activities depend on spontaneous optimism rather than on a mathematical expectation, whether moral or hedonistic or economic. Most, probably, of our decisions to do something positive, the full consequences of which will be drawn out over many days to come, can only be taken as a result of animal spirits—of a spontaneous urge to action rather than inaction, and not as the outcome of a weighted average of quantitative benefits multiplied by quantitative probabilities. Enterprise only pretends to itself to be mainly actuated by the statements in its own prospectus, however candid and sincere. Only a little more than an expedition to the South Pole, is it based on an exact calculation of benefits to come. Thus if the animal spirits are dimmed and the spontaneous optimism falters, leaving us to depend on nothing but a mathematical expectation, enterprise will fade and die;—though fears of loss may have a basis no more reasonable than hopes of profit had before.[1]

Keynes was a genius and polymath. He managed the portfolio at King's College (one of Cambridge University's wealthiest colleges), where he was a professor. He knew philosophy and art but also understood mathematics and what we call today analytics. He was convinced that human behavior had a subjective element that required going beyond data. He was an early behavioral economist who was interested in the psychology of individual and group decision-making. Keynes did not believe that we could explain the volatility of investment with interest rates alone. *Animal spirits* captured the instinctive, nonquantifiable, irrational forces that drive us.

There is no doubt about it: Investment is the source of the volatility in GDP. Investment is driving the business cycle. Figuring out how and why I is so volatile is at the top of the research agenda in modern short-run macroeconomics.

Takeaways

The key equation in national income accounting is

$$GDP = C + I + G + NX.$$

1. Source: Keynes (1936, chap. 12)

This says that total output can be measured by adding the spending of consumers, firms, and governments (with an adjustment for net exports).

National income accounting is all about categories and adding up subcategories into bigger aggregates. Investment, for example, is composed of spending by firms on new tools, plant, and equipment, plus new housing construction, plus changes in business inventories (a subcategory to handle goods sold in a later time period).

Long-run macroeconomics is about the path the economy is on, while short-run analysis focuses on the ups and downs of the business cycle.

Instead of computing a CAGR over long periods of time, the short run is about quarterly changes or predicting how the economy will be doing a few months from now.

A core question in the short run concerns the intense volatility of market economies. Booms are followed by busts in a wild roller coaster ride. The focus is on identifying the source of the volatility and how to manage it.

Investment is the culprit. It has much bigger ups and downs than C or G.

While interest rate movements contribute to investment fluctuations, animal spirits (defined by Keynes as a "spontaneous urge to action") often produce waves of euphoria and rapid upswings in the economy that are then followed by pessimism and recession.

If you want to see Keynes speaking from a 1930s newsreel and learn more about his most famous book, *The General Theory of Employment, Interest and Money*, visit vimeo.com/200367754.

References

The epigraph is from pp. 1–2 of "Concepts and Methods of the U.S. National Income and Product Accounts" (visited in November 2023 and available at www.bea.gov/methodologies/index.htm#nationalmeth). This document answers the question, How did the NIPAs originate? It is noteworthy that the person instrumental in setting up British national income accounts, Richard Stone, also received a Nobel Prize in Economic Sciences. Establishing a coherent, reliable methodology for aggregate measures of economic performance is not trivial.

Keynes, J. M. (1936). *The General Theory of Employment, Interest and Money*. Full text online at www.marxists.org/reference/subject/economics/keynes/general-theory.

U.S. Bureau of Economic Analysis, *Real Gross Domestic Product* [GDPC1], retrieved from FRED, Federal Reserve Bank of St. Louis; https://fred.stlouisfed.org/series/GDPC1.

U.S. Bureau of Economic Analysis, *Real Gross Private Domestic Investment* [GPDIC1], retrieved from FRED, Federal Reserve Bank of St. Louis; https://fred.stlouisfed.org/series/GPDIC1.

U.S. Bureau of Economic Analysis, *Real Government Consumption Expenditures and Gross Investment* [GCEC1], retrieved from FRED, Federal Reserve Bank of St. Louis; https://fred.stlouisfed.org/series/GCEC1.

U.S. Bureau of Economic Analysis, *Real Personal Consumption Expenditures* [PCECC96], retrieved from FRED, Federal Reserve Bank of St. Louis; https://fred.stlouisfed.org/series/PCECC96.

For a more modern take on the role of psychology in investment and human behavior, see Akerlof, G., and Shiller, R. (2010). *Animal Spirits: How Human Psychology Drives the Economy, and Why It Matters for Global Capitalism* (Princeton University Press).

8.2 International Comparisons

We know that national income accounting is grounded on this key equation:

$$GDP = C + I + G + NX.$$

Simple logic says that fluctuations in GDP must depend on its components, and the data for the United States show that investment is more volatile than consumption and government spending.

But what about other countries? Is investment responsible for the boom-and-bust nature of GDP in other economies?

Data from the Organisation for Economic Co-Operation and Development (OECD) answer this question. This international agency was created after World War II and serves, in part, as a hub for data gathered from member countries. They are online at oecd.org, but we will access the data through the FRED Excel add-in.

There is a data issue to address before we explore the volatility of investment in other countries. Instead of investment spending, the OECD reports gross fixed capital formation (GFCF) as a measure of investment activity.

There are several differences between I and GFCF, but the key one is that GFCF includes secondhand assets (think of used heavy machinery that is purchased by a manufacturing company). Investment, on the other hand, counts only new tools, plant, and equipment.

STEP Insert a sheet in your *GDPInvestment.xlsx* workbook. In the top row, enter GPDIC1 (this is real I) and NAEXKP04USQ652S (this is real GFCF). Enter 01/01/1972 in cell A4 (so both series start from the same date) and get the data. Widen column D if needed.

Investment spending is in billions of dollars, so to make it easier to compare the two, we need to convert GFCF to billions of dollars.

STEP Enter the formula =D8/1000000000 (carefully enter 9 zeroes) in cell E8. Fill it down.

It is easy to see that column E, GFCF (in billions), is greater than column B (I in billions). This is mainly because GFCF counts the resale of previously produced tools, plant, and equipment, and I does not. It also means that you would not get C + GFCF + G + NX to equal GDP.

It is not that GFCF is wrong, but we want to be aware that it is a different measure of investment activity than I. The OECD uses GFCF in its country reports and highlights it as their preferred measure of investment activity. We will compare the volatility of GFCF to C and G to answer our question.

OECD Countries and Series IDs

The OECD has data on real C, GFCF, and G for 39 countries. We will focus on the major economies in the OECD, called the G7: Canada, France, Germany, Italy, Japan, the United Kingdom, and the United States.

To get the data, we parse the *Series ID* we used to get GFCF for the United States: NAEXKP04USQ652S. To *parse* means "to separate something into its component parts."

The Series ID for OECD macro aggregates has five parts. We can show this using vertical line separators:

NAEXKP|04|US|Q|652S.

In the second part, the 04 indicates GFCF; 01 is GDP, 02 is C, and 03 is G.

The third part is a two-character country code. The table in Figure 8.4 shows the two-letter abbreviation for each country.

The last part is troublesome because it is different for different countries. This means that we cannot simply plug in the two-letter FRED code for each country because the last part of the Series ID (the part after the Q) is not always the same. As a work-around, we use FRED's search tool.

Country	FRED code	Country	FRED code	Country	FRED code	Country	FRED code
Australia	AU	**France**	**FR**	**Japan**	**JP**	Slovak Republic	SK
Austria	AT	**Germany**	**DE**	Korea	KR	Slovenia	SI
Belgium	BE	Greece	GR	Luxembourg	LU	South Africa	ZA
Brazil	BR	Hungary	HU	Mexico	MX	Spain	ES
Canada	**CA**	Iceland	IS	Netherlands	NL	Sweden	SE
Chile	CL	India	IN	New Zealand	NZ	Switzerland	CH
Czech Republic	CZ	Indonesia	ID	Norway	NO	Turkey	TR
Denmark	DK	Ireland	IE	Poland	PL	**United Kingdom**	**GB**
Estonia	EE	Israel	IL	Portugal	PT	**United States**	**US**
Finland	FI	**Italy**	**IT**	Russia	RU		

Figure 8.4: OECD country codes.

STEP Insert a sheet in your *GDPInvestment.xlsx* workbook and click the Data Search button. In the search box, enter the text NAEXKP02USQ and click the *Series ID* option (below the search box). Click the Search button. Select the series with units of US $ and click the Add Series IDs button at the bottom of the dialog box. Change the 2 to a 3 in the search box and repeat the procedure: search, select the series with units of US $, and add it to the spreadsheet. Change the 3 to a 4 and repeat again. Click *Close* and then get the data.

You have real C, G, and GFCF for the United States. But we want the annualized growth rate for each quarter, and we want to start from the same date.

STEP Change *lin* to *pca* in each cell in row 2, and set the start date in row 4 to 04/01/2002 (since that is the latest date for the series). Get the data.

We are ready to answer the question of which component is the most volatile for the United States, but this time using GFCF instead of I.

STEP Use FRED's *Build Graph* tool to put the three series on the same chart.

GFCF seems a little more variable than C and G, but the difference is not as dramatic as when we used investment spending. Also, there is a sharp increase in G in 2007 that is not in the NIPA data. That is an error in the OECD data.

The SD

Before we explore the other G7 countries, we offer a more objective measure with which to gauge volatility than the eyeball test we have been using.

The standard deviation, or SD, is a measure of dispersion in a list of numbers. if the numbers are bunched tightly together, the SD is low (if they are all the same, then the SD is zero). The more spread out the numbers, the larger the SD.

The SD has the same units as the numbers. If we measure the heights of 20 college students in inches, then the SD is in inches.

Think of the SD as a +/− number. The SD tells us the size of the typical deviation from the average. If the average height is 5 feet, 8 inches with an SD of 3 inches, that says most of the students are around 5 feet, 8 inches tall, give or take 3 inches. In other words, most of them are between 5 feet, 5 inches and 5 feet, 11 inches.

It would not make sense if the SD of the height of 20 college students was 4 feet, because then the range is from under 2 feet to almost 10 feet tall.

STEP Return to the sheet with GDP, C, I, and G (from the US NIPAs) and scroll down to the bottom row. In any row after the last row, in column B, use Excel's STDEV.P function to compute the SD of real GDP. Copy your formula and paste it in columns D, F, and H.

	A	B	C	D	E	F	G	H
313	07/01/2023	4.9	07/01/2023	4.0	07/01/2023	8.4	07/01/2023	4.6
314		=STDEV.P(B6:B313)		=STDEV.P(D6:D313)		=STDEV.P(F6:F313)		=STDEV.P(H6:H313)
315	SD -->	4.6		4.4		20.9		7.4

***Figure 8.5*: SD of GDP, C, I, and G.**

Figure 8.5 shows the result as of fall 2023 (so 07/01/2023 is the last value). Investment spending is in column F, and it has a much higher SD, or dispersion, than C or G. Does the same hold true for GFCF?

STEP Return to the sheet with the OECD measures of C, G, and GFCF. Scroll to the bottom and compute the SDs for the three series. Yes, GFCF has a higher SD than C or G, but not by a lot.

Discovery

What about the other G7 countries? Use the same steps applied to the United States to explore the volatility of C, G, and GFCF in the other G7 countries.

STEP Download OECD data on the annualized percentage change in real C, G, and GFCF.

Make a chart. Compute the SDs of the three series. What do you find with respect to the crucial question about volatility in GDP—is investment driving volatility in GDP for these economies?

Notice that the *Series IDs* can be tricky to work with in this case. Confirm that the *Series IDs* are correct and that they make sense. It is easy to make a mistake. A simple check is to click on the URL in row 5 of each variable and make sure it is the correct country and series.

9. Introduction to VBA

> Once you become acquainted with VBA, you'll wonder how you ever got along without it.
>
> Reed Jacobson

9.1 My First Macro in Excel

You have learned many new Excel functions, created a variety of different charts in Excel, and used Solver, Comparative Statics Wizard, Monte Carlo simulation, and FRED Excel add-ins. But those are all front-end Excel skills.

For computer scientists, the front end is the presentation layer or the user interface of software. The front end is that part of the restaurant, where the diner sits down and orders food.

The back end of a restaurant is the kitchen, where the meal is actually made. Excel's back end is built on a computer language called Visual Basic. Excel and other Office products such as Word and PowerPoint run a version called Visual Basic Applications edition—or VBA for short.

It is in VBA that we write code, also known as macros, to perform especially complicated tasks. The code is written and stored in *modules*. The resulting Excel workbook is a combination of spreadsheets and modules that must be saved as a macro-enabled workbook with the extension *.xlsm*. Without macros, an Excel spreadsheet has the file extension *.xlsx*.

> **EXCEL TIP** Excel warns you if you save a workbook with macros as a simple Excel workbook (.xlsx). If you ignore the warning, it will simply save the workbook without the macros, and your code will be lost.

There is no question that a macro-enabled workbook is more powerful than a simple spreadsheet, but this power comes at a cost. Not only do you have to know how to write code in

VBA, but your end user will probably have to enable macros when opening the file. Sometimes, security settings in a particular installation of Excel are set so high that the macros will not be allowed to run. The user has to change Excel's settings, adding another layer of difficulty, just to open the file.

> **EXCEL TIP** If you can accomplish a task without macros, *always* do so. Sometimes, however, VBA is the only solution.

Hello, World!

It is a tradition in computer science to introduce a new language by outputting "Hello, World!" Let's do it.

STEP Open Excel and save the file as *IntroVBA.xlsm*, making sure to save it as a macro-enabled workbook with the .xlsm extension by clicking *Save as type* in the save window and choosing *.xlsm*. Click the Visual Basic button in the *Developer* tab in the *Ribbon*. If the *Developer* tab is not visible, press *Alt*, *f*, *t* and click *Customize Ribbon*, then check *Developer* in the list. You can also access Visual Basic by pressing *Alt-F11* (you may need to use the *function* [*fn*] key) or right-clicking the sheet tab and selecting *View Code*.

You have a new window on your screen with a lot of things you have never seen before. Welcome to Excel's kitchen! You are in the Visual Basic Editor (VBE).

Across the top there is a familiar menu of items. The top-left panel should be the *Project Explorer* (press *Ctrl-r* if you do not see it). You may also see other panels.

STEP In the *Project Explorer* panel, scroll, if needed, to find your *IntroVBA.xlsm* workbook (it will be in parentheses after VBAProject), and select it (highlighted in blue). Click *Insert* in the top menu and select *Module*.

You now see a blank window. This is where you will write your code. Notice also that your workbook in the *Project Explorer* panel now has a new component, the module you just inserted.

STEP The cursor should be blinking in the blank window, but if not, click in the window. Enter the text *sub myfirstmacro* and press *Enter*.

The text is transformed. The S is capitalized and *Sub* is in blue, parentheses have been appended, and a new line *End Sub* has been added. Apparently, VBE is a high-level editor with a great deal of support.

Sub stands for subroutine, a set of instructions or lines of code. The statements between the *Sub* and *End Sub* lines are the *body* of the macro. You could pass *arguments* to your *Sub* by entering them in the () on the first line.

STEP In the middle line (where the cursor is blinking), enter the text *msgbox "Hello, World!"* and press *Enter*.

As you entered the text, you undoubtedly noticed the yellow pop-up showing the various options for the *MsgBox* object. This shows again the strong support offered in the editor in the VBA environment. Also, this example reveals that VBA is an object-oriented programming language. We write code to apply different methods and options to the objects.

We have finished our first macro and are ready to run it.

STEP Click *Run* in the top menu and select *Run Sub/User Firm* (or press F5).

You did it! You are returned to the Excel spreadsheet, and it displays a message box with "Hello, *World!*" on it.

This is exciting, but how can we run the macro from the spreadsheet?

STEP Press OK to close the message box and click the *Developer* tab. Click the Insert button and select the top-left *Button* icon. Click and drag in the spreadsheet to create a button. In the *AssignMacro* dialog box, select *myfirstmacro* and click OK. Click on an empty cell in the spreadsheet.

You have added a button to the spreadsheet and attached a macro to it. When you click the button, the macro will run. Try it.

STEP Click the button to see the message box pop up.

Now the user does not have to know how to run macros in VBA. By attaching the macro to the button, you have made it easy for the user to run your code.

> **EXCEL TIP** Regular (left) clicks enable you to use objects in Excel. Right-clicks select objects so that you can modify them.

STEP Right-click your button and replace the *Button 1* text with *Click Me*. Click the button to see that it works.

This shows that the caption of the button can be different from the name of the macro.

We used the *Scroll Bar* and *Combo Box* controls earlier, but they were not macro-enabled. By assigning macros to controls, we greatly expand the power of Excel.

Recording Macros

VBA is hard at first because beginning users do not know any of the objects or commands. It is like learning a new spoken language: You know the words exist for what you want to say, but you do not know what they are.

One way to start growing your VBA vocabulary is by recording macros. You turn on the recorder and do things in Excel, then examine the recorded code in VBA.

STEP Click the *Developer* tab and click the Record Macro button. Click OK in the pop-up dialog box. Select cell A1 and enter 100. Make the formatting $. Click the Stop Recording button. Press *Alt-F11* to go to VBA.

There is a new module sheet in your VBA project.

STEP Double-click *Module2* in the *Project Explorer* panel.

You are looking at the code needed to do the steps you did in Excel. You now know that *Selection.Style = "Currency"* applies currency formatting to the selected cell.

STEP Change the 100 in the recorded macro to 0.1 and change *Currency* to *Percent*. Return to Excel by pressing *Alt-F11* (this toggles you between Excel and VBA). Right-click your button and select *AssignMacro*. Choose *Macro1* (that you just recorded and edited) and click OK. Click an empty cell in the spreadsheet and click your button.

Your macro changed A1 to 0.1 and formatted it as percent! This demonstrates that you can definitely control Excel from VBA.

This example shows how you can record a macro to reveal the code needed to perform a task in Excel. The usual procedure is to record a series of steps and then edit the code, removing superfluous lines and changing values or other attributes.

STEP Use the macro recorder to write a macro that takes a random number from a cell and pastes its value into the cell below it. Assign your macro to your button and click the button to run it. If you need help, see the appendix.

Takeaways

In the late 20th century, Excel was in a race with other spreadsheets that you have never heard of because Excel completely overwhelmed them. In 1993, Excel 5.0 debuted with VBA, and Microsoft crushed the competition.

VBA is an implementation of Visual Basic that runs within Excel. Macros are written in VBA in modules and then assigned to controls (such as buttons) on the spreadsheet.

If you want to continue learning about VBA, Reed Jacobson's *Microsoft Office Excel 2007 Visual Basic for Applications Step by Step* is a great place to start. The files needed were originally on a CD (an older technology that could store "huge" amounts of data), but they are available for download at dub.sh/hbvba.

You can also look at open-source VBA code. For example, the Comparative Statics Wizard and Monte Carlo simulation add-ins are freely accessible. So are the macro-enabled workbooks we have used. You can open their modules and inspect the code to learn VBA.

References

The epigraph is from the first chapter of Reed Jacobson's *Microsoft Office Excel 2007 Visual Basic for Applications Step by Step* (Pearson Education), Kindle Edition. This book is out of print, but there are many copies available, and it remains a great way to learn how to write macros in Excel.

Appendix

STEP Click the Record Macro button and enter the formula =RAND() in a cell. Copy the cell, select another cell, and *Paste Special* as *Values*. Stop recording and go to VBA. The body of your recorded macro (the code between the *Sub* and *End Sub* lines) should look something like this:

```
'
' Macro3 Macro
```

```
'
'
Range("A3").Select
ActiveCell.FormulaR1C1 = "=RAND()"
Range("A3").Select
Selection.Copy
Range("A4").Select
Selection.PasteSpecial Paste:=xlPasteValues, Operation:=xlNone, _
SkipBlanks :=False, Transpose:=False
Range("A5").Select\\
```

These lines are the actual commands you gave Excel. Notice that an apostrophe at the start of a line comments out that line (it is not executed) and is displayed in green-colored text (e.g., the line Macro3 Macro). The underscore character, _, continues the current statement on the next line.

You could clean up this code so it looks like this:

```
Range("A3").FormulaR1C1 = "=RAND()"
Range("A3").Copy
Range("A4").PasteSpecial Paste:=xlPasteValues, Operation:=xlNone, _
SkipBlanks:=False, Transpose:=False
Range("A5").Select
```

You could comment out the first line, and it would still work since the *RAND()* function is already in cell A3. Running this macro replaces the contents of cell A3 without any warning. You do not notice this because the code writes the same formula that was there.

9.2 Functions in VBA

Attaching a macro to a button or other object allows you and your users to run VBA code, but there is another way to access code from an Excel workbook: a *user-defined function* (UDF).

Unlike a native function, like =RAND() or =SUM(cell range), which is part of the Excel application itself, UDFs are functions that you write in VBA and are stored in a module in a macro-enabled workbook (file name extension .xlsm).

To the user, UDFs work the same way as native functions, so they require no special knowledge. The only extra step is that the user has to enable the content in the workbook (or disable all security, which is not recommended).

To demonstrate how UDFs work, we will create two user-defined functions, the first without any arguments and the second allowing the user to pass information to the function, making it more flexible and useful.

UDF with No Arguments

Recall from our work on Monte Carlo simulation that we can create a 90% free throw shooter in Excel with the formula =IF(RAND()<0.9,1,0). Alternatively, we could create a function in VBA—say, FT()—that the user could enter in any cell. Ninety percent of the time it would produce a 1, and the remaining 10% would be 0.

STEP Open your *IntroVBA.xlsm* macro-enabled workbook and press *Alt-F11* to go to Visual Basic. Insert a new module sheet in this workbook. Type the text *function FT()* (uppercase FT) and hit enter.

Excel's Visual Basic Editor capitalizes the F in *function*, adds an *End Function* for you, and colors the text blue for the beginning and ending lines of the code.

Instead of the Excel function =RAND(), VBA has its own random number generator *Rnd*. It produces random numbers in the interval from 0 to 1. It is supereasy to make our UDF output a random number.

STEP Enter the text FT = *Rnd* and press *Enter*. Return to Excel (*Alt-F11* is a toggle) and click on cell H1. Enter the function =FT() and press *Enter*.

Congratulations! You just wrote your first function in Excel and accessed it from Excel.

> **EXCEL TIP** For UDFs, Excel remembers how you first entered the function. If you enter =*ft()* (lowercase), it will keep using lowercase (even if you enter FT in a different cell). This is not true for native functions: Enter =*rand()* and Excel converts it to =RAND().

There is, however, a problem with our UDF.

STEP Press F9 a few times. Nothing happens to cell H1. It is not bouncing like *RAND()*, generating a new random number each time we recalculate the sheet.

The problem is that UDFs, by default, are nonvolatile functions. This means they do not get recalculated unless they depend on other cells that have changed. We must add code to make our function recalculate when F9 is pressed.

STEP Return to your VBA code for the FT function. Click on the top line, after the close parenthesis, and press *Enter* so that you are on a new, blank line and enter the text *Application.Volatile True*. Press *Enter*. Return to Excel and press F9 a few times. Success!

But we do not want to simply output a random number; we want to see if we made (1) or missed (0) a free throw attempt. We need to add some code to do this. Like the Excel formula we used to model a free throw result, we need an *If* statement to separate made from missed free throws.

STEP Go to the FT code. Click after *True* and press *Enter* to create a new line after the volatile statement. Enter the text *if rnd* < 0.9 *then* and press *Enter*.

As usual, the editor capitalizes and colors the text for you. The next line of code defines what happens if the random number is less than 0.9. It is followed by lines of code for missed free throws.

STEP Press the *Tab* key to indent, type the text FT = 1, and press *enter*. Type the word *Else* and press *enter*. Press *Tab*, type FT = 0, and press *enter*. Type *end if* and press *enter*. Put a straight single quote (') in front of the FT=*Rnd* line to comment it out (so it does not get executed).

Your masterpiece of code should look like this (with color added to keywords and lines):

```
Function FT()
Application.Volatile True
If Rnd < 0.9 Then
    FT = 1
Else
    FT = 0
End If
'FT = Rnd
End Function
```

The macro draws a uniformly distributed random number on the interval from 0 to 1 (*Rnd*), and if it is less than 0.9, it goes to the FT = 1 line. Since the function is called FT, it outputs the number 1 if *Rnd* < 0.9. If the random number drawn is not less than 0.9, it goes to the FT = 0 line and outputs a 0.

The code is easy to read, but does it actually work? Let's find out.

STEP Return to Excel, fill cell H1 down to cell H10, and press F9 a few times.

That is pretty cool, but what if we wanted a more generalized version, where the user tells us the chances of success?

UDF with an Argument

In native Excel functions—like SUM, for example—the arguments are passed in the parentheses: SUM(A1:A3). UDFs work the same way. We will add an argument to our code in the parentheses and modify the code to enable it to incorporate the information provided by the user.

STEP Copy the FT code and paste it below the *End Function* line. Since you cannot have two functions with the same name, change the name of the newly pasted function to FTARG (for argument). In the parentheses, type the text *Shoot as Double*. Replace the 0.9 in the *If* statement line with *Shoot*. Return to Excel and enter the formula =FTARG(0.5) in cell I1.

Excel displays an error message in cell I1. Can you figure out what is wrong with the UDF and fix it? If you cannot, take a look at the appendix.

We can make the function even more flexible by having it accept a value in another cell.

STEP Copy the FTARG code and paste it below the *End Function* line. Change the name of the newly pasted function to FTARGCELL (for argument from another cell). In the parentheses, change the text to *myShootCell as Range*. Replace *Shoot* in the *If* statement line with *myShoot-Cell.Value*. Change the FTARG = 1 and FTARG = 0 lines to FTARGCELL = 1 and FTARGCELL = 0. To see how this works, return to Excel and enter the formula =FTARGCELL($K$1) in cell J1. Fill it down to cell J10. In cell K1, enter a number from 0 to 1, such as 0.25. Press F9 a few times.

With a 25% chance of success, your 10 numbers in column J are bouncing around every time you press F9, and you usually get 2 or 3 ones.

Is it better to allow the user to input a number as the argument or a cell address? That depends on the context of the problem, including the user's familiarity with Excel. In fact, if you do not need to change the success rate, our original UDF, FT(), might be the best choice.

Takeaways

VBA code can be accessed by users from Excel's front end by attaching macros to buttons and other controls.

Another option is a UDF. The user enters a formula that runs the UDF code to do computations or other manipulations that are not available in native Excel functions.

Like native Excel functions, UDFs usually require arguments. These variables are declared in the *Function* statement, inside the parentheses.

Writing code is science and art. Deciding whether arguments are needed and, if so, how to pass them (numbers or cell addresses, for example) requires knowledge of what needs to be done and who is going to do it. You need to know your audience.

Most people think of Excel as some kind of sophisticated adding machine or calculator. Excel can certainly do arithmetic and other mathematical operations, but its back end or kitchen opens up a whole new world of opportunities and possibilities.

Appendix

The FTARG function fails when you change the name of the function to FTARG but do not likewise update the name of the function in the code. You must change the FT = 1 line to FTARG = 1 and the FT = 0 line to FTARG = 0.

When you write a UDF, you always use the function name to output a result. If you need more than one cell to output results, you can use an array function.

10. Demographics

> If a series of nuclear explosions were to wipe out the material equipment of the world but the educated citizens survived, it need not be long before former standards were reconstituted; but if it destroyed the educated citizens, even though it left the buildings and machines intact, a period longer than the Dark Ages might elapse before the former position was restored.
>
> Lionel Robbins

10.1 Visualization and Population Pyramids

Demography is the quantitative study of human populations. Demographers analyze *vital statistics* about people, including total number, births, deaths, and health. *Vital* means "of the utmost importance," and it is true that the oldest and most fundamental statistics include counting the number of people in a place (called a *census*) and how many were born, died, got sick, or moved.

We will use a remarkable data visualization known as a *population pyramid*. By showing the number of people by age and sex, this graph not only conveys information about the current situation; it also predicts the future.

First, we will show how population pyramids are made and interpreted using hypothetical examples. Next, we will explore real-world population pyramids. Finally, we will take a close look at two key statistics: the male-female birth ratio and the dependency ratio.

Accessing the Excel Workbook

STEP Go to dub.sh/gbae and click the *Excel Workbooks* link (top right). Click *PopulationPyramid.xlsm* to download it. Move the file from the downloads folder to a safe place on your computer or network.

The file's *.xlsm* extension means it is a macro-enabled Excel workbook. When you open it, you must enable macros to get full functionality from the file.

STEP Open *PopulationPyramid.xlsm*, read the *Intro* sheet, and be sure to click the Click to Test button. You may have to adjust your security settings as described in the *Intro* sheet.

Population Propagation

STEP Click the Begin button at the bottom of the *Intro* sheet.

A new sheet is revealed called *PlanetX*. Here is the explanation for this puzzling name.

It is January 1 several centuries from now, and humans are once again populating a new world. A group of 600,000 adults have arrived on PlanetX. The chart and the data below it show that there are 20,000 people of each age from 15 to 44.

Not surprisingly, culture and language have changed a great deal. The people on PlanetX are androgynous—they wear the same clothes, and there is only one pronoun, *himo* (borrowed from Pulaar before it disappeared).

Although the Technological Revolution triggered by AI in the 21st century was breathtaking, science has been unable to grow humans outside a natural womb. What were called females are now productive (P) people. There are 10,000 nonproductive (NP) people and 10,000 P for each age cohort.

Over the course of a year, the population will change. The inhabitants will each age one year, and some of them will, sadly, pass away. On the other hand, new people (still called babies) will be born. This equation captures these events:

$$Population_{t+1} = Population_t + Births_t - Deaths_t$$

How many births and deaths will occur during the year? That depends on the age-specific fertility rate (ASFR) and age-specific death rate (ASDR).

STEP Hover your mouse over cells E15 and F15 and read the definitions of ASFR and ASDR in the comments that pop up. You can also *Show All Comments* in the *Review* tab. Scroll down to see that the values for ASFR are all 0.1.

A constant ASFR of 0.1 is not at all close to our fertility rates today. Usually, the age-specific fertility rate rises as females mature, reaching a peak in their 20s and then falling again. Women can and do give birth past age 45, so the zeroes after age 44 are also unrealistic.

Unlike the completely fake ASFR, ASDR is roughly that experienced by the United States in the early 21st century. The 0.006 value in cell F16 is called the *infant mortality rate*. It expresses the chances that a baby born will not survive to their first birthday. There is some good news in that the US infant mortality rate is much lower than it used to be, and this is also true all around the world.

We could have made this hypothetical example more realistic by giving different ASDRs for NP and P people. In our current times, females outlive males by several years, on average. We will assume, however, that on PlanetX, NP and P people experience the same age-specific death rates.

Notice how the age-specific death rate declines after the first year and then starts to rise after the teenage years. The value of 0.049 in cell F96 means that an 80-year-old has a 4.9% chance of not surviving to the next year. At the bottom row (101), the value becomes unrealistic—unlike on Earth, everyone on PlanetX dies at age 85.

Before we continue, note that the cells in column B are minus 10,000. The minus enables those values to be plotted in the blue rectangle (to the left of zero) on the *Clustered Bar* chart above.

STEP In cell H3, enter the formula = -SUM(C16:C101) + SUM(D16:D101) to add up all of the people at the beginning of the year.

Cell H3 should display 600,000, which is the starting number of people on PlanetX. To compute the number of people born during the year, we use Excel's SUMPRODUCT function.

STEP In cell H5, enter the formula =SUMPRODUCT(D31:D60,E31:E60).

SUMPRODUCT multiplies (hence the PRODUCT in the name) two or more arrays and then adds them up (hence the SUM). So it takes the value in cell D31 and multiplies it by E31. This is the number of children (1,000) produced by the 15-year-old Ps. Then it multiplies D32 by E32 and so on. Finally, it adds up the products—in this example, 30,000.

STEP In cell H6, use SUMPRODUCT to compute the number of deaths. You will need two SUMPRODUCT terms added together, and the NP term needs to have a minus sign in front of it. Unlike births, we use the entire range from row 16 to 101 because there could be deaths at every age.

STEP Check your work by clicking the Next button.

You are now in a new sheet called *Propagate* (which means, in general, "to spread out or expand" and, in biology, "the breeding of a plant or animal from parent stock"). The first few columns are the same—your computations for births and deaths are replicated (or you can see how to use SUMPRODUCT for deaths)—and we now see new data for Year 2.

Cell H7 applies the population propagation equation from above. It takes the starting population, adds births, and subtracts deaths.

The percentage change in the population of 4.89% in cell H8 is extremely high. The Rule of 70 tells us that we would get doubling in roughly 15 years (70/5 = 14, but we are a little below 5%). That is extremely fast for human population growth.

STEP Look carefully at the Year 2 chart. Do you see the thin red and blue strips at the base of the chart? Those are the 30,000 newly born babies.

We made another simplifying assumption in that half of babies are NPs and the other half are Ps. (Most people think there are equal chances of getting a boy or a girl, but this turns out to be incorrect.)

STEP You can also see the newborns in cells L16 and M16. Click on these cells to read the formulas used. By multiplying by 0.5, we split the babies into equal amounts of NPs and Ps.

Unlike the first year, the second year's population numbers are all based on formulas.

STEP Click on cells L32 and M32 to see their formulas.

Because their ASDR is 0.0002, 2 of the 10,000 15-year-olds in Year 1 did not survive to Year 2. The formula uses (1 – ASDR) to compute the number surviving. The other values in columns L and M are computed the same way.

It is extremely difficult to see on the chart, but the adults no longer form a rectangle. We need more years to make this clear.

STEP Click the 1 Year button.

A new year appears with the previous year's births, deaths, and net increase in population computed. A new layer has been added at the base of the chart, and last year's babies have moved up. The adults are also all moving up.

STEP Click the 1 Year button again.

There are fewer babies than the previous year because some of the Ps died during the year. The data below the chart make this clear.

STEP We can speed up the propagation by using the ? Years button. Click it, read what it says, enter 20, and then press OK. Scroll right, looking at the data and charts as you scroll, until you reach the final year.

EXCEL TIP Because the sheet uses formulas to compute the surviving number of people at each age from the previous year, recalculating the sheet gets increasingly slower as we add more years. Closing other apps (especially browsers) may help.

In year 24, your chart looks like Figure 10.1. It is now easy to see the tapering of the rectangle at the top as more of the older original settlers do not survive until 85. Also, the children of the original settlers have started having children. The space in the middle reflects the fact that there were no children (ages 0 to 14) at Year 0.

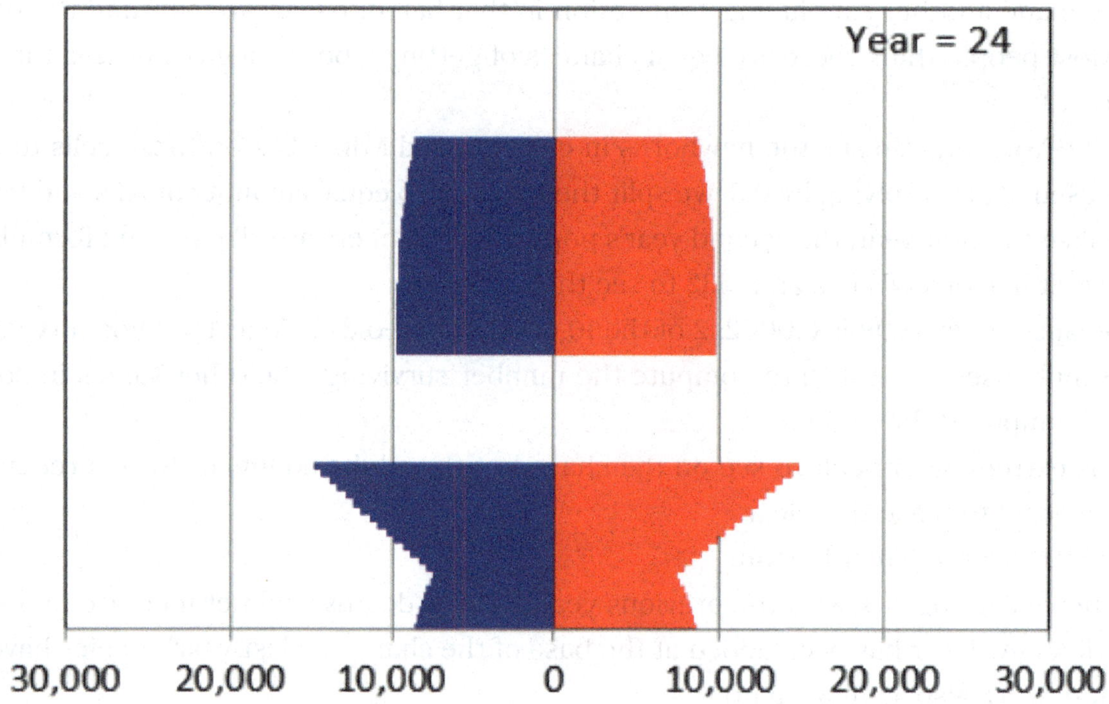

Figure 10.1: Population age distribution in year 24 on PlanetX.

Figure 10.1 also shows a baby boom after human arrival on PlanetX. Births fell for a number of years, but then a second baby boomlet starts to appear. The dynamics of the pyramid can be quite complicated.

STEP From any year, click the Animate button.

You are taken to the beginning of the sheet, and the years from 0 to 24 are displayed, like a moving picture. It is clear that the chart has an upward motion built into it as time goes by. Each age cohort begins at the bottom and makes its way to the top, getting shorter as it moves up.

STEP Add enough years to your sheet (using the ? Years button) to get to 100. Excel may take a while to display all these years, so you may have to be patient. Scroll right to Year 100. Your chart should look like Figure 10.2.

At Year 100, it is clear why this chart is called a *population pyramid*. The pyramid (or triangular) shape of many human societies, with few old and many young people, was quite common when it was first introduced by Francis Amasa Walker, an economist who was the head of the US Census in 1870.

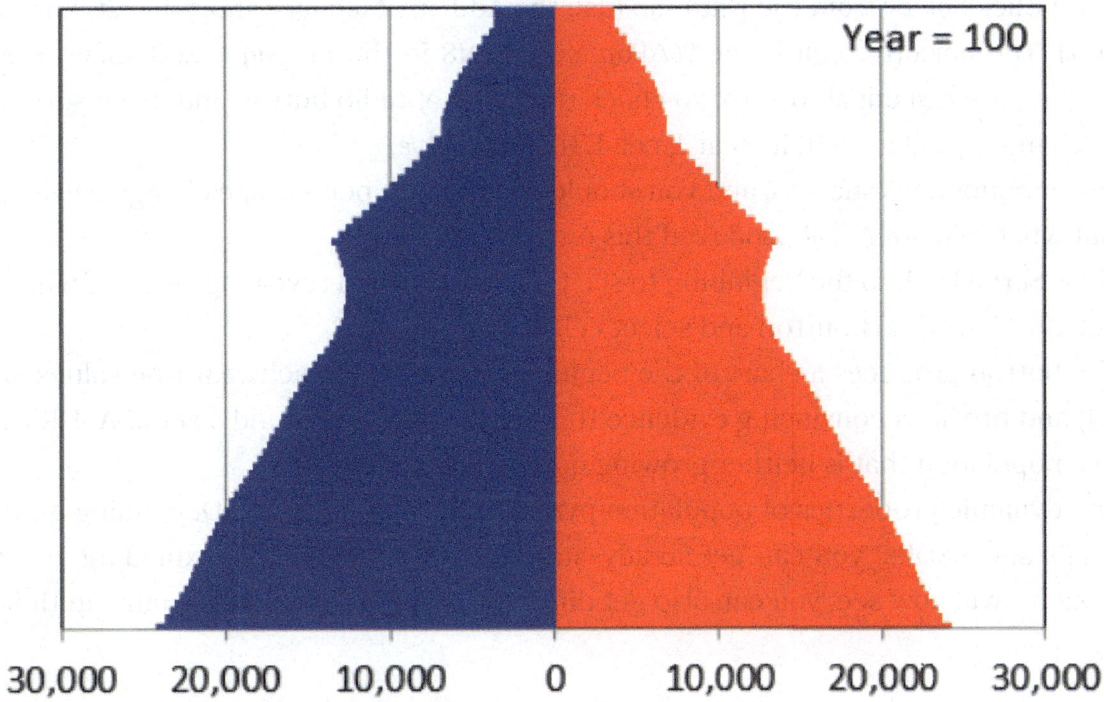

Figure 10.2: Population pyramid in year 100 on PlanetX.

The chart is also known as an age-distribution graph or age pyramid, and even more technically, it is a bilateral histogram. But no matter what you call it, the amount of information it delivers is impressive. Not only does it give a static snapshot, but once you know that it will scroll up as time passes, it provides insight into the future population age distribution.

It is important to understand that the pyramid shape was produced by the ASFR and ASDR values. Keep propagating and the pyramid shape will get ever more pronounced, and the population will keep expanding.

But this is not the only possibility.

STEP Return to the beginning of the sheet and change the ASFR values from 0.1 to 0.05 by changing cell E31 to 0.05, entering the formula =E31 in cell E32, and filling it down to cell E60. Scroll right to Year 24. That chart is quite different from Figure 10.1. Scroll right to the end. What shocking result do you see?

So with ASFR = 0.1, population keeps increasing, and with ASFR = 0.05, it shrinks. Is it possible to get some kind of balanced result where it does not grow without bound or collapse completely? Yes. To see this, we need more years.

STEP Propagate for 200 years or, if your computer is too slow, click the Propagate 200 button.

We want to find the ASFR that produces a constant population; in other words, its percentage change is zero. This sounds like a job for Solver.

STEP Click *Solver* from the *Data* tab (use the Add-ins Manager shortcut *Alt, t, i* if you need to install it). The objective cell is the *%ΔPop*, cell BQN8 in the *Propagate200* sheet. We want to make the objective cell equal to zero, so check the *Value of* radio button and make sure it is set to zero. The changing cell is ASFR in Year 1, cell E31. Click *Solve*.

Solver announces success, and you should see that the percentage change cell is displaying 0.00%, but what value of ASDR produced this outcome?

STEP Scroll back to the beginning to see the answer. For a revealing visual of what you have done, click the Time Chart button and select cell H3.

The button produces a chart of the beginning population each year (the values are in column BQN) and provides convincing evidence that we have indeed found a set of ASDR values that results in a population that is neither growing nor collapsing.

The dynamic properties of population pyramids are complicated. Depending on the values of the ASFRs and ASDRs, you can get steady-state (equilibrium), stable, exploding, or collapsing patterns. As we will now see, you can also get different shapes at particular points in time.

Real-World Population Pyramids

Now that we know what a population pyramid is and how to read it, we are ready to examine real-world data. Unlike PlanetX, today, babies are assigned a sex as male or female at birth. Most people identify as adults with their assigned sex, but some do not. The US Census Bureau's Pulse Survey asks about sexual orientation and gender identity (visit www.census.gov/library/visualizations/interactive/sexual-orientation-and-gender-identity.html). The International Database population estimates provide only male and female categories.

STEP Click any PopPyr button.

A new sheet appears. You select the country and years, then Excel acts like a browser and gets the data from the US Census Bureau. They maintain an international database of past and predicted population age distributions. You can access their website via the link under the chart in the *PopPyr* sheet.

STEP Click *Select a country* in the listbox and select Afghanistan. With 2024 in the yellow-background cells K3 and K4, click the Get IDB Data button. Excel downloads the data in columns B, C, and D and displays them in the chart.

The result is striking. You are looking at a classic population pyramid. Most low-income countries have pyramids like this, with very few old and many young people.

STEP Copy the sheet. This enables comparison of different countries. Change the country to the United States and click the Get IDB Data button. In seconds, you have a new pyramid. Double-click the sheet tab and make the name US.

Unlike Afghanistan, this pyramid is triangular at the top, but the sides are more vertical, like a stick drawing of a house.

STEP Copy the sheet and get Japan's population pyramid. Set the sheetname to *Japan*.

We get yet another new shape, like a hexagon (or benzene ring, if you know some chemistry). The three shapes are roughly drawn in Figure 10.3. The classic shape used to dominate, since most countries were poor, with high fertility and death rates. As countries became rich, they underwent what is now called the *demographic transition*, first with low death rates, followed by low birth rates.

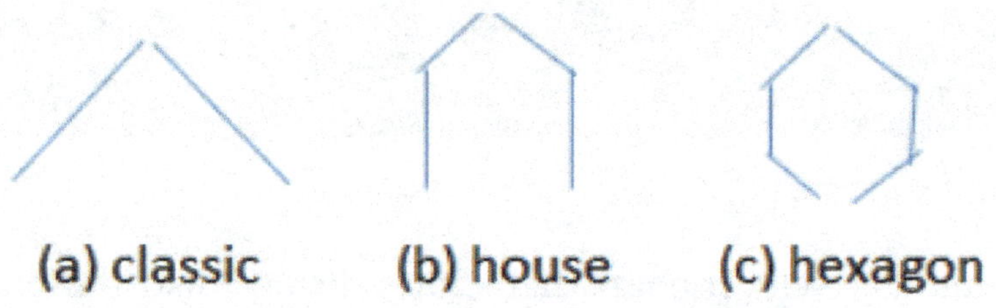

Figure 10.3: Three common population pyramid shapes.

Japan's hexagon shape hints at big trouble in the future for its economy and society. The narrow base means there are few children to grow up to become workers to support their aging parents.

The United States might be in this same position were it not for immigration. Native-born Americans have much lower fertility rates than do immigrants.

In fact, fertility rates are collapsing all around the world. This has been a stunning and completely unexpected reversal coming on the heels of explosively fast population growth in the decades following World War II.

We can see what the Census Bureau predicts by downloading more years.

STEP Return to your US (*PopPyr*) sheet and set the years to 1950 in cell K3 and 2060 in cell K4. Click the Get IDB Data button. This might take a little time, since you are downloading a lot of data. Click OK if you get an error message saying some years are unavailable.

The earliest year of available data for the United States is 1980.

STEP Click the Pick a Year button and enter 1980. Click OK.

The baby boom generation was much more noticeable back then. We can animate the chart to see the boomers and everyone else march up the chart.

STEP Click the Play button.

The Census Bureau is projecting a relatively stable population pyramid for the United States up to mid-century. Immigration will continue to play an important role, but the most difficult thing to predict is the fertility rate. Death rates fall slowly but steadily, while fertility can change quite rapidly.

STEP Get data for Japan from 1990 (the earliest year) to 2060. What is the demographic outlook for Japan?

And if you think that is mind-blowing, take a look at China or Cuba. In fact, almost every country's population pyramid has a story to tell. The gouges represent traumatic societal events (such as famines or revolutions), and you can get deep insight into economic and social issues from this chart.

Takeaways

A population pyramid is a clever chart that shows the age distribution of males and females.

Figure 10.4 shows original examples from Walker's 1870 Census report. These were some of the earliest data visualizations and an instant hit.

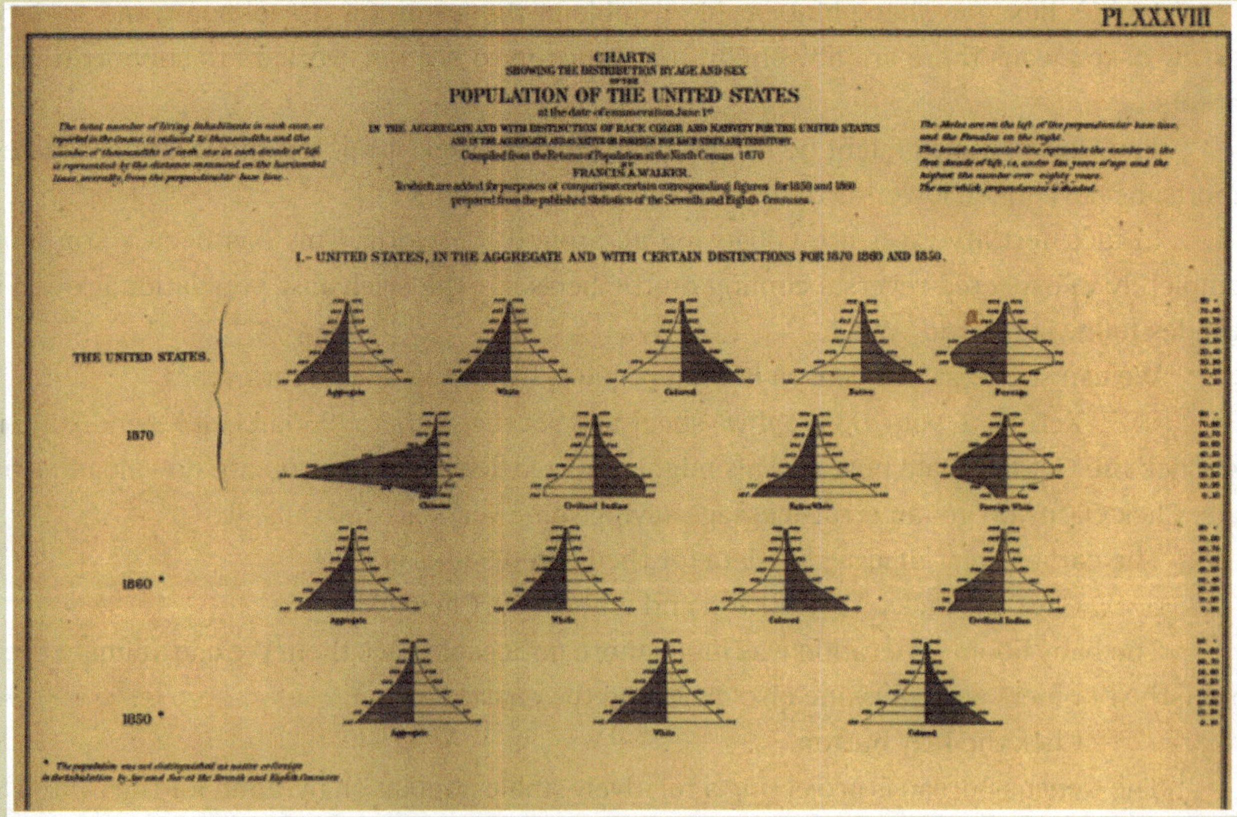

Figure 10.4: Population pyramids from the 1870 US Census.
Source: 1870 Census: Statistical Atlas of the United States / Public domain.

High birth and death rates (which used to be common for poor, developing countries) produce lots of children and few old people, yielding a triangular shape with a wide bottom and pointed top, so that's why it is called a population pyramid.

But there are other possible shapes. Many developed, rich countries have gone through a demographic transition, with death rates falling first, then fertility falling. At this time, they have roughly equal numbers of people at each age until finally tapering off for older folks, so it looks more like a house.

With really low fertility (and little immigration), we get a hexagon, a house with an added narrow base, like Japan. This has the potential to cause serious problems for the economy and society. Demographic headwinds help explain why Japan's economy has stumbled so badly after flying high in the decades after World War II.

Population pyramids depict historical events and calamities. Baby booms are easily seen as bulges in the pyramid. Indentations or gouges reflect traumatic events such as famine or political upheaval (China is a good example).

Population pyramids have a dynamic aspect. The cohorts (horizontal bars) march up the graph as time goes by.

Since the rapid expansion of humanity in the 1700s, we have worried and obsessed about having too many people. Today, we are undergoing an incredibly sudden slowdown in population growth, triggered by collapsing fertility rates.

References

The epigraph is from p. 205 of Robbins, L. (1963). *The Robbins Report: Higher Education Report of the Committee Appointed by the Prime Minister Under the Chairmanship of Lord Robbins* 1961–1963 (London: Her Majesty's Stationery Office), education-uk.org/documents/robbins/robbins1963.html.

On p. 16 of the second edition of *An Essay on the Nature and Significance of Economic Science*, Robbins gave a modern definition of economics as "the science which studies human behavior as a relationship between given ends and scarce means which have alternative uses." This book was originally published in 1932, and the second edition is available online at www.mises.org/books/robbinsessay2.pdf.

Walker's full report, published in 1874 by the US Congress, *Statistical Atlas of the United States* (1870), launched his career. He went on to a series of high-profile positions, including serving as president of MIT and the American Economics Association. Walker's pathbreaking atlas is available online at www.census.gov/library/publications/1874/dec/1870d.html.

10.2 Demographic Analytics

The data in *PopulationPyramid.xlsm* can be used to compute the male-female (M/F) birth ratio and the dependency ratio.

M/F Birth Ratio

STEP Use *PopulationPyramid.xlsm* (visit dub.sh/gbae to download the file, if needed) to get age-distribution data for the United States in 2024. In cell E4, enter the formula = -C3/D3 and press *Enter*.

The M/F birth ratio in the United States is around 1.045. If there were equal (50/50) chances of having a boy or girl, the M/F ratio would be 1.0. Thus, we see a bias toward more boys being born than girls.

In 2024, more than two million boys and two million girls were born, but there were about 4.5% more males born. Can chance explain that deviation from equal numbers of male and female births?

No. If it was 21 boys and 20 girls or even 210 to 200, luck could explain more males than females, but 2.1 million to 2 million would almost never happen by chance.

In fact, it took a while to figure out that the M/F birth ratio is not 1.0, and the story of how this was discovered takes us to the beginning of statistical theory.

John Arbuthnot (1667–1765) was a Scottish minister and Queen Anne's doctor. He published a paper in 1710 (see references) proving, he thought, that Divine Providence, not chance, determined a baby's sex.

Arbuthnot analyzed annual data on christenings from 1629 to 1710. In 1629, for example, there were 5,218 male and 4,683 female babies baptized. This kept happening—each year, there were always more boys than girls.

If sex determination was controlled by chance, Arbuthnot said, then having more males than females in a year would be 50/50 (like a coin flip). He used log tables to compute the chances of getting more males than females 82 years in a row. Arbuthnot argued that the ridiculously small number he came up with meant that something beyond chance was at work. Since boys are more likely to die, an uneven start was part of a Divine Plan that would ensure an equal number of men and women for marriage.

Arbuthnot defined chance as requiring an equal probability of males and females at birth, but randomness can operate with likelihoods other than 50% (like someone being a 90% free throw shooter). One thing, however, is sure: This was the world's first statistical hypothesis test.

Arbuthnot is important because he posed a question involving randomness and framed it as a claim that could be tested with data.

Arbuthnot's work led to a key vital statistic: the male-female ratio at birth. The evidence soon mounted for a small but real bias in favor of boys. Today, we know that the birth of boys is about 5% more likely than that of girls, but there are places around the world that deviate substantially from 1.05.

STEP Use *PopulationPyramid.xlsm* to find India's M/F birth ratio in 2024. This is easily done by downloading India's age distribution for 2024 and computing the ratio of males to females at age zero.

The result is surprisingly high. What is going on? Indians (like many other cultures) have strong preferences for boys over girls. Low-cost ultrasound can easily determine sex before birth. Pregnancies with females are terminated, while males are born. After birth, boys are treated much better than girls. The result is an M/F birth ratio over 1.1.

In a 1990 article on missing women (see references), Amartya Sen, who would go on to win a Nobel Memorial Prize in Economic Sciences in 1998, pointed out that "a great many more than a hundred million women are simply not there because women are neglected compared with men." Missing women remains as important a global public health issue today as when Sen first called attention to it.

Another country that we might suspect has a high M/F birth ratio is China. In 1980, responding to fears of a population explosion, the government instituted a one-child policy. As in India, ultrasound sex determination and selection for boys was quickly adopted, and this increased the M/F birth ratio. But by how much?

STEP Use *PopulationPyramid.xlsm* to find China's M/F birth ratio in 2010.

It is one thing to know that China's one-child policy led to more boys than girls being born, but the actual statistic, 1.17, is staggering.

There are, of course, serious social consequences for these kinds of imbalances in the population of males and females. In 2016, China rescinded its one-child policy, and more recently, it is actively encouraging fertility. The problem is no longer too many people but too few young people.

STEP Set the start year to 1950 and the end year to 2060 to download all available years. Get the data and click the Ratios button (under the chart). Make a chart of the M/F birth ratio.

Your chart shows that the US Census Bureau does not expect China's M/F birth ratio to remain abnormally high.

Dependency Ratio

Another demographic statistic that gives insight into societal and economic issues is the *depen-*

dency ratio. It can be computed in different ways, but a common method is young plus old divided by working-age adults:

$$\text{Dependency Ratio} = \frac{\text{Up to } 14 + 65 \text{ and over}}{15 - \text{ to } 64 - \text{year} - \text{olds}}$$

The idea is that children (defined as under 15 years old) and retired people (65 years and older) do not work and depend on the labor of adults ages 15 to 64. Obviously, this is a rough measure, since many people continue to work past age 65, and not all 15- to 64-year-olds work. The ratio tries to capture the number of dependents per working-age person.

STEP If needed, download data on the United States from 1980 to 2060. Click the Ratios button.

The sheet displays M/F and dependency ratios along with the components needed to compute these ratios for each year. Instead of simply plotting the dependency ratio, we will split the data into two parts, historical and projected.

STEP Make a *Scatter with Straight Lines* chart of the dependency ratio from 1980 to the present year. Copy the SERIES formula, paste it, and change the cell addresses to future years. Title the chart and label the *y*-axis.

Your chart should look like Figure 10.5. The dependency ratio is expected to increase in the United States from its previously stable level of 0.5 to over 0.6 in the coming decades.

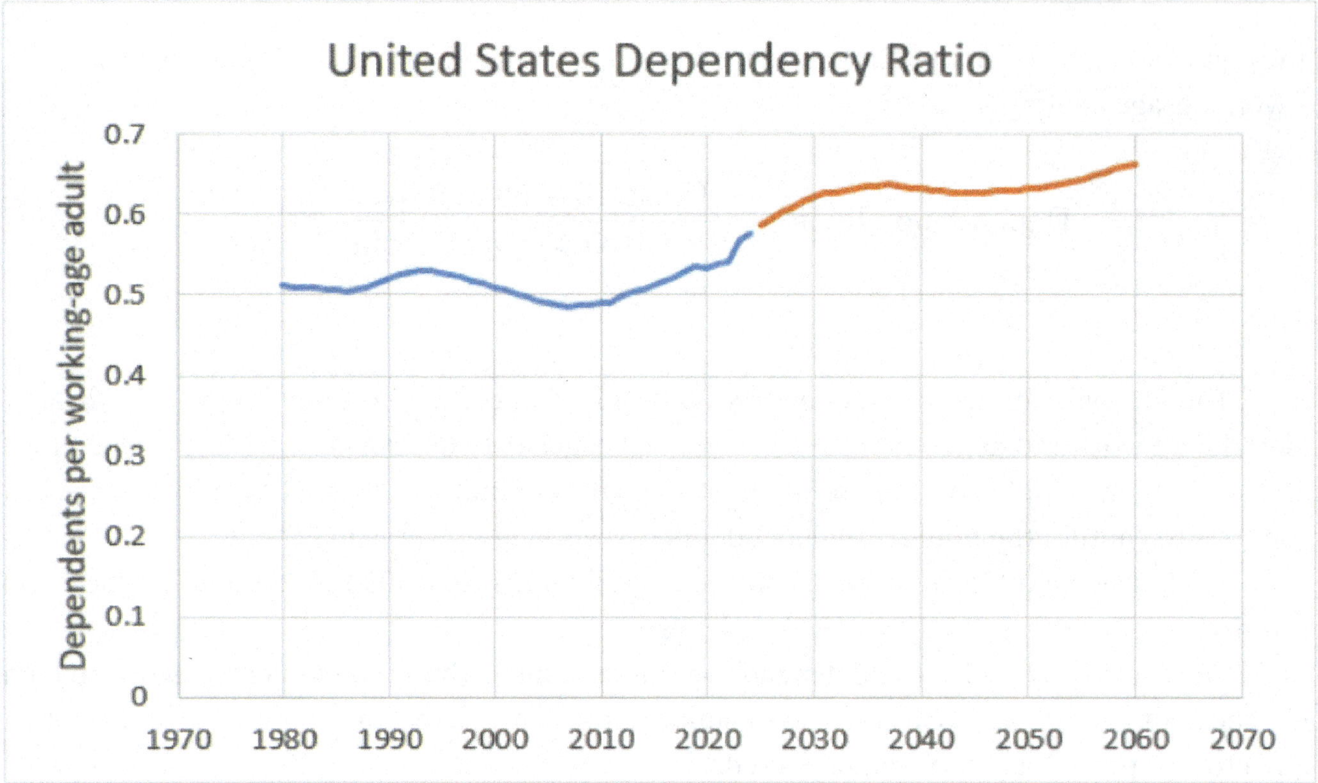

***Figure 10.5**: Rising projected dependency ratio in the United States.*

The dependency ratio is a function of the age distribution of the population and is affected by two opposing forces: Fertility is falling, but life expectancy is rising. We can focus on the share of elderly people by computing the *old-age dependency ratio*:

$$\text{Old-Age Dependency Ratio} = \frac{\text{65 and over}}{\text{15- to 64-year-olds}}$$

STEP Enter the label *Old-age dependency ratio* in cell O33. Enter the formula = M34/L34, in cell O34 and fill it down. Copy the chart, paste it, and edit the SERIES formula so it displays the old-age dependency ratio.

Figure 10.6 shows that the old-age dependency ratio in the United States is projected to reach 0.4 by 2060. Many other (typically rich) countries also face rapidly rising old-age dependency ratios, but none as extreme as Japan.

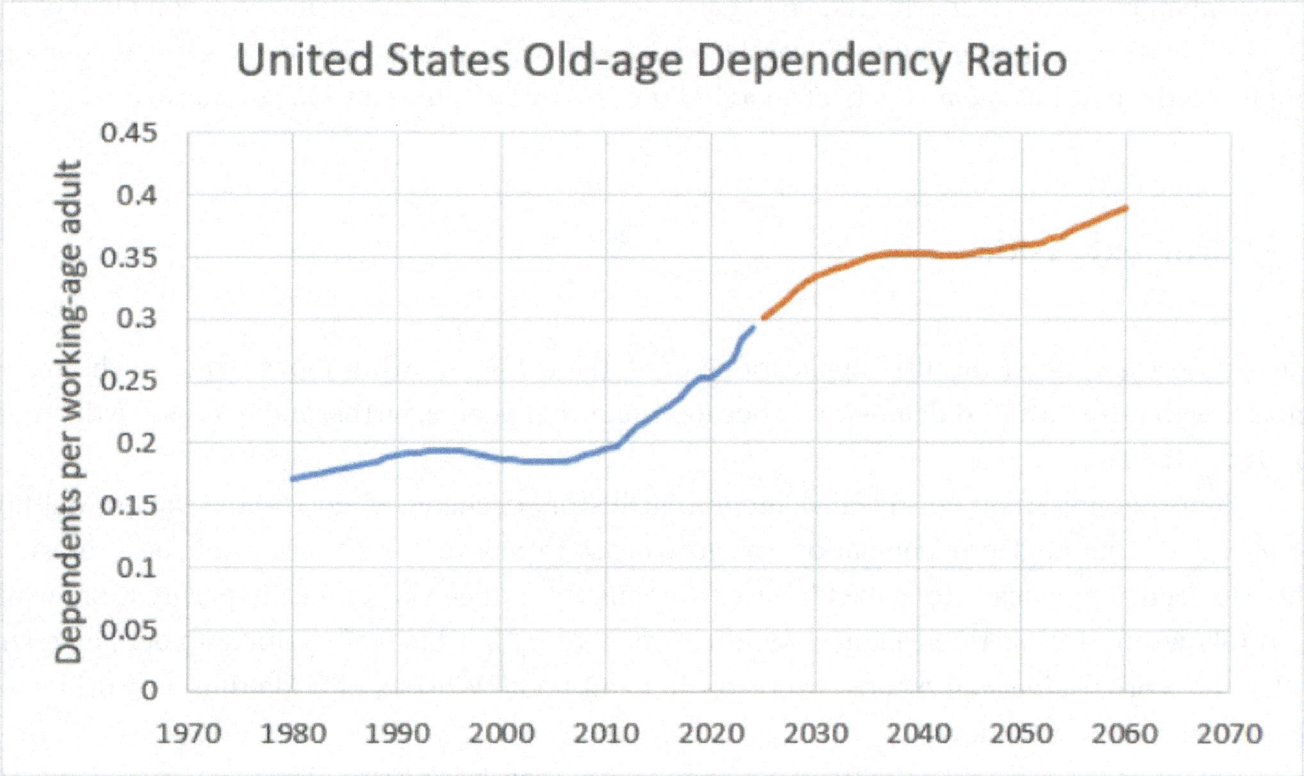

Figure 10.6: High future old-age dependency ratio in the United States.

STEP Download data and create dependency and old-age dependency ratio charts for Japan for all available years. What do you find?

Countries with traditional population pyramids can have high dependency ratios because there are many children, but no country has ever seen this statistic near 1.0 with low fertility. Japan's old-age dependency ratio above 0.7 in 2050 is simply staggering to contemplate.

Every country has a dependency ratio story, and some can be astounding. Cuba, for instance, faces strong demographic headwinds, with shockingly low fertility and an aging population. Old-age dependency ratios are made even worse by emigration of young adults. For more, see Barreto (2018).

High old-age dependency ratios and falling fertility spell social and economic trouble for two reasons. First, resources have to be reallocated and adjusted. For example, more assisted living and senior facilities are needed, while schools have to be consolidated and reorganized for fewer students. Labor markets are also strongly affected, with less childcare needed but more jobs for elderly services.

Second, and more important, an aging society can be a pessimistic place. Keynes (1936, chap. 12, VII) emphasized animal spirits, "a spontaneous urge to action rather than inaction," as the driver of investment. Optimism produces high levels of investment spending. Without it, a lack of business and consumer confidence stops economic growth.

Japan has been intensely studied because its high-flying economy in the second half of the 20th century has been stagnant for several decades. Thus far, no policies have worked. Its demography and the psychological effects of an aging society are undoubtedly part of the story.

A Historical Aside

It is fitting that one of the first applications of statistical logic, Arbuthnot's work on the male-female birth ratio, involved demography because counting people, births, and deaths are the most fundamental data.

Another important episode in demographic history occurred when Thomas Robert Malthus (1798) argued that England's population was growing so explosively that there would be a catastrophe. He used simple math to make his case: Humans reproduce via geometric progression, while food follows an arithmetic sequence. Malthus was wrong, but his fears gained an audience and today the word *Malthusian* means "overcrowded and poor." Worries of a Malthusian world continue to claim our attention.

More recently, Ehrlich (1980) wrote a book with a captivating title, *The Population Bomb*. He argued exponential population growth would produce famine and disaster. That did not happen.

In fact, unbeknownst to Ehrlich and everyone else, there was a sudden and deep reversal at play. Fertility rates have spectacularly cratered, crashing down from extremely high levels experienced in the decades after World War II.

The problem now is not too many people but how societies and economies can adjust to aging populations. The implications for business are tremendous. Not only investment but innovation and entrepreneurship are impacted by the demographic tides.

Takeaways

Demography is a quantitative discipline with its own analytics. Vital statistics involve counts, ratios, and other computations of human populations.

The *PopulationPyramid.xlsm* workbook enables downloading years of age-distribution data, which can then be displayed as a chart but also be used to compute statistics.

The M/F birth ratio is around 1.05, but it can deviate substantially from that in particular places and times.

Dependency ratios give information on the structure of the age distribution. Old-age dependency ratios are expected to rise substantially in almost every country as people live longer and fertility is much lower.

It is easy to think that the impact of an aging population involves mechanical adjustment in capital and labor resources, but the psychological effects are much more important.

You might think it odd to include demography in a book on business analytics, but there is no doubt that the study of human populations and their age distribution and movement are critical to economics, finance, and business.

There is a hidden sheet in the *PopulationPyramid.xlsm* workbook. Do the last step in this book to see a population pyramid of college graduates in the United States.

STEP Right-click any sheet tab and select *Unhide*. Select *PopPyrCollege* to reveal the sheet.

The red bar for 25-year-olds (the lowest bar) is longer than the blue bar. This shows there are more female than male 25-year-old college grads. The ratio, 0.8, is quite low, don't you think? What are the implications of this?

References

Arbuthnot, J. (1710). "An Argument for Divine Providence, Taken from the Constant Regularity Observed in the Births of Both Sexes." www.york.ac.uk/depts/maths/hist-stat/arbuthnot.pdf.

Barreto, H. (2018). "Cuban Demography and Economic Consequences." Working Papers 2018-01, DePauw University, School of Business and Leadership and Department of Economics and Management, ideas.repec.org/p/dew/wpaper/2018-01.html.

Ehrlich, P. (1968, 1st ed.). *The Population Bomb* (New York, NY: Ballantine Books), www.google.com/search?q=ehrlich+population+bomb.

Keynes, J. M. (1936). *The General Theory of Employment, Interest and Money*, www.marxists.org/reference/subject/economics/keynes/general-theory.

Malthus, R. (1798, 1st ed.). *An Essay on the Principle of Population*, oll.libertyfund.org/titles/malthus-an-essay-on-the-principle-of-population-1798-1st-ed.

Sen, A. (1990). "More Than 100 Million Women Are Missing." *New York Review of Books*, December 20, 1990, www.nybooks.com/articles/1990/12/20/more-than-100-million-women-are-missing.

Afterword

Gateway to Business Analytics with Microsoft Excel®

Pressbooks URL: https://doi.org/10.59319/FMVH4866

Website URL: https://barretoh.github.io/busanalytics/

Shortcut: dub.sh/gbae

This text uses Microsoft Excel® to deliver a sampling of topics in business analytics as an introduction to the field. There are no prerequisites, and the target audience is first- or second-year undergraduate students who have used a spreadsheet before but have no specialized training in Excel, calculus, statistics, or programming.

Readers acquire sophisticated Excel skills and a solid foundation for further work in business analytics. With concrete examples, novel applications, and eye-catching visualizations, engagement is guaranteed as the user creates spreadsheets, manipulates live graphs, and analyzes data.

Humberto Barreto is Professor of Business Analytics at DePauw University. He earned his PhD from the University of North Carolina at Chapel Hill. Professor Barreto has lectured around the world on teaching economics with computer-based methods, including in Cuba, Brazil, Canada, Scotland, Spain, Poland, India, Myanmar, Japan, and Taiwan. He was a Fulbright Scholar in the Dominican Republic and has taught National Science Foundation (NSF) Chautauqua short courses using simulation. He has received several research and teaching awards. His book The Entrepreneur in Microeconomic Theory was translated into Arabic in 1999. He has written numerous articles and books on using Excel to teach economics (including introductory-level material, micro- and macroeconomics, and econometrics). He offers an annual workshop for faculty on teaching economics. Visit his Teaching Economics with Excel website for more information: dub.sh/hbhome.

Contributors

Author

Humberto Barreto
DEPAUW UNIVERSITY

Humberto Barreto is interested in using computers (especially Microsoft Excel) to improve the teaching and learning of quantitative methods. He is Professor of Business Analytics at DePauw University and has published papers and books on pedagogy, including (with Frank M. Howland) Introductory Econometrics using Monte Carlo Simulation with Microsoft Excel (Cambridge University Press, 2006), Intermediate Microeconomics with Microsoft Excel (Cambridge University Press, 2009) – now freely open-access – and Teaching Macroeconomics with Microsoft Excel (Cambridge University Press, 2016). Prof. Barreto has been a Fulbright Scholar, won several teaching awards, and given presentations on teaching economics and quantitative methods at many colleges and universities around the world.

https://orcid.org/0000-0003-4822-038X

Contributors

Victoria Peters (Project Manager)

Scribe Inc. (Copyeditor)

Reviewers

Nelson Altamirano
NATIONAL UNIVERSITY

Nolan Taylor
INDIANA UNIVERSITY INDIANAPOLIS

Made in the USA
Monee, IL
02 November 2026

67384322R00144